Test Tube Families

Test Tube Families

Why the Fertility Market Needs Legal Regulation

Naomi R. Cahn

NEW YORK UNIVERSITY PRESS

New York and London

NEW YORK UNIVERSITY PRESS
New York and London
www.nyupress.org

Library of Congress Cataloging-in-Publication Data
Cahn, Naomi R.
Test tube families : why the fertility market needs legal regulation /
Naomi R. Cahn.
p. cm.
Includes bibliographical references and index.
ISBN-13: 978-0-8147-1682-3 (cl : alk. paper)
ISBN-10: 0-8147-1682-2 (cl : alk. paper)
1. Fertilization in vitro, Human—Law and legislation—United States. I. Title.
KF3830.C34   2009
346.7301'7—dc22   2008037014

New York University Press books are printed on acid-free paper,
and their binding materials are chosen for strength and durability.
We strive to use environmentally responsible suppliers and materials
to the greatest extent possible in publishing our books.

Manufactured in the United States of America

10 9 8 7 6 5 4 3 2 1

Contents

Preface

THE CREATION OF families—legally, emotionally, and functionally—has always fascinated me both personally and professionally. This book explores the creation of technological families, the processes by which biology, medicine, human determination, and the law bring babies into being. Although some of what we now think of as the reproductive technologies, such as artificial insemination, have existed for centuries, others have only come into being over the past several decades or years—or months. Indeed, during this book's gestation, the technology for freezing human eggs has, for example, become far more efficient and effective, and the first embryo bank opened—and closed—for business. Writing about such a rapidly changing field is exciting, challenging, and intimidating.

Consequently, what I have tried to do is to examine the fundamental legal issues that underlie reproductive technology, issues that will not change even as the technology transforms how we think of the means of reproduction. So long as we have families, we will want to determine who the parents are. So long as children have questions about their origin, issues surrounding the identity of their biological progenitors will arise. And whenever we deal with technology, we will have concerns about the safety and regulation of that technology, and the protection of those individuals who engage with it. This triptych of legal issues—defining families, forming identities, and regulating markets—provides the framework for this book.

Over the years, as I have struggled to develop conceptions of family relationships, I have explored these topics with numerous colleagues, friends, and family members. Thank you to June Carbone, Martha Ertman, Tony Gambino, Michele Goodwin, Joan Hollinger, Helena Michie, Mary Lyndon Shanley, Jana Singer, and Bob Tuttle. Without Debbie Gershenowitz, my editor at NYU Press, this book would not exist. Her hand appears on every page. I would also like to thank Rachel Hull for her perceptive independent study paper and her permission to use it; my research assistants, Kathie Carroll, Alexis Chapin, Talita Kiper, Kristalyn Loson, and Lauren Valden; my gratitude to Christy Zlatkus for her research and excellent index preparation; and Kasia Solon, my library liaison, who has answered all of my questions. And I would like to express my gratitude to Fred Lawrence, who so ably supports faculty development.

I cannot figure out how to thank my family enough.

Introduction

PRODUCING FAMILIES TODAY is a paradox. It is, for some, the most intimate of intimate acts and, for others, a multibillion-dollar business that simultaneously creates our closest relationships. Although 90 percent of Americans do not have fertility problems, 10 percent do. Each year, about one million people seek some sort of fertility treatment, and three hundred thousand go as far as undertaking in vitro fertilization. The infertility statistics are real and scary. A woman's fertility drops off beginning in her late twenties, continues to fall even more dramatically after the age of thirty-five, and plummets when she reaches forty. Once a woman turns thirty, her chances of getting pregnant decrease about 3–5 percent each year. By the age of thirty, 7 percent of couples are infertile, and by the time they reach the age of forty, 33 percent of couples are infertile.

An industry—albeit with comparatively little legal regulation—has developed to help, with almost five hundred fertility clinics nationwide. Fertility drugs constitute a $3 billion yearly business. In 2005, there were more than 130,000 in vitro fertilization (IVF) cycles in the United States, with over 50,000 babies born.[1] There are more than half a million frozen embryos in storage, and the Society for Assisted Reproductive Technology, an industry group, estimates that nine thousand donor-egg children were born in the United States in 2005, the most recent year for which statistics are available. In vitro fertilization accounts for about 99 percent of all assisted reproductive technology, and 18 percent of women using artificial reproductive technology (ART) services were over the age of forty in 2004.

Does IVF work? IVF success rates (the birth of a healthy baby) vary with the parents' age, but the most successful fertility clinics report pregnancy rates higher than 30 percent. After months or years of a couple's not conceiving, these statistics provide promise, although for any individual, the odds of having a baby are either 0 percent or 100 percent.

About fifteen years ago, after my third failed IVF attempt, my husband's and my reproductive endocrinologist suggested that our fertility problems resulted from my eggs. They just were not good, he explained. I was thirty-five, had experienced an early miscarriage, and was stunned when he recommended donor eggs to us. It had simply not occurred to me, even after years of infertility, that we might be candidates for using someone else's gametic material to create "our" child. Even though we briefly considered trying to search for a suitable candidate to provide the necessary eggs, we decided, instead, to try another fertility clinic, where, on our first try, I produced beautiful eggs, one of which became our first daughter. Our second daughter was conceived completely outside the fertility industry.

In writing a book about reproductive technology and other-provided gametes, my physician's words, and my initial shock, have constantly guided me. How do we navigate this world of thoroughly modern family-making? What guides—legal, emotional, and sociological—are there for us as individuals and as a society?

In my dual roles as a lawyer who teaches family law and as a player in the fertility game, I have learned that there is comparatively little legal regulation of any aspect of this industry and its participants. Although the fertility trade potentially affects millions of people—as consumers and producers, as physicians and patients—the regulation that does exist is piecemeal; purchasing eggs or semen involves entirely different regulations from those involved in determining whether the seller or purchaser is the parent or whether donor-conceived offspring have any rights to information about their donors. To a large extent, legal regulation of the fertility market, of the identity needs of resulting children, and of the determination of parenthood, have developed separately, and the legal approaches have evolved well after the technological innovations appeared. Indeed, the law has been in a catch-up mode, not in a shaping mode. The law has only minimally responded to the legal conundrums posed by ARTs, rather than guiding their expanding uses, and individual cases rather than broader legislation have more typically provided legal signposts.

The Continental philosopher Jürgen Habermas has suggested that "new technological developments have created new regulatory needs," and he challenges existing regulations that ensure that "freedom of science and research is entitled to legal guarantees."[2] Instead, he argues that there is a need to "moralize human nature" and assert "an ethical self-understanding of the species."[3] In responding to this challenge and examining the morality of our current approaches to the new reproductive technologies, my intent is to promote an ethical approach to developing new laws that respects human dignity.

The promise of the reproductive technologies—producing babies—now goes beyond curing infertility and challenges our conceptions of natural families as families that are static and unchanging.[4] Creating a family, regardless of whether you are an infertile husband-and-wife couple, a same-sex couple, or a single person, now involves deliberate choice. Indeed, approximately two-thirds, or four million, of all pregnancies in the United States are "wanted"[5] (although only a very small portion of these are to the millions of people defined as infertile). We can imagine a continuum of procreative choices, ranging from birth control at one end and the advanced technologies at the other end, with a range of decisions on childbearing in between and a variety of legal protections for each of these decisions.

Of course, as discussed in chapter 9, the possibility of choosing to form a family outside the traditional heterosexual married couple is controversial both practically and legally. And use of the technologies is not equally available to all, regardless of sexual orientation, class, or race. Moreover, the possibility of purchasing eggs, sperm, or embryos from another person has engendered its own controversies. Finally, although the law clarifies some of the resulting legal, social, and personal relationships, there are multiple gaps.

This book examines three distinct issues and their relationship to the law: the market in gametes, the creation of familial relationships through ART, and the identity interests of the resulting children. Legally, each of these issues has developed at different times, responding to different pressures. The gamete market, which began with sperm and now includes surrogacy, eggs, and embryos, has been subject to little regulation, reflecting the secrecy that was integral to early sperm provision. Recognition of the legal relationships that resulted from the creation of families through ART has similarly developed in reaction to the stigma of illegitimacy; on the other hand, early cases pondered whether a married woman's use of donor sperm, even with her husband's consent, constituted adultery that would render any child illegitimate. In many cases, of course, only the doctor knew, and neither the mother nor father had any reason to air the issue in public; many children are unaware that they are "donor babies" and may never find out without DNA tests. Finally, the identity interests of resulting children have been camouflaged by the traditional secrecy that attended use of ART as well as by analogy to adoption, for which, for roughly the past half century, most birth records have been sealed. These diverging and overlapping origins have helped ensure that laws pertaining to each aspect have been viewed as relatively independent.

The politics of reproductive technology are deeply intertwined with the politics of reproduction. This is a message that conservatives understand profoundly and that accounts for many of the legal and policy debates discussed in chapter 9. On the other hand, many feminists have not connected the two movements, and, although the reproductive rights issue has a long feminist genealogy, infertility does not. Much of the feminist history of reproductive politics involves an examination of attempts to control fertility and sexuality by women, such as through contraception or the power to say no to sex, and by others, such as through eugenics. This history has typically included neither an examination of the need to enhance fertility nor an examination of the laws surrounding conception support. *Test Tube Families* joins the nascent discussion of legal approaches to reproductive technology, proposing that the law respond comprehensively to the issues involved in market regulation, parenthood determination, and identity needs.

Infertility has always existed (many people list Abraham's wife, Sarah, from the Bible as the first historical example of infertility), but over the past several decades, as the secrecy surrounding adoption has dissolved and as science has learned more about fertility, reproductive politics has expanded to include the politics of contraception and conception. For feminists, however, discussion of infertility may be threatening on two levels: first, it reinforces the importance of motherhood in women's lives, and second, the specter of infertility reinforces the difficulty of women's "having it all."

When the American Society for Reproductive Medicine (ASRM)[6] decided to launch an infertility-awareness campaign in 2001, emphasizing that a number of factors—ranging from smoking to age—affect infertility, it was concerned that a discussion of age might be seen, on the one hand, as encouraging adolescent pregnancy and, on the other hand, as castigating women. And when the ASRM rolled out these "Protect Your Fertility" advertisements, the National Organization for Women viewed it as a "scare campaign."[7] Advertisements like those involving a baby bottle shaped like an hourglass (see figure 1.1) were viewed as giving the impression that younger women must "hurry up and have kids" or give up and never have them, claimed Kim Gandy, the head of the National Organization for Women.[8] Others saw the message as telling women that they should not be too ambitious and should return to their homemaking roles.[9] Lisa Marcus, a thirty-seven-year-old professor of women's studies undergoing infertility treatment, asked in the *Women's Review of Books*,

ADVANCING AGE DECREASES YOUR
ABILITY TO HAVE CHILDREN.

While women and their partners must be the ones to decide the best time when (and if) to have children, women in their twenties and early thirties are most likely to conceive. Infertility is a disease affecting 6.1 million people in the United States.

GET THE FACTS   WWW.PROTECTYOURFERTILITY.ORG 1-866-228-6906
AMERICAN SOCIETY FOR REPRODUCTIVE MEDICINE   The space for this public service message is provided by *IDI*source*

Figure 1.1. Courtesy of the American Society for Reproductive Medicine

"Do I blame my infertility on my desire to divorce destiny from biology, to nurture a career rather than a child? Not for a minute. But the popular press is doing a number on women who've delayed motherhood."[10]

Shunning information about the relationship between infertility and age, however, ignores biological facts and, ultimately, does a disservice to women both in terms of approaching their own fertility and in providing the legal structure necessary to provide meaning to reproductive choice. The feminist classic *Our Bodies, Ourselves* is designed to provide accurate and clear information so that women can become experts in managing their own health.[11] Particularly in light of the premises of the feminist health movement, information about controlling fertility must range from the means for preventing conception to the means for promoting conception. It is only with this information that reproductive choice becomes a meaningful concept; choice cannot mean only legal control over the means *not* to have a baby but must include legal control over the means to have a baby.

Even the discussion of the technology itself is not always a celebration. Feminists are divided over the multiple legal and policy issues posed by the new reproductive technologies, thereby providing inconsistent and incomplete guidance on how the law in this area should develop. In its starkest terms, the basic scholarly debate goes like this: for those who have access to it, reproductive technology exploits women because it reinforces a pronatalist ideology; for those who do not have access to it, reproductive technology provides evidence of privilege, allowing wealthy white women to reproduce themselves; and the mere concept of reproductive technology encourages women to live men's lives.[12] With donor eggs or surrogacy, the process involves the transfer of money from wealthier couples to poor women, who do not freely choose their participation. It is a market transaction that resembles a sale. Indeed, as one legal writer has charged, it is difficult to control the "rapaciousness of U.S. baby consumers."[13] The money and energy spent chasing reproductive technology could be better spent on reforming the child welfare system both here and abroad and paying for basic access to reproductive services for all women.

For example, Elizabeth Bartholet, a professor at Harvard Law School, regrets the years she spent on the "treadmill" of infertility treatment, pursuing yet one more cycle of in vitro fertilization in her desperate hope for a biological child. She believes that the trend toward insurance coverage of IVF is destructive because it will encourage women to continue often-futile treatment. In Bartholet's view, the increasing use of IVF conditions women to want only biological children and renders adoption a rather undesirable option.[14] She suggests that, rather than encourage fertility treatments, as a society we should improve counseling for the infertile so that they understand the risks of various treatments, remove the hurdles in the adoption process, and create incentives to adopt. Although the information that Bartholet provides suggests that these may be important measures, her analysis reflects the notion that women cannot make appropriate reproductive choices because of the strong, socially constructed imperative toward biological childbearing. For example, while mandatory counseling ensures informed consent to undergo invasive medical procedures, it is also paternalistic to impose such a requirement. Ultimately, Bartholet advocates restricting women's options to undergo infertility treatments because she believes that women's decisions to pursue such treatments cannot be freely and validly made.

In this area, Bartholet draws heavily on some feminists' analysis of the new reproductive technologies. Some have suggested a "patriarchal reproduction" position, which fears that women are unable to choose the new technologies voluntarily and that, instead, male doctors simply appropriate women's bodies to produce children.[15] Gena Corea, one of the leading proponents of this perspective, has argued that the concepts of "choice" and "consent" with respect to women's participation in assisted reproduction are artificial on two levels: women's actual understanding of the technology and the patriarchal structuring of women's lives. According to Corea, women are victimized by a society that values them for producing children; they do not choose the new reproductive technologies so much as they are socially coerced to choose. Catharine MacKinnon has made similar arguments with respect to the authenticity of women's voices, emphasizing that women are unable to make valid choices under patriarchy. In other words, infertile women are socialized into wanting biological children, and therefore, the law should foreclose the possibility of choosing the new technologies so that women are not victimized. Bartholet makes a related, and more practical, argument that IVF may eliminate the possibility of parenting because, by the time they have finished their medical treatment, some patients are too old and too exhausted to adopt. She provides no statistics or studies for this conclusion; it appears to be speculation based, perhaps, on her own experiences. In addition, by focusing on reproductive technology and the pressures for biological parenting, or even on the empowering possibilities of adoption, Bartholet leaves unchallenged the more general social discipline on women to become mothers. A celebration of adoptive parenting still does not question a gendered socialization process in which women are expected to become mothers and to perform the appropriate caretaking roles.

Although this "patriarchal reproduction" analysis presents a significant and cautionary perspective, it nonetheless both denies women any agency and reinforces the restrictions on options by income and class. By denying the possibility of choice under existing social conditions, this view treats women as passive victims, disempowered from making their own legal choices concerning the reproductive technologies. Philosopher Karey Harwood, who is concerned about the "overconsumption" of the new reproductive technologies and about the way ART encourages women to delay their childbearing, has nonetheless suggested that "the charge of pronatalism is overly simplistic"[16] and that the focus should shift to how our culture can support caregiving.

Another account is more celebratory, suggesting that reproductive technology allows both traditional and nontraditional families the opportunity to create children. This alternative perspective suggests that women may have helped to shape the new technologies or that women have, at least in some sense, chosen to undergo the risks associated with them. It may even be, as Martha Ertman argues, that women and men change roles when it comes to consumption of donor sperm.[17] That is, men are the mere sperm providers, and women, the discerning consumers who want men only for their bodies. Indeed, although women's experiences are mediated through a culture that reinforces biological motherhood, women may still look to technology as means of empowerment.

The dichotomy between women as victims of technology and women as agents in needing and demanding the technology is false. Instead, while women make choices constructed by and within a social ideology that values childbearing, they are still able to exercise some control over their options within these social constraints. Arguing that women are unable to make their own decisions about reproductive technology reflects an outmoded view of women as dependent, passive creatures, without a corresponding recognition of the context in which these choices are constructed. Instead of taking away options for women, the focus should be on reforming the surrounding social ideology: motherhood at any cost.

A related issue focuses on legal access to reproductive technologies for poor and middle-class women, who have generally been unable to afford this technology. The expense of the new technologies—a single IVF cycle may cost upward of ten thousand dollars—has generally denied poor women even the opportunity to "choose" them; restricting access further essentially prevents poor women from ever being able to use them. Indeed, continuation of existing methods for funding IVF reinforces a situation in which the technology allows only rich white women to bear biological children.

Ironically, antiabortion activists have pursued a similar class-based legal strategy, believing that denying funding for abortion will discourage women from choosing abortion. The impact of such a policy is, however, most clearly felt by poor women, who cannot afford abortions, while middle-class and wealthy women are more easily able to exercise their abortion choices. Likewise, decreased funding for infertility treatment will not affect wealthier women, who will still be able to afford the treatment. As we discuss the parameters of public or private funding for infertility treatments, we must recognize that limiting insurance coverage will affect poorer women and will have a disproportionate effect based on race.

Because reproductive technologies develop and exist as part of a larger culture, they must be evaluated within that context. In general, the notion that women should not have access to the reproductive technologies (or that such technologies should not even be developed) is paternalistic and seems to echo an outdated belief that the infertile do not deserve medical treatment. On the other hand, the medicalization of fertility, pregnancy, and childbirth, and the consequent usurping of a woman's choice not to avail herself of the techniques for motherhood, all raise legitimate fears. As technology becomes more accessible, there is certainly more pressure on women to use it. One challenge, then, is to reconstruct the choices women (and men) confront when they seek to become parents. A second challenge is to add into this discussion the interests of the other participants:

the children who are ultimately produced, the medical profession, and the gamete providers.

This book adopts a feminist perspective on these developments, but as is clear, there is no one feminist approach to fertility. The basics, examining the impact of gender, race, sexual orientation, and class of any particular approach or policy, are a given. Beyond that, however, how to measure those impacts, how to assess those impacts, how to accommodate those impacts, there is no agreement. Consequently, I respect insights from the divergent perspectives within feminism to craft my approach, one that examines the potentially conflicting rights of all involved in the reproductive technology area, of women and men wanting babies, of women willing to provide eggs, men willing to provide sperm, and couples willing to give embryos, of the middle people who facilitate gamete transactions, and of industry representatives, as well as examining the needs of the fertile and infertile and their children.

The book is organized according to three interconnected legal themes: market regulation, parenthood determination, and identity formation. Part 1 of the book has two chapters. The first chapter provides background information on the problematic and complicated status of legal regulation of each of these three areas. By contrast, the second chapter provides a more sociological and psychological approach to the contemporary usage of reproductive technologies, analyzing the meaning of infertility in contemporary culture and its impact on individuals seeking fertility treatment. Part 2 continues to expand on the three themes concerning market, parents, and identity, through four chapters, each of which examines the legal parameters for one set of participants in the reproductive technology world. Chapter 3 explores the technology market, including the fertility clinics and gamete suppliers. Chapters 4 and 5 explore the second set of themes, the different adults involved in technology who might have any legal claim to be parents: the intending parents and the donors. Chapter 6 examines the third theme, the complicated set of issues involved in identity disclosure. Part 3 provides theoretical frameworks for analyzing the three interconnected themes. Chapter 7 examines the structural and cultural barriers to using ART, barriers based on marital status, sexual orientation, and racial and ethnic background. Chapter 8 explores the cost barrier, articulating the jurisprudential and practical issues surrounding the commodification of sperm, eggs, and embryos. Chapter 9 turns to the cultural clashes affecting future regulation of ART, clashes ranging from the potential of ART to challenge the traditional two-parent heterosexual family to the ability of technology to allow parents to engage in prenatal screening. Finally, part 4 sets out recommendations for future regulation, with chapter 10 focusing on the market, chapter 11 on parenthood determination, and chapter 12 on identity claims. These chapters establish a preliminary framework for further regulation of the reproductive technology field, a framework that is sensitive to race, class, and sexual orientation issues and that includes parameters for market transactions, for certainty of parenthood determination, and for mandatory access to identity information.

A final note on terminology: There are a series of linguistic choices that reveal much more than language. Egg and sperm are typically bought and sold. Yet the rhetoric of the fertility markets suggests that gamete providers are engaging in altruistic acts and so refers to egg and sperm "donors." Injecting sperm into a woman's vagina other than through sexual intercourse has generally been called "artificial insemination," contrasting it with the "real" type of insemination. Some have begun to call this process "alternative insemination," attempting to make it more value-neutral. And the children produced through donor gametes remain "donor children," regardless of their age or the fact that parents *always* donate their gametes to their children. They are also called "donor offspring" or "donor-conceived adoptees." Although I use all these terms throughout the book, I carefully considered each of these "linguistic choices" and further discuss their implications in other chapters.

PART I

Initial Conceptions

1

The Treatment Plan for Legal Issues

Sperm

In May 1995, when Brittany Johnson was seven years old, she was diagnosed with an unusual genetic disorder that affects her kidneys.[1] Neither of her parents, Ronald and Diane Johnson, had kidney disorders in their family history. Instead, Brittany inherited the kidney disease from Donor 276, who provided the sperm to California Cryobank that ultimately resulted in her birth.

California Cryobank opened in 1977. Like other early sperm banks, California Cryobank focused on freezing the sperm of men who were considering sterilization, ensuring that the men would be able to have biological children with their partners. But it soon expanded its services to include freezing sperm that could be sold to strangers for artificial insemination. Today, it advertises itself as a leader in sperm banking, offering one of the largest selections of donors; its online donor catalogue is updated hourly. Customers can purchase vials of sperm for $315. The bank exercises strict quality control over its samples and provides a list of diseases for which donors are screened on its website.[2]

In his initial application to become a sperm provider in the mid-1980s, Donor 276 indicated that his mother and his aunt had kidney disease. He also signed an agreement with California Cryobank that stated that his identity would not be disclosed except with a court order based on good cause.[3] Over the next five years, Donor 276 provided 320 vials of sperm to California Cryobank and was paid $35 per visit. Ronald and Diane purchased the sperm that resulted in Brittany's birth in April 1989. Although California Cryobank knew about Donor 276's family history, the bank (for unknown reasons) did not initially provide this information to Ronald and Diane. It was not until the couple tried to get another vial of Donor 276's sperm several years later in order to have a second child that they found out about their donor's medical history. At that point, Cryobank told Ronald and Diane that sperm from Donor 276 was no longer available because of, according to the subsequent deposition of a Cryobank genetic counselor, "new medical information" about the donor.[4] Even after this disclosure, Ronald and Diane trusted California Cryobank enough to purchase sperm from another Cryobank donor, and Diane gave birth to a second child.

But then, Brittany was diagnosed with autosomal polycystic kidney disease. Ronald and Diane tried to get more medical information about Donor 276 to help them care for their daughter. They were able to obtain his initial application, but California Cryobank refused to provide enough information to enable them to get a more complete medical history. Indeed, California law supports the position of Cryobank, providing that any records relating to an insemination can be inspected only with a court order based on good cause for releasing the information.[5] And the Johnsons had agreed to an even stricter limitation when they first obtained the sperm by signing a form in which they acknowledged that the bank would destroy any records concerning the donor's identity, "it being the intention of all parties that the identity of said donor shall be and forever remain anonymous."[6]

Ultimately, the Johnsons sued California Cryobank for fraud, negligence, and breach of contract, claiming that the bank's initial failure to disclose that Donor 276 had a family history of kidney disease had caused their legal injury. During several years of legal proceedings, the Johnsons kept trying to learn the identity of Donor 276, but California Cryobank continued to refuse to disclose it. Finally, the lawyers for the Johnsons believed that they had found Donor 276 themselves, identifying him as "John Doe" in the court records. ("John Doe" often appears in legal proceedings as a fictitious name to protect the identity of the real person.) John Doe never admitted to being Donor 276, however. When the Johnsons' lawyers sought to depose him, asking him questions under oath in a meeting outside the courthouse, both John Doe and California Cryobank objected, claiming that a deposition would violate Doe's right to privacy. Donor 276 grounded his claims of privacy in the contract between the Johnsons and Cryobank, which stated that his identity would not be disclosed, as well as in the California and federal constitutions. California Cryobank also claimed that breaching the confidentiality that had been promised to a sperm provider would decrease the availability of sperm.

The court split the baby. It decided that the absolute prohibition on disclosure in the contract was contrary to public policy, which allowed for disclosure based on "good cause," thereby trumping the anonymity promised in the Johnsons' contract. Although the court recognized a limited constitutional right to privacy under the California constitution, it held that this right does not prohibit disclosure. Under the particular circumstances of the case, however, the court then crafted a compromise and directed that the donor be deposed without revealing his identity.

Johnson is the first case to allow for breach of the promise of confidentiality to a sperm provider. And, so far, it is the only reported case regarding the circumstances under which a sperm donor can be identified. But it is certainly not the last. Consider the following events reported in May 2006. Severe congenital neutropenia is a rare disease that affects one in five million births.[7] So, when five children, all born in Michigan, developed the same disease, physicians searched for what the children had in common. They found that all the children had been "fathered" by the same sperm provider. Mary Ann Brown, who was the director of the sperm bank, explained that there was no way of preventing this situation because, although sperm banks test for common genetic diseases, it is unrealistic to test for all genetically transmitted disorders.[8]

Egg

E.G. and K.M. met in October 1992 and became involved in 1993. Although the two women could not marry each other, they registered as domestic partners in San Francisco the following year.[9] Even before E.G. began her relationship with K.M., she had considered motherhood and had applied for international adoption before deciding to try to become pregnant herself. She continued her efforts toward parenthood once she became involved with K.M. Despite using donor sperm a dozen times and trying in vitro fertilization, E.G. was childless and frustrated.[10]

E.G.'s physician suggested that she consider using K.M.'s eggs, but she was hesitant; she wanted to be the only legal parent, not forced to share any legal responsibilities with anyone else. After numerous discussions with K.M., however, E.G. asked her lover to donate eggs. In March 1995, K.M. signed a standard ovum donation agreement, in which she stated that E.G. "may regard the donated eggs and any offspring resulting therefrom as her own children" and that K.M. would "specifically disclaim and waive any right in or any child that may be conceived."

E.G. gave birth to twins in late 1995. For the next five years, while E.G. and K.M. lived together, they shared parenting responsibilities. The twins even called K.M. "Momma."[11] But when the couple split up, E.G. moved to Massachusetts and cut off K.M.'s relationship with the girls.

K.M. filed a lawsuit in the California courts to establish a parental relationship with the children. Although it was clear that K.M. and the children were emotionally attached, two lower courts found no enforceable legal relationship.[12] They relied on K.M.'s egg agreement form, in which she waived any rights as a parent; the courts analogized her relationship to that of a sperm donor, who would similarly have no parental rights under California law. California's parentage law, which is based on model legislation that is in effect in several other states, provides that an anonymous donor who provides sperm to a physician is not the legal father.[13]

In August 2005, however, the California Supreme Court conferred the legal status of parent on K.M. K.M.'s genetic relationship to the twins was evidence of a mother-child relationship, and, as a parent, any agreement in which she waived parental rights could not be enforced against her. This was unlike the typical sperm-donor case involving an anonymous provider because, in the court's language, "K.M. supplied ova to impregnate [sic] her lesbian partner in order to produce children who would be raised in their joint home."[14]

The court ignored an explicit contract between two women, ultimately basing a parentage decision on actions, genetic relationship, and intent. Contract law typically upholds agreements unless they were the product of fraud or coercion. Nonetheless, the scrambled biological relationships between the two women and the twins resulted in the court's respect for functional parentage over a written agreement. By using language such as "impregnate" to describe K.M.'s egg donation, the court also analogized two lesbians' actions in creating a child to the actions of a man and a woman, coming close to labeling K.M. as the father.

State of ART

For at least one hundred years, women have become pregnant through insemination by "donor" sperm. The sperm donor may be someone known to the woman, or she may have gone to a sperm bank and selected the perfect donor. Sperm bank donors are often promised anonymity by the sperm bank or under state statute.

Artificial insemination is the oldest of the alternative reproductive technologies (ART). Under newer reproductive technologies, women can donate eggs so that other women may become pregnant, and couples can donate embryos. In 2004, the most recent year for which data is available, there were more than fifteen thousand cases of egg embryo donation and more than five thousand babies. As with sperm, recipients can choose donors based on a series of characteristics, ranging from hair color to body build to interests and hobbies. Children created through the new reproductive technologies now have the option of at least eight different "parents": two intending parents; a sperm provider (with a partner); an egg provider (with a partner); and a surrogate (who may have a partner) who carries the egg.

Enhanced by the development of IVF, the gamete provision industry has grown dramatically over the past thirty years. Because the new ARTs enable clinics to transfer eggs and embryos created with both donor sperm and eggs, and because of improved infertility diagnostic techniques, the demand for donor gametes has increased significantly. The distinguishing characteristics of this rapidly developing industry have been secrecy and little regulation. There is only minimal legal oversight over much of these market practices. The economic forces supporting the current lack of regulation are strong and well entrenched. Infertility is an approximately $3–4 billion-per-year business whose participants include surrogate mothers and major drug companies; families using donor gametes are so focused on having a child that their budgets are quite elastic.

Use of someone else's genetic material raises complex legal and public policy issues that touch on technological anxiety, eugenics, reproductive autonomy, identity, and family structure. How should the use of gametic material be regulated? Should recipients be able to choose the "best" genetic material? Should a child ever be able to discover the identity of his or her gamete donor? Who can claim parental rights?

Although these issues are fundamental to the increasing use of alternative reproductive technologies, there are few definitive answers provided by the law, ethics, or cultural norms. Although the law helps in framing the questions to ask about the new reproductive technologies, the lack of legal answers makes these questions especially thorny. Indeed, there is a regulatory void outside of minimal requirements for gametic testing and limited protection against deceptive marketing.

The ethical issues that are intertwined with gamete provision provide context but do not answer fundamental policy questions about how to regulate this area. What makes the use of gametic material so complex and difficult for formulating legal responses is not just its test of our contemporary scientific capabilities but the creation and preservation of life-producing material. Among the serious dilemmas for bioethics are the possibilities of engineering transhumans, humans whose abilities have been genetically enhanced—think Neanderthal v. Modern human. Bioethicists are also worried that we may become trapped by genetic essentialism, a concept that suggests that a person is merely the sum of his or her genes and that the parent-child relationship is primarily genetically, rather than functionally, based.[15]

The possibility of designing families is quite real. Gamete seekers can choose based on the appearance, profession, education, and even voice of the potential donor. The forms that gamete providers must fill out are extremely detailed with respect to their family health histories, and much of this information is disclosed to potential recipients. Sperm providers frequently undergo extensive screening as well as a complete physical examination.[16] Consequently, without fear of legal intervention, gamete seekers can specify race, ethnic ancestry, height, weight, physical build, hand coordination, vision, approximate IQ score, and college grade-point average for egg providers.[17] Cryogenic Laboratories offers the following: "Simply send us a photo of the individual you would hope for your offspring to resemble. Our staff will then rank the resemblance of the donors you've selected."[18] The bank may even be able to offer an audio interview of the providers. Sperm banks report that many of their clients are looking for a good genetic match. According to a study of 148 couples that had used donor eggs or sperm to create their children, almost everyone observed that resemblance was an important consideration.[19] In an HBO television program, Ellen DeGeneres expressed frustration with the process of seeking a sperm donor who looks like her.[20]

Bioethicists provide differing answers to these dilemmas of choosing children's genetics heritage. Many are concerned about interfering with nature. Choosing characteristics in this way has "undertones of eugenics," in the words of Jennifer Lahl, who is the national director of the Center for Bioethics and Culture.[21]

The law provides no definitive answers concerning the ethics of choosing characteristics. Federal law regulates the health of donated tissue, which includes sperm and eggs, by requiring that donors undergo certain tests for diseases such as AIDS, and it requires fertility clinics to report their success rates. Federal law does not otherwise regulate the process in any significant way. It does not preclude the sale of eggs, sperm, or embryos, nor does it even require that clinics minimally verify the veracity of donors' statements concerning their characteristics. Even observers who believe that there are "numerous" legal mandates concerning ART acknowledge the fragmentary nature of the regulation.[22]

A minority of states currently addresses some aspects of the gamete provision process, typically requiring additional donor screening or clinic reporting data, and about fifteen states require insurance coverage for some aspects of infertility treatment and diagnosis. Consequently, gamete donation remains a largely private transaction that is handled through contract and intention with virtually no uniform regulation.

As for legalization of the resulting relationships among donors, parents, and children, states have adopted varying approaches that generally attempt to facilitate transactions in gametes and embryos by allocating parental rights to the intending parents, rather than the gamete providers. However, there are gaps in existing state regulations; not all states address circumstances involving unmarried parents or the use of donor eggs or embryos.[23] Moreover, there is no uniformity among states concerning the laws of gamete donation or surrogacy or concerning the application of parentage statutes to define family relationships established through the reproductive technologies.[24] Thirty-five states have addressed, albeit not fully, the parental rights and responsibilities when gamete provision is involved.[25]

Disputes over gametes can be resolved through either private agreements or public regulation by courts or legislatures. The providers may draft a document setting out their intentions (e.g., a contract) with respect to their interests in gametic material. States may enact legislation establishing either override rules that mandate certain outcomes, such as a prohibition on destruction of the material, or default rules that control in the absence of an expression of contrary intent. Generally, as in the *Johnson* and *E.G.* cases, donors sign an agreement waiving all parental rights and responsibilities with respect to any child conceived from their eggs or sperm,[26] yet as of 2003, only five states had enacted specific legislation assuring the validity of those agreements by assigning parental status after egg donation. Statutes typically provide that a married recipient and her husband are the parents of a child from an egg donation but fail to address legal paternity for children conceived by single women using egg donation.[27] Legally, then, as discussed in chapters 4 and 5, single women may be uncertain about the potential claims of sperm donors.

Donors, recipients, banks, clinics, and physicians have little incentive to push for public regulation that might result in additional restrictions on their activities. Buyers want to buy, donors want to sell, banks want to market—and, as Arthur Caplan, a bioethicist at the University of Pennsylvania, explains, "The doctors don't want regulations. The couples who want the treatments don't want regulations. And politicians don't want to go in and regulate because it puts them right smack in the middle of discussions of things like embryos."[28] Even the occasional highly publicized reproductive snafu involving switched embryos or genetically questionable gametes[29] has not inspired the public to push for legislation. Although there is much more oversight of the industry in other countries, many of them (England, Australia, and France) have government-provided medical care, so the population may be more accustomed to government regulation of its health care. In the United States, unlike those other countries, individual states, rather than the federal government, are primarily responsible for regulating the medical profession and the family law issues posed by ART.[30]

Jurisprudentially, we lack a coherent framework for addressing issues involving human gametic material that unites both the technological and relational aspects of using the material. Gametes differ from other body parts in that their function is to create human life, rather than to sustain it. Much of the existing legal analysis relies on the property/privacy framework, attempting to categorize the material as protected by a property or privacy or "quasi-property" framework.[31] In general terms, privacy protects identity interests and provides freedom from invasion, whereas property protects ownership interests. Reproductive autonomy, such as the right to an abortion, has been categorized within the legal right to privacy. Identifying a property interest in gametes might allow an individual to sell eggs and sperm, while privacy interests might recognize the intending parents' right to familial autonomy, a donor's right to be let alone, or a donor-conceived child's right to know the identity of a donor. This analysis provides useful insights into the sale of gametic material and starts to uncouple genetic connection from parenthood; mere contribution to the creation of an embryo does not necessarily translate into parental rights and obligations.

The property/privacy distinction does not, however, resolve many issues concerning gametic material. There are, for example, conflicting privacy interests in the right of the donor who chooses anonymity, the rights of recipients to keep their use of the material confidential, and the rights of any resulting child to know about his or her donor-conceived state and to discover identifying information about the donor. Indeed, the whole notion of privacy—the right to be let alone—has developed as protection for individuals from state interference. The right of privacy protects against government overreaching and against undue state interference with fundamental personal decisions and beliefs, but it is incidental to the multiple interests involved in gametic donation. Although using a property rubric protects the marketing of gametic material, the law imposes multiple restrictions on other property interests and on the operation of the market in the interests of equity, access, and nonexploitation.

An alternative perspective on families formed through the new reproductive technologies adds the need to focus not just on liberty and equality but also on "relationship and care" and connections among family members.[32] But what happens when a gamete provider's privacy interest conflicts with a connection that a child, or a recipient, would like to establish?

Reproducing Dilemmas

This book focuses on the dilemmas of applying conflicting values to egg and sperm donation, arguing that the law must develop an integrated approach to the otherwise distinct aspects of technology and family, market and relationship. The parameters and appropriateness of the state's role in this context depends on a series of (overlapping) "conceptual categories," to use George Lakoff's terminology.[33] The metaphors that we use to describe these transactions in gametes reveal our actual attitudes and preferences. As an example, eggs and sperm are often sold, yet the most powerful and popular label refers to "donation," a word that is also used for blood and organs provided by third parties. Nonetheless, the places where gametes are stored are "banks," not "facilities" or "charities."

Analyzing these conceptual categories as they apply to the gamete transfer process determines the mode of regulations. If we conceive of gamete donation as a sale, then we will use market-based concepts enforcing private contracts and applying cost-benefits economics analyses; if we consider gamete provision as an altruistic act, then we will use philanthropic concepts that emphasize charitable donations and that are anticommodification; and if we classify it as provision of identity, then we will use family law and constitutional law terminology. None of these conceptions is, in and of itself, satisfactory. Later chapters in this book clarify how to coordinate these three categories to develop a system that respects both the market and the interests of the individuals involved. The book addresses two fundamental issues: market regulation and relational regulation of gamete provision.

As an example of how these two areas overlap, consider the use of "known" versus "anonymous" gamete donors; known donors may have been solicited by the recipients, and their identity is never concealed. The concept of anonymity is both a market and a relational marker. Known donors, who often donate their gametes without receiving any money, may come back and assert parental rights to the child despite an agreement not to do so.[34] In California, egg donors may be able to assert parental rights, regardless of their private contracts.

Without some definitive means of terminating the parental rights of sperm or egg providers, in a contract-based system, there are problems with identified donors who may return to claim rights.[35] In a few states, it may be possible for a known gamete donor to waive parental rights through contract, though the long-term enforceability of these agreements remains doubtful in the absence of a broader legal structure regarding gamete donation.[36] For lesbian mothers, for example, if known sperm donors claim paternity, then the men are often successful, regardless of the existence of a written agreement providing otherwise.[37]

When there is an anonymous donor, by contrast, given the collection practices of many sperm and egg banks, there may be little information available about the potential gamete provider. Individuals may search for information on donors for many reasons, including critical medical information, as in *Johnson,* or for more profound psychological reasons. If and when gamete offspring search, they generally want identifying information about the gamete providers, which may include names. Although not all children will seek this information, it is important to many of them to have the option of accessing it.[38] Children want to know why they have a certain eye color, where their musical talent comes from, whose sense of humor they have. An article in the women's magazine *Redbook* describes the search of one woman who tracked down her sperm-provider father to the OB/GYN office where he practiced medicine. He refused to talk about whether he might have provided the sperm. But, she explained, "it still bothers me. There are a lot of identity issues. Who am I? Who do I take after?"[39] One woman expressed uncertainty about what language to use to describe herself: "I'm unsure about what words to use. Do we refer to ourselves as DI [donor insemination] adoptees: do we say conceived or produced? There is an element of being produced."[40] When I partici-pated on a panel to discuss legal comparisons between adoption and re-productive technology, Bill Cordray, a donor-conception activist, used the term "medically assisted adoptees" to describe his status. Some gamete offspring search crowds, looking for half siblings, knowing that the same sperm donor could have helped in the birth of many children.[41]

There are a few sperm banks, such as the Rainbow Flag Health Services bank, which recruits gay and bisexual sperm donors and which calls itself "A Known Sperm Bank,"[42] that have well-thought-out policies on anonym-ity. As part of its services, the bank asks that the mother contact the sperm donor by the time the child turns one year old; such a requirement may be onerous and cause legal problems, however, particularly if the sperm donor seeks to establish a relationship with the child. Indeed, many sperm providers want to be involved with the resulting children. The Sperm Bank of California has a known-donor/yes program through which do-nors agree to let any resulting children learn their identity when the chil-dren are eighteen years old.[43] Similarly, Pacific Reproductive Services, which describes itself as "lesbian and single-women friendly,"[44] includes in its donor profiles whether the donor has indicated an interest in willing to be known when the child turns eighteen, or at least allowing the child to see a video of him.[45]

In the overwhelming majority of cases involving an unknown donor, however, when children begin searching for genetic information, they will be unable to receive any. Although some banks, such as the California Cryobank, allow for the release of donor information with mutual con-sent,[46] even this process is difficult, as it requires the bank to find the sperm providers many years later. A reporter who tried to track down California Cryobank Donor 5027, whose sperm had been used within the past sev-eral years, was unable to find the donor, even though the bank requests that sperm providers keep the bank apprised of their moves.[47] Donors themselves may be interested in meeting "their children" but may be pre-vented from doing so because of seemingly legal guarantees of anonymity, or because they have not kept all the information about their donations or have received very little useful information.[48]

The anonymity issue presents a series of other dilemmas that concern the relationship between parenting, technology, and markets. In a 2003 Maine case, involving guardianship of a child named I.H., several courts struggled with whether they were required to notify an anonymous sperm donor of the proceeding. Typically, any "parent" must be informed before the court can appoint a guardian, but here, the probate court found that the "biological father" was an unknown sperm donor. The Maine Supreme Court ultimately decided that nothing in Maine law prevented the sperm donor from being called a parent. Nonetheless, the court also decided it would be useless under these circumstances to try to notify "the child's father" of the guardianship proceedings if he was an anonymous donor.[49] The linguistic construct of calling the sperm provider both the "donor" and the child's "father" shows the awkwardness of current approaches to this situation.

In *Johnson, I.H.,* and *E.G.,* the courts had to identify the rights of gamete donors, balancing public policy, children's rights, and privacy rights. In *Johnson,* the court concluded that a private contract could not protect a sperm donor's identity; similarly, the *E.G.* court found that a private contract could not cut off parental rights. In *I.H.,* because of the lack of Maine law in this context, the court was required to apply parental rights notions to an unknown sperm donor.

If sperm is a marketable commodity, then, subject to public policy concerns, private contracts should be enforceable. If sperm is, instead, identity producing, then relationships and connection should be the primary considerations.

In this country, at least, a provider's privacy claims are generally based on promises made in connection with a sale. There are actually two sales transactions: a sperm bank typically pays some money for each ejaculation and, in turn, sells that sperm to the intending parents. A woman can sell her eggs to an in vitro fertilization program for thousands of dollars, and some women may receive tens of thousands of dollars. By allowing the sale of sperm and eggs, we are, in a sense, treating them, and their ultimate "product," as a commodity.[50] The *Johnson* court rejected the donor's claim to a physician-patient privilege because there was no evidence, it asserted, that the donor ever consulted the Cryobank for medical diagnosis and treatment; the donor instead sought merely to make money from the sale of his sperm and was thus not subject to the protections offered by the privilege. Sale of the good did not entitle him to the same privacy rights.

Children for Sale?

It is the thesis of this book that sperm and egg donors are not simply selling "spare" body parts but are instead providing hope to recipients, genetic identity to the resulting children, and profits within the marketplace. Accordingly, this book argues that, notwithstanding the predictions of various law and economics scholars, private regulation has not responded to these competing demands and that the government, at the federal and state level, must regulate the gamete donor process. This regulation must ensure that donors are adequately protected against exploitation, that recipients receive their promised "goods," that children are guaranteed access to their genetic information, and that the market functions efficiently. This does not mean a ban on the sale of gametic material, an issue that is quite contentious. On the one hand, the Ethics Committee of the American Society for Reproductive Medicine has defended payment for eggs, explaining that payment does not discourage the provider's altruistic motivations and also promotes fairness to the providers.[51] On the other hand, the President's Council on Bioethics advocated against the sale of human embryos and, although unwilling to recommend against the sale of eggs and sperm, did not indicate approval of the process.[52] There is, however, no federal legislation concerning the sale of gametic material.

The current lackadaisical approach to legal regulation of the gamete market derives from several sources unique to the reproductive context. First, the historical stigma of infertility—still with us today—has often helped keep the use of other-provided gametes a secret between an individual and her physician. Despite the increasing public attention to the potential use of donor gametes—women over the age of forty-five are highly unlikely to conceive using their own eggs, notwithstanding the births to celebrities over that age, such as Holly Hunter, who gave birth to twins at the age of forty-seven; Geena Davis, who gave birth to twins at the age of forty-eight; or model Cheryl Tiegs, who gave birth to twins at the age of fifty-two—there is virtually no disclosure of whether individuals have actually used their own eggs and sperm to create a baby.

Second, no one in the world of reproductive technology has any incentive to advocate for more openness and regulation, aside from the children, some disgruntled gamete providers, and the occasional unhappy patient. Reproductive technology is a multibillion-dollar business that is thriving on its own terms. Although the number of multiple births in the United States is increasing exponentially, and the industry's self-regulatory organization has adopted guidelines on the number of embryos to be transferred, there is no binding limit on how many embryos can be transferred into a woman's uterus, nor are there any limits on the number of times a man can provide sperm or a woman can provide eggs. Many of us who have used reproductive technology do not want to disturb the machine that has given us our children.

Third, reproductive technology reflects our deepest emotional and biological desires to have a child and touches on highly politicized issues. As evolutionary biology has shown, our genes seek to replicate themselves; and our social and cultural norms reinforce a pronatalist ideology. Reproductive technology has now become enmeshed in highly controversial debates about abortion and stem-cell research, and it raises issues of access based on race and class and family form. Subsequent chapters explore the legal disputes over the parameters of reproductive rights for all.

The secrecy, the lack of incentive to open up the processes, and the fundamental nature of wanting a child provide compelling explanations for the status quo. Nonetheless, I argue that the law must assert more control over the fertility market and the resulting familial relationships in three ways. First, the industry itself needs regulations concerned with the sale of gametes and quality control. Second, although providers may choose to remain anonymous until a child reaches the age of eighteen, at that point, the anonymity should end. Third, the parenting issues need further resolution to ensure the enforceability of private relational contracts that establish who may claim the title of "legal parent."

On the first issue of markets, federal law should regulate the sale of gametes, providing an incentive, but not a bonus, to the producers. Of course, even as we permit eggs and sperm to be sold, there remain additional concerns about the "purveyors" of these "goods" as well as the underlying validity of permitting their sale. Just as in the surrogacy context, the providers may be devaluing themselves[53] (as well as their commodities). Prohibiting the sale of sperm and eggs may be the appropriate response that prevents exploitation and that also acknowledges the significance of providing gametes. Although commodification may be useful conceptually in allaying privacy concerns, I remain concerned about allowing the unfettered sale of these particular commodities. Limiting or even removing the financial incentive may cause donors to embrace more fully the significance of their actions to their offspring.

Second, when it comes to anonymity, there are fundamental legal issues of identity and privacy that must be balanced against the background of ensuring adequate supply of gametic material. In recognition of the potential connection between gamete providers and the recipients and their children, federal and state law should ensure that the identity of each person can be disclosed once a child turns eighteen and that gamete donors update their medical information every five years. States should guarantee the release of such information to mature adults through laws that would preempt private agreements to the contrary (such as between the gamete provider and the intending parents or between the gamete provider and a gamete bank). Although all states have addressed this issue for adoptees, few states have considered legislation on disclosure of the identity of gamete providers.

Even under a system of full disclosure, there remains a distinction between "parenting" a child and contributing to the creation of the child.[54] Parents have a fundamental right to the control, care, and custody of their children;[55] allowing information disclosure to adults respects parental rights to raise children as they see fit while the children are minors but respects the children's rights once they are mature. The rights and interests of biological parents and gamete providers should be accorded respect, but a child should be entitled to receive information about the people who helped to create him or her. Such a right should be established both retroactively and prospectively, such that adult offspring who today want information about their biological backgrounds should be able to obtain it, and prospective adoptions and gamete provision arrangements should proceed in a legal context in which it is understood that offspring will have access to information once they become adults. States need to enact legislation, and courts need to establish precedent for allowing disclosure. Legal scholar Barbara Bennett Woodhouse has suggested, in the context of transracial adoption, the need for a child to be able to "claim her 'identity of origin,' defined as a right to know and explore, commensurate with her evolving capacity for autonomy, her identity as a member of the family and group into which she was born."[56] Applying this notion more generally in the adoption and gamete-provision context, mature offspring in these families similarly need access to the ability to explore their biological families of origin.

Finally, states should adopt legislation specifying the relationships that result from gamete transfer. This means that contracts in which gamete donors waive parental rights must be enforceable. This does not preclude courts from finding that the gamete donor has established the functional relationship of parenthood with any resulting child, but this relationship exists apart from the genetic contribution. Moreover, the intending parent or parents of children produced from gamete transfer should be the only ones who can exercise parental rights.

In developing new legal approaches to the reproductive technology market, it is critical to examine both the technological and the relational aspects of donated eggs and sperm. Regulating the gamete providers, both the individuals and the businesses, is only one component; the relationships between sperm and egg providers, recipients, children, and the state is integrally connected to how we think about the technology.

2

The Treatment Plan for Creating Babies

HOW DO YOU know if the new reproductive technologies are right for you?[1] There is the technical answer: if you are infertile or if, clinically, you need gametes from another person because you are single or gay; and there is the psychological/moral answer: if you are emotionally, mentally, and perhaps spiritually prepared to begin.

The medical definition of infertility applies to a couple that has been trying to conceive and been unsuccessful for six months to one year, depending on their age. But you can find out about your fertility long before one year. Walk into any drugstore and, next to the pregnancy tests, a woman can buy an ovulation predictor kit to help her know what time of the month is her most fertile. There are multiple Internet sites, such as storknet.com or fertilitynetwork.com, that help a woman measure her basal body temperature, another indicator of fertility.

In 2007, Genosis, a British company, began marketing a new product, Fertell, in the United States. Its launch was heralded in the *New York Times* under the not entirely complete headline "With New Test, Men Can Have At-Home Fertility Screening"[2]—Fertell helps women too. The first FDA-approved home fertility test, Fertell contains two kits, one that tests the quality of a woman's eggs and another that tests the motility of a man's sperm. Unlike visits to reproductive endocrinologists, which may cost hundreds of dollars (even if the initial consultation is free), Fertell costs under one hundred dollars. It advertises that results are available within ninety minutes. According to Genosis, the company is hoping to tap into the more than eighty million couples worldwide that may have problems conceiving, positioning Fertell as providing "early confirmation" of an individual's fertility; "convenience, economy and privacy"; the "ability to ease the psychological stress and reduce anxiety" associated with the uncertainty of fertility; and "control" without the intrusion of an infertility expert.[3]

Regardless of what Fertell tells you, you may want additional advice. For that, you can browse Amazon.com or walk into any bookstore to the self-help section, or even to the parenting and childbirth section, to look for books on infertility. Through a web search, the interested user can find books on many different aspects of infertility, can look at lists on infertility books that others have compiled, and can see that other consumers have continued their searches by purchasing books on fertility and pregnancy or adoption. In a bookstore, these books may be harder to find: they can nestle up beside books on breastfeeding, on autistic children, on addictions to food or to sex. There is a pattern in the titles of advice books on infertility: *Conquering Infertility, Infertility Survival Handbook, The Fertile Female: How the Power of Longing for a Child Can Save Your Life and Change the World, Taking Charge of Your Fertility, Choosing Single Motherhood, Fertility for Dummies,* and *Having Your Baby through Egg Donation.*

Many of the books suggest what they call a proactive approach to diagnosis and treatment, which encourages a woman to diagnose her condition, manage and chart her treatment, and continue to read more self-help books. Many of these books will tell her that she can help to change the condition that she herself will define: she can begin with "home remedies" like having her husband wear boxer shorts instead of more restrictive jockey shorts, and she can, as recommended by several books published in 2005 and 2006, use traditional Chinese medicine to help her enhance her inner harmony and control her hormones. She can learn about "fertility foods" in a 2006 book by Jeremy Groll and Lorie Groll, or, using a 1999 book published by Peanut Butter and Jelly Press, she can attempt to follow the demands of the Infertility Diet. For exercise, she can purchase the DVD for Fertility Yoga. And to help her find humor about a situation that may have her frequently bursting into tears as her body fails to respond to various treatments, she can read *Laughin'fertility.* Online, customer reviews and comments contain testimonials to the utility of each of these various measures.

Should the self-diagnostic remedies fail, the books and chatrooms can help her find the most qualified doctor, the clinic with the best success rate for one of up to a dozen different high-tech treatments and variations on treatment: IVF, AID (artificial insemination by donor), ICSI (intracytoplasmic sperm injection), and so on. The woman will be told that she must learn statistical analysis and relearn the alphabet so that she can understand all the possible treatments. And she can also learn about the promises and pitfalls of using donor eggs and gametes.

The books will be cautiously optimistic. If the reader flips to the end of each, she will see that most of them conclude with chapters about adoption and/or learning to live "childfree." But none of them begins this way. Almost all of them start with descriptions of the relatively uninvasive procedures and move toward an increasingly elaborate, expensive, and technological menu of treatment choices. If the woman reads chronologically, she might begin to get a sense of impending doom, of increasing complication. She might hope that her infertility story will end with chapter 1 and with the early diagnostic test of a hysterosalpingogram (HSG), which is described as causing only mild discomfort and which involves x-rays being taken as a dye is inserted through her vagina into the uterus.

The more that she reads, the more familiar she will become with the books' tone, with their emphasis on her choice, her responsibility. Most of them will acknowledge that she, not a male partner, will be the primary treatment manager. Indeed, so absent are the male partners in this world that the 2007 annual meeting of the American Society for Reproductive Medicine included a course for health-care professionals titled "Men and Art: The Missing Voice."

The books will suggest that infertility treatment is indeed a maze but that she will, she must, learn her way around it if she is to be rewarded with a biological child. She will be told that the primary site of diagnosis, treatment, and management will probably be her body. She will be taught new words about her body, names for parts she has never heard of but might soon see on a screen or a diagram.

And she will be encouraged by the information about the possibilities of the new reproductive technology. Usage of ARTs is increasing. Indeed, the number of IVF cycles has more than doubled since 1996, as table 2.1 shows, and transfers are increasingly likely to result in live births for all kinds of cycles. In 2005, there were 134,260 ART cycles, with 38,910 live-birth deliveries and 52,041 babies born, and the success rates for the different types of IVF cycles are tantalizingly high, as shown in table 2.2.

All this reading, all this learning, will be framed in the idiom of control. The woman will be told that the more she reads and the more she finds out about her condition, the more likely it is that she will become pregnant. She will be told that she can "overcome" infertility, "overcome" the odds, "overcome," in many cases, her own reluctance to proceed further with treatment and into the infertility maze. She will read over and over again that she can put up with discomfort; with pain; with interrupted work days, weeks, and years; with a mechanical sex life; with obsessively

Table 2.1

Increasing Use of ART

	ART Cycles	Live-Birth Deliveries	Infants Born
1996	64,681	14,507	20,840
1997	72,397	17,186	24,785
1998	81,438	20,126	28,851
1999	87,636	21,746	30,629
2000	99,629	25,228	35,025
2001	107,587	29,344	40,687
2002	115,392	33,141	45,751
2003	122,872	35,785	48,756
2004	127,977	36,760	49,458
2005	134,260	38,910	52,041

Source: U.S. Department of Health and Human Services, Centers for Disease Control and Prevention, *2005 Assisted Reproductive Technology Success Rates: National Summary and Fertility Clinic Reports* (2007): 61 (table 49).

Table 2.2

	Total Number[a]	Percentage of All Cycles	Success Rate
Nondonor IVF cycles—fresh	97,442	72.4%	34.3%
Nondonor IVF cycles—frozen	20,657	15.3%	28%
Donor IVF cycles—fresh	10,620	7.9%	52.3%
Donor IVF cycles—frozen	5,541	4.1%	30.9%

[a] New treatment procedures constituted 0.3 percent of (358) cycles.

Source: U.S. Department of Health and Human Services, Centers for Disease Control and Prevention, *2005 Assisted Reproductive Technology Success Rates*, Figures 2, 42, 48 (2007), available at http://www.cdc.gov/art/ART2005/index.htm.

reviewing catalogues of donor profiles and synchronizing intimate bodily functions with those of a stranger; and with financial sacrifice. She will learn to put up with these things because these are choices: she will have chosen these things in the name of a greater, a canonical, reproductive choice: the choice to become pregnant.

Choice and control are recurring themes in infertility definition, diagnosis, and treatment. If initially a diagnosis of infertility would seem to move a woman out of what has traditionally been the culture of reproductive choice, the popular discourse of infertility implicitly promises to reinstate choice under the sign of its sister term, control. The popular treatment accounts, which draw on self-help theories, offer the potential of liberation because they posit women as agents of change in controlling their own fertility, making the necessary changes in their lives. Browsing these accounts in hard copy or online, the reader is comfortingly and tantalizing lulled into thinking, "If only I can eat brown rice everyday, and visualize healthy ovaries, then I too will become pregnant, just like the author." And there is always more to read and discuss. A Google search in August 2007 for "infertility chat room" yielded almost 1.5 million results. The burgeoning field of Repro Lit helps provide even more community.[4]

The discourse of control within infertility treatment is doubly paradoxical. Ultimately, the discourse of autonomy, which appears to create the potential for liberation, instead reiterates the theme of confining and blaming women for failing to have children by making it women's fault for being unable to conceive or for not realizing, until it was too late, that they wanted a child. And the paradox of reproductive choice has yet another twist: as mentioned in chapter 1, apart from the politics of eugenics and sterilization, the history of reproductive control has paid scant attention to facilitating women's options to become pregnant, focusing instead on women's options not to become pregnant or on how to manage children, once they are born, with the rest of a woman's life.

Infertility is famously one of the few "self-diagnosed" medical conditions. Although it is usually suggested that one should not seek treatment for infertility until after one year of unprotected intercourse, infertility manuals are quick to point out that, especially for women over thirty-five, it is the couple (and usually, in practice, the woman) who decides when to take on the label "infertile." The manuals, then, imagine diagnosis in the context of individual choice; an individual can decide to be—that is, to identify as—infertile or not. Moreover, the manuals suggest that individuals within couples often identify differently with respect to infertility.

These varying instructions about when to consider oneself infertile are helpful in that they provide a great deal of latitude for self-definition; yet they also create even more pressure to make the correct self-diagnosis while providing conflicting guidance on how to do so. The omnipresent story is that women should be able to evaluate, and then to control, their own reproductive capabilities and that, if they do not, they are, in part, to blame.

The specific diagnostic tests and treatments that a woman will learn about, once she moves beyond diet, visualization, and yoga will probably begin with the various evaluations of her reproductive system to make sure that her hormonal levels are appropriate and that her reproductive organs are functioning. Approximately 25 percent of infertility is due to a woman's problems with ovulation (egg production); another 35 percent is due to structural factors, such as closed fallopian tubes; and then there is the possible diagnosis of "unexplained infertility," when egg and sperm production do not display any problems.

The first treatment option may be Clomid, perhaps the most commonly used fertility drug, which is a pill that stimulates the ovaries to produce eggs on a more consistent basis. Clomid may be enough. Peggy Orenstein describes Clomid as "my gateway drug; the one you take because, why not—everyone's doing it. . . . Just five tiny pills."[5] If Clomid does not work, then a woman will learn about stronger hormones that stimulate the production of more eggs. These drugs, marketed as Follistim or Luveris or Repronex, must be injected throughout the first phase of a woman's menstrual cycle and are followed by another shot designed to trigger the release of the eggs. These stronger drugs may be used with either inseminations or, more commonly, IVF. There may be more shots after ovulation to support the uterine lining and make sure it is hospitable to implantation and, hopefully, the growing embryo, and then a pregnancy test ten to fourteen days after ovulation.

Although sperm problems (or "male factor") is the partial or complete explanation for infertility in approximately 40 percent of all infertile couples, there are fewer diagnostic tests and treatment options. The process generally begins with a semen analysis to determine the quantity and quality of sperm; the quality is assessed by looking at movement and shape (motility and morphology). If there is no physical obstruction to sperm production, then treatment consists of either intrauterine insemination (IUI) or, if the couple is undergoing IVF, then insertion of a single sperm into the egg (ICSI). Third-party reproduction—using another person's egg, sperm, embryo, or, for surrogacy, body—is generally the last treatment option.[6]

For some people, of course, the decision of whether to engage with the new reproductive technologies is not a choice. Gay men must find a source for eggs, and a woman to carry any resulting embryo. Single women and lesbians must find sperm. These women may need to delve further into the infertility literature if, after several months of "trying" with various forms of insemination, they do not become pregnant. Consequently, another set of books goes beyond medical infertility to help single women or gay men and lesbians decide what forms of reproductive technology are appropriate. Although medical infertility may also be a problem, clearing a single woman's fallopian tubes will not help her conceive unless she has access to sperm, nor does information on infertility help a gay male couple hoping to have a child. Books such as Brett McWhorter Sember's

Gay and Lesbian Parenting Choices: From Adopting or Using a Surrogate to Choosing the Perfect Father (2006), the *New Essential Guide to Lesbian Conception, Pregnancy, and Birth* by Stephanie Brill (2006), and Mikki Morrissette's flatteringly titled *Choosing Single Motherhood: The Thinking Woman's Guide* (2006) provide guidance and resources on various aspects of structural infertility with the same theme of enabling potential parents to take charge of their reproductive lives.

The label "infertile" signifies in a very specific way in relationship to class. Since infertility treatment is extremely costly and only rarely covered by insurance, self-labeling as infertile is medically meaningless for a large percentage of the population. Infertility manuals rarely comment on the class implications of self-diagnosis. Although many of them take up the problem of finances, they do so, perhaps predictably, *within* the idiom of choice; paying for infertility treatment is acknowledged to be difficult, but only in the context of the redistribution of family resources.

Infertility itself, of course, has no class boundaries, notwithstanding stereotypes of "welfare moms" with dozens of children and college-educated women with few or none. The infertility epidemic appears to respond to the dilemmas of white middle-class couples that have put off childbearing until after both partners have established careers, rather than to the needs of infertile people throughout the population. Indeed, there is some speculation that poor women have a higher rate of infertility than wealthier women because of their inadequate access to medical care that might prevent sexually transmitted diseases and other causes of infertility. Indeed, many causes of female infertility stem from problems with access to medical care.[7] For example, if sexually transmitted diseases such as chlamydia or gonorrhea are not properly treated, they can lead to cervical infertility, a condition that prevents the sperm from passing through the mouth of the uterus because of cervical damage. Almost a quarter of all people with annual incomes under twenty-five thousand dollars do not have health insurance (23.5 percent), whereas less than 10 percent of people with annual incomes over seventy-five thousand dollars do not have health insurance (8.2 percent).[8] It is reasonable to conclude that lack of insurance coverage precludes people from receiving proper medical instruction and care, which, in turn, results in higher rates of infertility. Nonetheless, the historical rates of infertility have not changed; it is as older women have begun having children that infertility has become an increasingly public and tortured issue.

Infertility diagnosis and treatment are expensive; the bill for a basic postcoital test can be several hundred dollars. Clomid costs about thirty-five dollars per cycle, not including doctors' visits or inseminations. For the drugs leading to higher increases in the number of eggs, such as Repronex, the cost can be fifty dollars per ampule; a woman may spend somewhere between two and five thousand dollars per cycle just for the drugs, assuming no insurance coverage. In addition, there is often daily monitoring, including ultrasounds, which significantly increases the expense. As a result, the full range of infertility treatments is accessible to very few people in this country.

Consequently, the primary audience for infertility guides is the economically privileged. Books almost invariably target people with at least a middle-class income; poor people have no place in these books. Many of the infertility books include class-specific images:

> "I would advise every couple to have a 'what are your limits conversation' right at the start," says forty-two year old Laura, married to Evan for seven years, and finally pregnant with IVF twins.
>
> After much cajoling on Laura's part, Evan finally admitted that it was paramount to him to have his own biological child and he was willing to spend up to $100,000 to achieve that goal. . . . The couple put a second mortgage on their house, borrowed the rest from their parents, and began intensive fertility treatments.[9]

In this vignette, and later in the same 2005 book, we learn a great deal about class. First of all, Evan and Laura have a house on which they can take out a second mortgage and parents with enough disposable income that they can lend the couple the money that they need. Second, Laura is a lawyer who intends to become a stay-at-home mother when their babies are born, so presumably Evan, who is a wine salesman, earns enough to support a family of four. At this point, prior to the babies' births, they are a DINK: double-income, no-kids couple. Third, they have been married for seven years. Fourth, Laura seems to have relatively easy access to a doctor and a fairly flexible work schedule given the intensity of the infertility work-up and IVF process.

Each of these factors is a class marker. People with a college education earn more than those with less education. Access to decent medical care increases by class: from the brief description, the couple is not concerned about paying off their debts. Considering the possibility of being able to spend a hundred thousand dollars requires a certain class position.

Notwithstanding this pervasive image of upper-middle-class infertile couples, money is an important topic in the infertility books. Money buys choices in infertility treatment. Several of the guides note that money is one of the most common causes of stress for infertile couples. But money in these books is itself imbricated in the idiom of class and choice: it always appears in the context of decisions about how to allocate it, or how to get insurance coverage, rather than in the context of what can be done without it. Some clinics even offer money-back guarantees. Perhaps most pervasive is the idea of infertility treatment as a consumer object for which high-ticket items must be exchanged or sacrificed or for which other savings may be exchanged. *What to Do When You Can't Get Pregnant* provides advice for when you "plan to pay for your treatments with money you and your partner have carefully stashed away or borrowed" and tells the story of Cesar and Christine, who "had quite a lot of money saved, needed a new home and car, but ultimately decided to "tr[y] again.""[10] In *Having Your Baby through Egg Donation*, authors Ellen Glazer and Evelina Sterling note that one egg-donation cycle can cost between twenty thousand and thirty thousand dollars and then warn that "once you start, it is very easy to get caught up in all the reproductive technologies that are available. You may say to yourself after some unproductive cycles, you just spent $50,000, what's another $10,000 or $20,000?"[11] What indeed!

Class also becomes explicit in the context of access to infertility treatment for the poor. Whereas choices concerning treatment for the comparatively wealthy are made privately, through insurance coverage or other personal financial limitations, the fertility choices of poor people are publicly marked and discussed. In April 1994, *Newsweek* reported that almost twenty states had provided funding for infertility drugs through the state Medicaid programs. In New Jersey, where women on public welfare received no additional money for additional children, the state nonetheless funded infertility treatment for welfare recipients. *Newsweek* claimed that this financial support raised the following questions: "Is every woman entitled to bear a child, even if she can't afford to raise one? Can the government deny people the chance to have children, simply because they are poor?"[12] More than a decade later, these questions remain. For example, at theangrypharmacist.com blog, there are numerous complaints concerning the efforts of people on public welfare to use infertility drugs.[13]

Having children is depicted as an opportunity, a choice that can be restricted based, initially, on one's own fertility and then on one's own finances. Class becomes significant to both the definition and treatment of infertility, and it serves to restrict one's options for a "cure." Class is not, of course, the only factor that is significant to the choices surrounding infertility. Poor infertile women are considered financially irresponsible for seeking to have additional children; but all infertile women are signified as responsible when it comes to their inability to have children.

Once infertility is created as a woman's responsibility, the next step is the placing of the causes of infertility on women. The concept of women's responsibility for causing infertility appears, again, in a series of texts as well as in a set of myths that establish women's control while they, simultaneously, blame women for not having done the right thing.

The myth that infertility is due to a woman's decision to have a career and defer childbearing occurs in two distinct locations: in discussions about the contemporary infertility crisis and in speculation about the type of woman who is infertile or voluntarily childless. Discussions of the contemporary infertility crisis claim that women have deferred childbearing for too long and are now paying the price. Here, too, the paradox of choice reappears in the image of women who choose to have careers and defer childbearing, in the midst of a culture that fostered this choice but then, later, blamed the women for having made this choice.

More women made this particular choice as the liberating potential of the Pill and the promise of workplace equality encouraged middle-class women increasingly to enter the workforce over the past several decades (poor women have always worked at much higher percentages). These same women also appeared to have increasing control over their fertility. Until enactment of the Pregnancy Discrimination Act in 1978, becoming pregnant could, legitimately, be the basis for a reduction in benefits or, worse, could jeopardize a woman's job. The Pill, of course, allows women to have sex without the risk of pregnancy; it is a medicine that simultaneously gives women more control over their bodies and encourages a focus on *contra*ception, rather than on conception.

All these advances by women have triggered a cultural anxiety about maternity. Our culture has discovered an "infertility epidemic" of crisis proportions, allegedly caused by a delay in (women's) childbearing. The choice of career over motherhood has become sinister. At the same time, there is a solid scientific basis for this concern over women's fertility; striking the right balance in providing information without blaming has proven quite difficult, as is clear from the discussion in chapter 1 about the publicity surrounding the image of the hourglass/baby bottle.

Although the term "biological clock" refers, in scientific terms, to various physiological systems, including sleep rhythms, in the public mind, it most commonly refers to a fertility clock, the appropriate time for women and men to have children. As women age, they have fewer eggs and the egg quality of the remaining eggs is lower, and they have a diminished response to fertility medications; they also have a higher rate of miscarriage. There are diagnostic blood tests to measure a woman's "ovarian reserve," a sign of her potential ability to conceive. Doctors have even developed a computer program designed to predict a woman's remaining years of fertility.

Consider Cara Birrittieri's 2005 book, *What Every Woman Should Know about Fertility and Her Biological Clock.* The book promises to help women in their planning for children, marriage, and a career. Although the author acknowledges that this goal is unrealistic, she hopes that she can help women plan to have children at a younger age but warns, "The relentless clock will continue to tick, while countless numbers of you, due to life circumstances, will be unable to start a family in time."[14] She observes that most women do not know enough about their own fertility and suggests that the medical profession is somewhat complicit because of its reluctance to discuss private issues, such as planning for a family.[15] Ironically, as discussed in the introduction, publicity about women's aging ovaries may be deemed antiwoman.

When women do obtain information about their fertility, they often express anger and betrayal. Martha Stewart's daughter Alexis explained in a 2007 interview with *People* magazine that she figured she would be pregnant after a couple of months of trying but that she has now "learned a few things" about women's fertility. "Take all these movie stars we see on magazine covers who are having babies in their 40s. . . . a fertility doctor . . . [will] tell you bluntly, 'It's not her egg.' But no one says that in these articles."[16] Instead, there is almost a cover-up of the use of reproductive technology, keeping secrets lest the twinned stigmas of age and infertility are revealed.

Being unaware of declining fertility is part of the narrative for many older women who use donor eggs or sperm, according to a study of seventy-nine couples that was published in 2006. As part of the effort of the study's authors to understand how women viewed their "old eggs," they found that many women were upset that they had not learned all the facts about their age-related decline in fertility and often took it upon themselves to educate other women about the relationship between age and fertility.[17] The study identified two different ways in which women who had used donor eggs thought of themselves: they were either "eleventh-hour moms," women who were shocked and felt cheated that their fertility was declining so quickly, or "miracle moms," who were delighted at the ability of medical technology to allow them to give birth using someone else's eggs, even though their own eggs were old.[18] There is so much emphasis on women controlling their fertility by preventing conception that controlling fertility to enhance conception receives scant attention. As a legal reflection of these issues, most states have enacted laws affecting contraception, whether it be through restrictions on abortion, protecting adolescents by limiting access to birth control, or promoting abstinence education, but have enacted few regulations concerning infertility education, insurance, or marketing tactics.

PART II

The State of ART

3

Market Regulation

IN JUNE 2007, viewers of the soap opera *The Bold and The Beautiful* watched as characters struggled with a case of "scrambled eggs." In July 2006, viewers of the soap opera *Days of our Lives* learned that vials of eggs had been switched in a fertility clinic, so the wrong sperm fertilized the wrong egg. Is this just the stuff of soap operas, or is it real life?

For anyone seeking sperm, there are thousands of possibilities. In the United States alone, there are dozens of sperm banks in a business that accounts for about $75 million per year.[1] Consumers can let their fingers do the walking online, all in the privacy of their own home. You can search for banks that provide differing levels of screening, that comply with applicable state regulations, that provide videos, that ship frozen sperm in special canisters, or that offer particular donor characteristics. There is even a site that will help you do the shopping so that you do not have to search each website yourself. Although frozen-egg banks are relatively new, there are countless means for finding egg providers, ranging from special matching services that are part of larger fertility clinics to stand-alone options. And the number of physicians offering assisted reproductive services has increased exponentially. The main trade group, the Society for Assisted Reproductive Technology, reports that it has 392 member practices within the United States that offer reproductive technology services, accounting for more than 95 percent of all fertility clinics.[2]

So what guarantees do you have about the safety of sperm that you buy? The eggs that you use? The success rate of the fertility clinic that you choose? Or even that the embryo created with your egg and your partner's sperm is the embryo that will be transferred into your body? The answer, somewhat shockingly, is very little. In one of the only studies to look at quality of sperm from commercial providers, Douglas Carrell and his coauthors found that more than a quarter of the participating sperm banks could be providing "suboptimal" sperm.[3] And researchers at New York University published a study in 2006 finding that egg donors frequently understated their weight. The authors looked at charts for more than three hundred patients and then compared the weight that donors reported when they first came to the clinic with the donors' actual weights at their first physical exams, concluding that "donors do not give accurate measurements of their body weight."[4] Yet there are no requirements that clinics verify the information submitted by donors; the only federal requirements concern the safety testing of the gametic material.

Although reproductive technology is today a multibillion-dollar business, the amount of state and federal oversight of any of the participants is limited, as is the amount of self-regulation. In regulating the use of sperm and egg donation, there are two distinct sets of legal issues: first, what are the laws that should govern the provision and use of this material? and, second, what is the resulting relationship between donors, recipients, and the child? Although there is some overlap between these issues—a provider who signs up with a bank might be legally required to undergo counseling and to agree to be contacted once any child reaches a certain age—this chapter focuses on the first issue of market regulation, examining the laws that apply to providers and intermediaries; the next chapter addresses relational regulation issues, such as how to define "parent."

There has been comparatively little regulation of the market from external and internal sources until the past several decades. The lack of market oversight has repeatedly been traced to the comparatively limited use of the technology until the 1980s, as well as the contested nature of the technology's relationship to parenthood and other social issues. The technologies and their uses have radically changed and expanded over the past several decades, with, for example, commercial sperm banks supplanting doctor-chosen sperm and the increasingly successful use of donor eggs. Many of the controversies in this area have appeared, and have been temporarily resolved, outside the law: in doctors' offices, in scientific advances, or in philosophical inquiries. It may well have been appropriate, as one legal scholar suggested, "to allow non-legal institutions such as 'science' or 'medicine' to be the primary forum for policy debate and resolution,"[5] particularly in light of the secrecy surrounding individuals' use of the technology and the legal consequences of coming forward. The current status of regulation also reflects differing cultural views not just of technology but also of family forms and the embryo itself. Finally, as this chapter argues, most market participants have had no incentive to advocate for further regulation, and the aura of secrecy attached to using reproductive technology has further inhibited participants from seeking controls.

Market regulation can be both internal and external. Internal regulation refers to supply and demand—what consumers want and providers sell—and also includes efforts at self-regulation within the industry; external regulation refers to governmental efforts to exert control. Both forms of regulation have been quite limited. Until the mid-1980s, the market for sperm was very small; clinics that performed artificial insemination rarely used sperm other than the husband's. Donor sperm was typically provided by friends or family of the recipient and did not involve payment to the donor, and doctors did not frequently counsel patients to use donor sperm. As infertility physician Barry Verkauf explained in 1966, the medical literature contemplated only three uses for donor sperm: when the husband was infertile (Verkauf assumed a married couple), when children had died from Rh incompatibility, and when the husband had a heredity disease that should not be passed on to the children.[6]

Professor Gaia Bernstein has suggested that, in examining the acceptance of a new technology, it is important to distinguish between three different aspects: first, the technology itself, that is, what it actually does; second, its cultural implications, in this case, the ability to create families outside heterosexual intercourse; and third, how the technology is actually used, for example, with respect to who has access to it and what types of families are created. As Bernstein points out, understanding the workings of the technology itself does not explain how it becomes—or does not become—accepted; an appreciation of the technology must be supplemented by an examination of the social and legal forces affecting the acceptance of the technology.[7] With respect to artificial insemination, it was not, Bernstein argues, the technology's usage in resolving infertility, but its social implications—a threat to the traditional, biological family—that has fundamentally affected its acceptance.[8] Her observations provide background to the complexities of policy choices concerning sperm and egg donation and, taken together with an analysis of the economics of the infertility industry and an understanding of the biological and emotional dimensions of having a child, provide a perspective on the contemporary regulation of the fertility market. To understand the paucity of legal regulation, and the need for new laws, this chapter provides an overview of the development of the fertility industry.

Donating to History

Artificial insemination has a long history that predates Anton Van Leeu-wenhoek's description of sperm in 1677. The idea that a woman could be impregnated outside of the act of intercourse was known as early as the second century, and there are stories of an Arab sheik who, in the four-teenth century, used artificial insemination to weaken the bloodline of his enemy's horses.[9] The first recorded artificial insemination of a woman occurred in 1785, when Dr. John Hunter impregnated the wife of a Lon-don linen merchant with her husband's sperm.[10] Another hundred years passed before Dr. William Pancoast performed the first artificial insemina-tion using donor sperm, the sperm of someone besides the patient's own husband, in 1884.[11] In that particular case, the woman never knew that she had been inseminated by a stranger's sperm. Even if the husband had consented, artificial insemination by a donor was somewhat scandalous, because it might expose the woman to a charge of adultery.

Although artificial insemination was almost certainly used by small numbers of women throughout the late nineteenth century and early twentieth century, it was not until the 1930s that it received significant publicity. Articles appeared in the popular press in greater numbers dur-ing this time, but, according to Gaia Bernstein, "the reports . . . were not limited to informative accounts of the procedure, [and] included intimi-dating references to the possible eugenic effects of the technology and po-tential legal difficulties."[12] For example, a 1943 article in *Newsweek* maga-zine reported on the plans of the National Research Foundation for the Eugenic Alleviation of Sterility to repopulate Europe. According to Dr. Frances Seymour, the medical director of the foundation, women would be inseminated with sperm donated by "superior men . . . [which offers] the only positive hope of improving racial quality." To support its claims about the viability of this method, the foundation reported that more than nine thousand babies had already been born in the United States through artificial insemination.[13]

A series of events in the 1940s served to overcome these scare tactics, however. The devastation of World War II starkly emphasized the problem of infertility in the minds of many Europeans and Americans as the me-dia emphasized the need to repopulate their countries.[14] At the same time, according to Bernstein, "advances in the parallel technology of birth con-trol" and a liberalization of social norms (in part because of the increasing number of women in the workforce) combined to create both greater acceptance and greater demand for artificial insemination.[15]

Until 1949, sperm generally had to be freshly collected shortly before the insemination. In that year, scientists discovered that glycerol, a colorless sugar alcohol, could be mixed with sperm to protect it from damage during freezing and the subsequent thawing.[16] Scientists continued to work on the freezing technique over the next several decades. At first, this new technology was seen primarily as an aid to animal (rather than human) husbandry, and the use of frozen sperm for human insemination was not yet a commercial proposition.[17] This may have been because producing fresh sperm for inseminations when a husband was involved was generally not too difficult, the use of donor sperm remained highly secret, and donors (typically medical students) were easy to attract. In 1948, the influential physician and lawyer Alfred Koerner, who was the executive secretary to the National Research Foundation for Fertility, wrote one of the first articles in a law journal addressing donor insemination. He observed,

> The tastes and mental level of the family group into which the artificially inseminated child is to come must be carefully considered. It would be disastrous to place an artistically inclined child into the home of a hard-headed businessman. Controlling one-half of the genes, the physician or surgeon must choose the donor for the mental qualities most likely to be salutary to the group. The I.Q. of the donor should be high so that he may bring to the family group mental qualities of a high order. As has been said so often, the donor should be a man who has demonstrated the effects of a favorable genealogy, salutary environment and superior mental capacity.[18]

What is striking about this passage to us today is, of course, both the assumptions concerning eugenics so characteristic of this era and the presumption that the physician, rather than the recipients, had the right to choose the appropriate donor. Koerner also noted that it was important for the recipient woman to trust her physician to choose the right donor as well as not to disclose her use of donor sperm.[19] This need for complete confidence in physicians typifies other commentary from the same time period.

Although the first insemination of a woman with frozen semen was performed in 1953,[20] its successful use was not reported until the eleventh International Congress of Genetics in 1963, and the first wave of sperm banks finally opened in the 1970s.[21] When sperm banks first appeared, they were far more likely to sell only to physicians, rather than directly to the patient-recipients.[22] According to a 1977 survey undertaken by the University of Wisconsin, most physicians were choosing donors themselves, not using sperm banks.[23]

By the late 1980s, more than four hundred sperm banks were in operation.[24] Yet banks still sold their wares primarily to doctors; in 1987, 60 percent of sperm banks in a federal survey claimed that they would sell only to doctors, and none would sell only to recipients.[25] According to the same survey, physicians wanted to continue their practices. When they were asked about potential involvement of different organizations in quality assurance, two-thirds believed that the role of federal public health authorities should remain the same, and more than half believed that the role of the courts should be eliminated.[26] On the other hand, virtually all were in favor of national standards for screening donors and recordkeeping.[27] They generally believed that professional standards were adequate to protect donors' privacy, but 40 percent thought they were inadequate to protect against physician liability.[28]

Sperm banking became increasingly patient-oriented throughout the 1980s. In a series of articles for *Slate* magazine, journalist David Plotz credits the Repository for Germinal Choice (also known as the "Nobel Sperm Bank"), created in the late 1970s, with transforming the sperm-banking business by requiring rigorous testing and providing increasing amounts of information to consumers.[29] Other banks began offering the same services, and the AIDS epidemic added more incentives for additional safety tests.[30]

Fertile Appearances

Using donor sperm facilitated a couple's appearance of fertility. Unlike adoption, which, although surrounded by secrecy, involved legal procedures and multiple parties outside the newly formed family, using donor sperm simulated the expected familial relationships. In a 1964 book, Dr. Wilfred Finegold, the head of the Division of Sterility at the Planned Parenthood Center in Pittsburgh, explained the advantages of artificial insemination: "The husband's infertility is a secret in A.I. To his friends, the husband has finally impregnated his wife. . . . In A.I., the child is never told."[31] The donor's characteristics should be, he observed, similar to those of the husband's, and the two men must be of the same religion.[32] Further,

Finegold explained that "all" physicians require an anonymous donor and listed a series of precautions for preserving the sperm provider's anonymity.[33] Even today, many recipients of donor gametes are reluctant to disclose this information to family, friends, and the children themselves, and most donors do not reveal their identity.

Sperm banks are a resource for the one-third of couples for whom male factor is involved in their infertility diagnosis, as well as for single women and lesbian couples. Sperm banking, however, became less critical to couples with male infertility with the development in the early 1990s of ICSI, or intracytoplasmic sperm injection. Until then, IVF required that a man produce hundreds of thousands of sperm for an egg to become fertilized. ICSI allows doctors to insert one sperm directly into the egg, meaning that men with extremely low sperm counts can use their own sperm for IVF. In 2005, although male factor was present in approximately 37 percent of infertility cases, ICSI was used in 60 percent of all IVF cycles, indicating widespread use beyond male factor. Indeed, ICSI was used in almost one-half of all IVF fresh nondonor eggs without male factor infertility.[34] Although there are no reliable figures on who uses sperm banks, anecdotal evidence suggests that their usage by heterosexual couples is declining because of the availability of these new technologies for sperm manipulation but that usage by single women and lesbians is increasing.

The Incredible Egg

Egg provision has a far more recent history. The first documented egg donation occurred in 1983, when an IVF patient donated her eggs; by 2005, clinics used donor eggs in almost fifteen thousand fertility procedures.[35] Egg donation began with identified donors, who were often related to the recipients. Today, identified donors constitute a much smaller part of the donation pool, and recipients are more likely to use specifically recruited donors. Eggs are typically available under two circumstances: first, women already undergoing an IVF cycle may agree to provide their eggs to other women in exchange for a reduced IVF fee; and second, women from outside the clinic may be recruited specifically to provide eggs.[36]

Until recently, most donor eggs had to be "fresh." Because of the novelty of the freezing process, frozen eggs remain less available and more expensive. Unlike the technology for freezing sperm, a process that is more than fifty years old, the possibilities for freezing eggs have been far more limited. The technology for freezing embryos improved dramatically in the mid-1980s, but the technology for freezing eggs has lagged far behind even that. Although a woman did become pregnant using a frozen egg in 1986, it was not until the early twenty-first century that the technology had advanced sufficiently to make cryopreserving eggs commercially viable. Worldwide, in 2006 there were only about two hundred children who had been born through the use of frozen eggs, and egg banks were just beginning to be established.[37]

The slow freezing technique that has been used for sperm and embryo freezing does not work as well on eggs because of the potential for forming ice crystals, which can crack and harm the internal structure of the egg. Fertility clinics have looked for alternative methods of freezing, such as vitrification, a much faster freezing procedure that provides less opportunity for the formation of ice crystals. Even with the older method, however, younger women are increasingly freezing their eggs for later use. Extendfertility.com, a company whose mission is to help women preserve their fertility, explains that it can help women "slow down their biological clocks."[38] And the cost for egg freezing is *only* about fifteen thousand dollars.[39]

Because of the practicality of fresh eggs, an egg provider and her recipient must synchronize their reproductive schedules, a hormonally intensive procedure, to ensure that the eggs are transferred at the optimal time. With frozen eggs, however, this elaborate synchronization is unnecessary, thereby further separating the donor and the recipient.

Clinically Speaking

According to Yale sociologist Rene Almeling, programs for both egg and sperm donation are structured similarly, with comparable stages for donors and recipients.[40] All programs must, first, recruit donors. Recruitment may be done through word-of-mouth, media advertising, or the Internet. Indeed, clinics typically use several strategies to find donors. According to a 2006 survey of egg-donor recruitment that was sent to the almost four hundred member clinics of the Society for Assisted Reproductive Technology (and to which more than one-half of the clinics responded), almost all clinics use their own patients to recruit donors, three-quarters of clinics have their own donor-recruitment programs, and almost the same number of clinics use donors already screened by other donor recruitment agencies.[41]

A second stage involves screening donors. The screening typically includes both medical and personal history profiles. The American Society for Reproductive Medicine has even issued extensive guidelines for psychological screening that asks donors not only to explain their reasons for donating but also to detail their sexual histories, their personal relationships, and their "life stressors and coping skills."[42] Aside from the few laws governing the various contractual relationships, this is perhaps the only other stage at which the law plays a direct role in the reproductive industry, mandating certain safety tests of the donated gametic material.

Third, the agency helps the donor prepare a personal profile and then advertises the profile. Clinics vary considerably as to how much information is included in this profile. Egg and sperm banks differ as to when they publicize this profile: for sperm banks, the donor's profile is not posted until there are enough samples ready for sale, whereas egg-donor information is listed as soon as the profile is ready, well before eggs are provided. Egg donors may be identified through a picture and a first name, whereas sperm donors are more typically identified by number.[43]

Once the profile is publicly available, the next stage involves matching donors and recipients—and collecting fees. As Almeling describes the matching process, agency staff members often provide help, framing the characteristics of various donors to the potential recipients, effectively serving as matchmakers. Although egg donors may be given some information about the recipients, sperm donors—outside of the known-donor programs—receive virtually no information. Egg donors' feelings about potential recipients appear to affect their willingness to participate. In one study of more than one hundred potential egg donors who discussed possible scenarios involving recipients of their gametes, most were willing to trust the clinic's screening process, even though they would prefer the exclusion of certain potential recipients. The possible scenarios included recipients who were married, single, physically challenged, older than forty, or involved in a gay or lesbian relationship. Nonetheless, 6 percent indicated that they would not donate if the clinic were to use their gametes for recipients about whom the donors had reservations.[44] On the other hand, many donors have no knowledge of what ultimately happens to their eggs. Contact between egg donors and recipients ranges from ensuring complete anonymity to agreeing to be contacted once the child reaches a certain age, meeting several times, or arranging for ongoing contact throughout a pregnancy and once a child is born.

The final step involves monitoring the donation process, a stage that is far more onerous for egg donation. The sperm is ready to be shipped when it is selected, whereas egg donors start the process of production only once they have been chosen. Although clinics may construct egg donation as a job, they encourage feelings of altruism by emphasizing that the donation involves caring and helping others. The monitoring process occurs over an extended period of time, as women must take hormones, sometimes giving themselves shots; report for regular, if not daily, medical examinations; and then undergo a retrieval process that requires some anesthesia. By contrast, sperm donors have relatively few demands. They must sign a contract with the bank and abstain from ejaculation for several days before producing a sample. Programs are now required by federal law to do some minimal follow-up with sperm donors, such as making sure that they are tested for HIV once they have stopped providing samples altogether.[45]

Inspecting Gametes

Although today there are various federal and state laws concerning gamete providers, and industry groups have adopted their own self-policing standards, initially there was little regulation of these technologies by the federal or state governments. In 1947, after a group of entrepreneurial donors in New York City advertised the availability of their sperm, the city Department of Health's Sanitary Code was amended to allow only doctors to collect, market, or provide for the transfer of sperm, and donors were required to undergo medical examinations and tests.[46] No other city or state had comparable laws at the time.[47]

Regulating Success

The medical profession is typically regulated by the states or is self-regulated through physicians' professional organizations, not by the federal government. The American Board of Obstetrics and Gynecology, which is a nonprofit organization, administers both an oral and a written test to doctors who want to become certified as obstetricians or gynecologists. Once successful applicants become board certified, they also have the opportunity—following more examinations and a mandatory research thesis—to become certified in the subspecialty of Reproductive Endocrinology and Infertility. Urologists, physicians who specialize in the male reproductive tract, undergo a similar certification process administered by the American Board of Urology. There are continuing obligations imposed on physicians to maintain their certification.

States are generally responsible for any additional oversight of health professionals and procedures, and, in addition to their board specialties, doctors must be licensed to practice in a particular state, rather than nationally. Over the past several decades, however, the federal government has taken a few tentative steps toward the regulation of reproductive technology. Today, it regulates clinical laboratory services, drugs, and medical devices that are used in IVF treatments, it has established standards for the use of human tissue, and it provides monitoring of fertility clinic success rates.

As an initial phase, Congress carefully and thoroughly studied the issue of artificial insemination in the late 1980s, issuing a comprehensive report in 1988. The report identified nine different policy areas for potential federal government action and set out potential courses of action within each of these areas: the collection of public health data; prevention of infertility; provision of information to consumers; mechanisms for access to infertility diagnosis and treatment; expansion of infertility care for veterans; federal regulation of gamete and embryo transfers; retention of nonidentifying records; federal regulation of surrogacy; and support for additional research. The report cautiously evaluated the implications of federal action in each of the areas.[48] (Relatively little has changed since then, and more than thirty years later, a comparable report would identify these same areas.)

That same year, Congress enacted amendments to the 1967 Clinical Laboratory Improvement Act (CLIA) in order to improve the quality and reliability of testing at any type of medical lab.[49] Although CLIA requires federal certification for any lab that handles semen or blood, its application to IVF centers is uncertain. When the American Association of Bioanalysts sued the federal government in 2000 to require certification for any lab procedures involved with ART and for any labs that created embryos, a judge found that the association had not suffered a legally recognized injury and so dismissed the suit.[50] According to the President's Council on Bioethics, even semen and blood tests are not covered by CLIA's requirements when they are performed as part of the lab's ART services.[51]

Spelling Success: Clinical Style

It was not until 1992, however, that Congress enacted legislation that applied explicitly to the reproductive technology industry itself through the Fertility Clinic Success Rate and Certification Act. (The act was designed to prevent fertility clinics from reporting misleading data about their pregnancy success rates.) Witnesses at the hearings on the bill testified about some clinics' use of deceptive advertising by, for example, reporting on the number of embryos created rather than the number of pregnancies achieved.[52] The law does not regulate the safety or uses of sperm or eggs or embryos but, instead, is designed simply to provide access to information about the success rates of fertility clinics. As with other legislation in this area, the 1992 law provides only minimal safeguards concerning the potentially deceptive practices of clinics.

A second portion of the law required the government to establish a voluntary model program that states could use in certifying embryo laboratories as having satisfied certain safety and other professional quality standards. And, as an example of its extreme deference toward the industry, Congress also refused to let either the federal government or states interfere with doctors' authority over reproductive practices in developing the embryo-certification program.[53]

Moreover, implementation of both aspects of this law has not been particularly speedy or protective of consumers. The first set of data on success rates was not even published until December 1997, five years after Congress passed the law, and that report included information from 1995.[54] If fertility clinics do not provide data about their programs, there are no sanctions beyond the clinic's listing as "nonreporting" in the annual compilation of data. The Model Program for the Certification of Embryo Laboratories was finally released in 1999,[55] and it does not appear that any state has actually adopted it.[56] The legislation is hortatory rather than protective; it does not require embryo labs to apply for state certification, nor does it require states to enact the Model Act. And it does not even apply to sperm banks or to clinics that only involve artificial insemination. Instead, it covers only programs that provide treatments involving embryos or eggs.

The Department of Health and Human Services administers the data reporting system, requiring that clinics report their pregnancy success rates to the Centers for Disease Control (CDC).[57] For the first decade after this law was passed, the CDC, in turn, requested that the Society for Assisted Reproductive Technology (SART), a professional association for reproductive technology clinics, collect the information.[58] Clinics are supposed to provide information on whether the clinic belongs to SART, whether its services include surrogacy, the total number of ART cycles that year, demographic details about the patients including their medical history and reasons for using ART, the source of donor eggs, and information about the success of the procedure.[59] SART audited approximately 10 percent of all clinics that reported data and found minor discrepancies between actual practice and recorded data.

Beginning in 2006, the CDC contracted with Westat to collect and verify the data.[60] Unlike SART, Westat is not an industry-based group but an employee-owned organization, with a so-called main campus just outside Washington, D.C., that specializes in statistical survey research. Westat has a long record of working with a variety of government agencies on a series of issues, ranging from child abuse and neglect to customer satisfaction assessments.[61] Each clinic reports data for the annual survey, including a patient's medical history, medical information concerning the ART cycle, and the numbers of pregnancies and births, to Westat's National ART Surveillance System (NASS). For quality review, once clinics have submitted their data and their medical directors have verified (by signature) that the data is accurate, Westat engages in an in-house review of the data and visits a small number of clinics to review a sample of their medical record data. In 2004, Westat visited 28 of the 411 clinics that reported their data, or approximately 7 percent of all reporting clinics.[62] After the visits, Westat analyzes the discrepancy rates (the proportion of treatment cycles for which there was actually a difference on a particular piece of data). In 2004, Westat found, for example, a 1.4 percent discrepancy rate on reports of whether or not the patient became pregnant, but it concluded, "validation indicated that the clinic success rates presented in this report are valid."[63] Because it is based on visiting less than 10 percent of the reporting clinics and relies on self-reported data, however, the data-collection verification process seems inadequate.

Each December, the CDC issues a report available online that provides a national summary of success rates, data on each of the individual clinics that has reported, and a listing of the nonreporting clinics. As explained in the report, its purpose is "to help potential ART users make informed decisions about ART by providing some of the information needed to answer the following questions: What are my chances of having a child by using ART? Where can I go to get this treatment?"[64] The report is a comprehensive compilation of information, but its purpose is not to establish uniform standards for ART programs or to ensure compliance with various safety standards.[65]

Cell Safety

In 1997, the federal government proposed new regulations covering the safety of "human cell, tissue, or cellular or tissue-based products," including donor gametes. Not until 2005 did these regulations become fully operative; today, they apply to all clinics, banks, or other facilities that handle sperm and egg. All gamete providers must be screened, and by federal law, all their "products" must be tested. Some states have gone beyond these federal laws with even tougher standards. By contrast, SART proudly proclaims on its website that is has tried to protect against "inappropriate external intrusion and regulations" and that, indeed, it has "worked successfully to mitigate many of the somewhat onerous requirements that had been initially proposed by the Food and Drug Administration, including the need to quarantine all embryos derived from donor eggs."[66] Rather than advocating for more stringent standards and more federal regulation, SART played a role in toning down the standards that had initially been proposed.

One fertility practice evaluated the cost of additional tests and audits in order to implement the new egg-donor requirements at $228,180 for the forty egg-donor cycles performed at the clinic in the first year following the mandatory new regulations.[67] The researchers observed that, particularly in light of the fact that no cases existed of infectious disease transmission via egg donation, the cost-effectiveness of the new regulations was difficult to evaluate; on the other hand, they did recognize the value of providing reassurance to the public concerning more rigorous testing.

Notwithstanding—or perhaps because of—all the delays, the FDA guidelines are somewhat limited; they do not regulate the practice of ART, only the collection, processing, storage, and distribution of human gametes as the "articles" of ART. The regulation requires screening of donor semen, eggs, and embryos within seven days of donation for sexually transmitted diseases, including HIV, hepatitis B, syphilis, chlamydia, and gonorrhea,[68] and it imposes penalties for HIV-positive persons who knowingly donate or sell semen.[69]

Once a potential donor arrives at a clinic, the clinic must take certain steps to determine the donor's eligibility. To decide on eligibility, the clinic is supposed to review an applicant's medical records for various communicable diseases, such as chlamydia and HIV.[70] Not only must the clinic look to see if the applicant has already experienced one of these diseases, but also the clinic must decide whether the applicant shows risk factors for these diseases. Potential risk factors range from hemophilia to a man having had sex with another man during the previous five years.

If the donor passes the medical records examination, then the clinic must test the actual specimen collected for communicable diseases. The rules generally apply to both egg and sperm donations, with a few minor variations. Beyond the initial screening for various diseases, there must be tests for HIV Type 1 and 2, hepatitis B and C, syphilis, chlamydia, and gonorrhea (although the last two may be omitted if the specimen is collected in a way that ensures freedom from contamination).[71] All tests must be done using FDA-licensed or approved screening tests.[72] Further, anonymous sperm donors must be retested at least six months after the date of donation, which means that the specimens are collected, tested, quarantined for six months, and then tested again before use.[73] Interestingly, the same stipulation does not apply to donated oocytes, which are only required to be withheld until donor eligibility is established, without the comparable necessity of retesting.[74] It may be that, as some researchers have suggested, when this regulation was initially proposed, fresh eggs were the standard, with few frozen oocytes used; consequently, a single test determining eligibility was considered sufficient to allow egg donation.[75] What remains unclear is why such regulation has not yet been amended to apply the same standards to both sperm and egg donors. Regardless of these small requirement discrepancies, however, the most important precautionary measure applies equally to both donor sexes: it is only after both screening and testing (and quarantine, for anonymous donors) that the determination of donor eligibility is made. There are no testing or screening requirements, of course, if the donor and the recipient are already "sexually intimate," so existing partners are exempt from this elaborate screening and testing process.[76]

When specimens are deemed eligible, they are then released for use. Repeat donors need not be completely rescreened; instead, an abbreviated process can be used that focuses on any changes in the donor's medical history or relevant social behavior.[77] However, this leniency is only pertinent to donors who have been submitted to complete testing within the previous six months.

In addition to implementing standards for testing donors, the federal regulations require that donation facilities maintain sufficient staff to ensure that they can comply with the federal regulations, and personnel must be competent based on measures of education, experience, and training.[78] Clinics must establish their own internal quality-control program to make sure that any corrective actions are documented, personnel receive proper training and education, periodic audits are performed, and computer software is validated for its appropriate use.[79] Clinics must also set up procedures for all steps involved in the screening, testing, and determination of eligibility.[80] A list of the procedures must be "readily available to the personnel" and must be kept in the area where each step is performed.[81] The regulations are thorough and specific concerning clinics' requirements.

To help in explaining how clinics should implement these mandatory screening requirements, the Food and Drug Administration has also issued a "guidance" document that suggests how to determine donor eligibility. It has the enticing title "Guidance for Industry: Eligibility Determination for Donors of Human Cells, Tissues, and Cellular and Tissue-Based Products (HCT/Ps)."[82] Guidance documents such as this one are designed to reflect the FDA's "current thinking on a topic," but they are not legally binding. Although clinics are not legally required to follow the guidance, many of them do. Indeed, sperm banks and even officials at the FDA itself are sometimes confused about the difference between mandatory regulations and advisory guidance documents.[83] This evidence of confusion together with the clout of the FDA reveals that the guidance document is quite important in establishing industry norms. The document does provide useful information on how to comply with the law, but it is stricter than the regulations, for example, when it comes to sperm donated from gay men. Although the regulations require that donors whose medical histories indicate "risk factors" for diseases such as HIV must be deemed ineligible, the specific risk factors are not actually identified in the regulations;[84] the FDA guidance document, however, suggests several risk factors, including a man having had sex with another man in the past five years.[85] Similarly, examples of "high risk behaviors" are identified in the guidance document and include physical evidence of anal intercourse, needle tracks, oral thrush, and blue or purple spots that may indicate Kaposi's sarcoma, a common symptom of AIDS. This blanket prohibition on men who have engaged in sexual relations with another man has been highly controversial. One reason for such intense controversy is that although gay men are not explicitly barred from anonymous donation, the focus on sexual activity gong back five years is tantamount to suggesting that their sexual orientation prevents them from donating their "product" and is highly prejudicial. Critics argue that under these guidelines, "a heterosexual man who had unprotected sex with HIV-positive prostitutes would be OK as a donor one year later, but a gay man in a monogamous, safe-sex relationship is not OK unless he's been celibate for five years."[86] Kevin Cathcart, the executive director of Lambda Legal Defense and Education Fund, agrees and, in fact, goes even further, asserting that "this rule is based on bad science because the AIDS epidemic is an increasingly heterosexual epidemic" and suggesting that the policy is due to "bigotry."[87] Still, supporters of these guidelines seem unconvinced. UCLA professor Eugene Volokh argued in his blog that the guidelines are extremely sound, basing his support on the fact that homosexual males are more likely than their heterosexual counterparts to acquire HIV.[88] Moreover, advocates for the guidelines point out that the suggested prohibition applies only to anonymous sperm donors and that gay men are not prohibited from donating to women who knowingly and voluntarily choose their sperm.[89]

One possible solution, much less draconian than the one chosen by the FDA, would be to concentrate on sexual conduct rather than on sexual orientation. Indeed, the Lambda Legal Defense and Education Fund has suggested that prospective donors be rejected if they have engaged in unprotected sex in the previous twelve months with an HIV-positive person, an illegal drug user, or an individual of unknown HIV status outside a monogamous relationship, regardless of sexual orientation.[90] This proposal is further supported by the elaborate screening process that applies to sperm: HIV tests are about 99 percent accurate, and in addition, the specimens must be collected, tested, quarantined for six months, and then tested again before being available for use.

Other than through these procedures for safety, federal law does not, however, regulate the medical procedures involved in donation. Clinics are not required to meet additional standards (other than, perhaps, with respect to "tissue"), by preventing discrimination against certain potential recipients or donors, by mandating any ongoing obligation for donors to report health information, by regulating the disclosure of information to any subsequently born children, or by limiting the number of embryos transferred per cycle or even the number of times that one person can provide sperm or eggs to another. As one journalist accurately charged after a thorough report in 2007 on California Cryobank, the largest sperm bank in the world, "the industry has operated almost completely unmolested. Outside of a mostly inept series of somewhat bizarre FDA rulings, there is no top-down governance in the field. It is, as it has always been, self-policing."[91] And the industry often resists further regulation, claiming that it restricts patient choice by creating market constraints.

The State of the States

As on the federal level, there is "a marked void" in state regulation of egg donation.[92] States, with few exceptions, have not filled the gaps in federal oversight, although almost half the states do have some legislation concerning medical practices applicable to sperm donation.[93] Some states have enacted legislation requiring limited forms of reporting and/or clinic certification. Unlike the federal government, states have also addressed access to such services and whether and to what extent ART will be covered by insurance benefits. There is, not surprisingly, enormous variation in scope and coverage among states, but, very generally, they regulate either the clinic or the commercial transfer process. In turn, these types of regulations can be usefully thought of in three different categories: those affecting clinics, suppliers, and recipients. To be sure, these categories are interrelated, and the goal is generally to ensure marketing safety.

Some states regulate clinics and their procedures directly through mandatory reporting or training requirements; some states limit supply with law relating to the disqualification of certain donors or a limitation on compensation; and some states, as discussed in chapter 9, prevent certain potential recipients from using ART based on their social identity or traits such as sexuality, age, or marital status, or guarantee funded access by mandating insurance coverage.[94]

A few states, including Virginia and New Hampshire, require that egg and sperm donors be screened. New Hampshire is the only state that requires detailed medical history for sperm donors and imposes age and health requirements for gamete and embryo recipient qualifications.[95] States have been more successful in regulating sperm-donor screening, although heightened screening is optional in most states, given the economic interest of cost saving and the widespread practice of nongovernmental self-regulation.[96]

Several states have enacted their own reporting laws for clinic success rates, requiring limited reporting about certain types of ART procedures. On the state level, a law similar to the federal Fertility Clinic Success Rate Act has been enacted in Virginia, where individual clinics must disclose their success rates to patients. Virginia law requires that fertility patients be provided with information including the total number of live births, the number of live births as a percentage of completed retrieval cycles, and the rates for clinical pregnancy and delivery per completed retrieval cycle bracketed by age group.[97] In Virginia and Massachusetts, ART can be undertaken only after a patient has given informed consent on a form specifying the success rates of the particular clinic.[98] In Virginia, doctors cannot perform in vitro procedures until they have disclosed to the patient the success rate for the process together with the tests used to ensure that the gamete providers do not have AIDS.[99]

The concern in some states is to provide patients undergoing fertility treatment with enough information to allow them to make an informed decision regarding the disposition of any embryos that are left over.[100] If the people undergoing such treatment choose to do so, then they can donate the remaining embryos to another person attempting to conceive through assisted reproduction.[101] In Massachusetts, anyone who performs IVF must give the patient information about how to dispose of excess reproductive material after treatment; and anyone who is involved in providing egg extraction must give patients an informational pamphlet about the procedure and must ensure that the patient has given informed consent after reviewing the pamphlet.[102] Although this requirement appears to be directed at stem-cell research, it also applies to IVF patients.

As self-regulation for members of professional agencies is the most common practice and is praised for its ability to respond to emerging issues in a more flexible and reflexive manner than legal regulation,[103] only a few states require clinic certification.[104] Pennsylvania, however, requires ART clinics to file reports on clinic management and operation. Anyone involved in IVF must file quarterly reports with the state that include information on the number of eggs fertilized, of fertilized eggs that are destroyed, and of women implanted with fertilized eggs, and the state imposes a fine of fifty dollars per day for failure to comply.[105] Only fourteen states have laws concerning the preservation of records related to ART.[106]

No regulations govern the number of implantations an infertility clinic may perform per IVF cycle. The ASRM has set forth a recommended limit on embryo transfers, advising that doctors implant only two to five embryos in a woman, depending on the patient's age and the probability for a successful pregnancy, but no law requires observation of this voluntary limit.[107] Some clinics voluntarily limit the number of donations per donor, although no laws exist with respect to this. Similarly absent are laws that regulate advertisements, limit the price for donations, or place constraints on the grounds on which intending parents might choose donors.[108] Disclosure of donor identity is also unregulated, leaving the decision of anonymity to sperm banks, fertility clinics, and people who use their services.[109]

States have developed a patchwork of additional laws, with, for example, New Hampshire establishing comprehensive regulation of the ART process. All gamete providers must be medically evaluated.[110] Maryland requires that banks have distinct spaces for processing, quarantining, and labeling sperm.[111] Louisiana prohibits using fresh sperm for anonymous donation, and Delaware requires that sperm banks register with the state, with a five-thousand-dollar fine for a failure to do so.[112]

In Ohio, the physician must give the recipient detailed information about the donor, such as the donor's race, the color of his eyes and hair, his educational achievements, and his religious background—but only if the doctor knows these facts.[113] There is, however, no requirement that the doctor actually obtain this information. Idaho law specifies that only doctors and the people they supervise can perform artificial insemination or even choose potential donors.[114]

A few states have dealt with the regulation problem by relinquishing to outside groups the responsibility for setting up regulations that apply to gamete banks. Both Kentucky and Maryland require tissue banks to follow aspects of rules promulgated by the American Association of Tissue Banks (AATB), a nonprofit peer group that issues standards for tissue banks and also inspects and accredits them. Kentucky law requires tissue banks to test for HIV and other communicable diseases as specified by AATB.[115] Maryland has developed a sort of hybrid regulation system, writing many of its own regulations regarding licensing and inspection while mandating that sperm banks follow certain AATB standards.[116] Maryland also requires each tissue bank to have a governing body "consisting of individuals from various professions" to determine the scope of activities to be pursued by the tissue bank.[117] This same governing body is also responsible for any liability, ethical, fiduciary, and compliance issues that might arise.[118]

The State of Industry Regulation

Long before the federal standards became effective, the reproductive technology industry had undertaken self-regulation. This process is still ongoing, and the industry has established its own voluntary standards and processes of accreditation that coexist with the federal and state regulations. The industry has also developed a series of ethical guidelines that, again, are not binding but that contain advice and standards on a variety of topics that go beyond basic ART medical practice, including patient screening and preimplantation genetic diagnosis (PGD), which involves screening embryos prior to implantation for genetic diseases.

To become a member of the Society for Assisted Reproductive Technology, the main industry group that represents more than 85 percent of fertility clinics, the clinic must have its embryology laboratory accredited by one of three organizations, including the College of American

Pathologists/American Society for Reproductive Medicine accreditation program (CAP/ASRM), the Joint Commission on Accreditation of Healthcare Organizations (JCHO), or the New York State Tissue Bank Program.[119] As the CDC emphasizes, however, the federal government does not provide any oversight of these programs, and their standards vary.[120] SART has recognized the need for some interventions and has, for example, developed a program to attempt to reduce the number of triplets at member clinics.[121]

While all sperm banks in the United States are required to conform to the FDA's rules regarding communicable diseases, many banks have also been aggressive about screening for genetic abnormalities and developing various safety mechanisms. Guidelines for sperm banks seeking to go above and beyond state and federal regulations are produced by nonprofit scientific peer groups like the American Association of Tissue Banks (AATB) and the American Society for Reproductive Medicine (ASRM). The AATB accredits sperm banks that conform to their guidelines and membership requirements, and some states defer to this accreditation.[122] Sperm banks may also choose to develop their own set of safeguards instead of seeking accreditation, taking into account the particular needs of their client and donor populations. Guidelines developed by either an accrediting body or an individual sperm bank are not, of course, enforceable by law, and families using these services are dependent on the good-faith effort of the sperm bank to comply and to fulfill the screening, testing, and use requirements promised by the banks.

Although most sperm banks in the United States are not accredited by the American Association of Tissue Banks (fewer than ten of the several hundred sperm banks in the country are certified), the AATB guidelines are highly influential.[123] The guidelines emphasize patient safety, which must be accomplished through a combination of personnel training, structured oversight, and precise screening, storage, and recordkeeping methods. The eleventh edition of the AATB's "Standards for Tissue Banking," which was published in October 2006 and is frequently updated, establishes guidelines, including for the types of tests that must be performed, records that must be maintained, and the assessments of donors.[124] AATB accreditation requires an on-site inspection of the facility to ensure compliance.

The banks themselves understand that consumers want guarantees of the safety of the sperm they are purchasing. When they are accredited, they make sure that the public knows. For example, Northwest Andrology and Cryobank, which is headquartered in Spokane, Washington, includes an extensive list of genetic and pathology tests applicable to all donor sperm and advertises, "Our donor screening meets or exceeds the standards set forth by the FDA, AATB, ASRM. (Food and Drug Administration, American Association of Tissue Banks, American Society for Reproductive Medicine)."[125] In its comparison of services offered by other sperm banks, Fairfax Cryobank lists a series of donor screening tests that it performs, unlike its competitors, which go beyond the FDA's required regimen.[126] It also advertises that it is licensed in California, Maryland, and New York and that it is registered with the FDA.[127]

In 2003, the Practice Committee of ASRM revised its minimum standards (which had previously been revised in 1998) for clinics offering fertility services. The comprehensive standards provide recommendations on the types of personnel required for each ART program, the minimum amount of specialized training and experience for personnel ranging from the medical director to an embryology laboratory technologist, record-keeping and data collection, and informed consent.[128] Although the standards are thorough and concrete, they remain voluntary, with no sanctions for noncompliance.

Who Can Give?

Providers can be any age, although some banks do have limitations; men who donate sperm to California Cryobank must be at least eighteen years old, and women who donate eggs to Egg Donor, Inc., must be twenty-one.[129] But there are no legal limits on the number of times that individuals can provide their gametes for use by others; there is no requirement that banks make sure an individual donor has not already donated material at multiple other banks.

Most sperm banks explain that they reject more than 90 percent of their potential applicants.[130] The reasons for rejection may vary from concerns about disease to concerns about physical appearance, as banks can establish their own qualifications beyond the federal minimum safety standards. On its website, Cryogenics Laboratories (CLI) boasts,

> American Association of Tissue Banks Inspected and Accredited semen cryobank, CLI performs testing and screening of donors in accordance with the AATB Standards. In addition, we conform to the

New York State Regulations and the American Society for Reproductive Medicine (ASRM) guidelines. Donor screening consists of questionnaires, blood screening, specimen screening, genetic analysis and a physical examination.

Candidates undergo vigorous, lengthy interviews involving personal questions concerning sexual behavior, family background and reasons for participating in our semen donor program. A minimum of 3 generations of family history is taken and evaluated.[131]

Although federal law now ensures minimal testing, and some states expand on these minimal requirements, there is little governmental oversight and no comprehensive regulation of the gamete-donation process. Gamete donation remains a largely private transaction that is handled through contract and intention with virtually no uniform regulation.

Is Less Enough? Judges and Courts

Even if legislatures did not exert pressure, the judicial system might have served as a force for change when lawsuits resulted from market failures. There have been plenty of cases involving so-called wrongful reproduction, defective sperm, and switched eggs.

Indeed, even with better regulation, there will be cases in which the results are not what the recipients wanted. Consider that *American Jurisprudence Proof of Facts,* a legal reference book on litigation, contains an almost one-hundred-page article just on the liability of sperm banks for transmission of AIDS through donor sperm.[132]

There are three different kinds of cases in which reproductive mistakes occur that might then result in lawsuits: first, gametic material may be lost or damaged; second, the wrong gametic material may be used in the wrong person, either because the plaintiff's intended material is used for someone else or someone else's material is wrongly used in the plaintiff's treatment; and third, clinics may make mistakes in genetic screening, such as failing to require certain tests of gamete providers or failing to report the outcome of the tests that have been administered, leading to injuries to the resulting child.[133] Of course, not all mishaps in reproductive clinics have any effect on patient care, but mishandling gametic material can certainly have an impact. When these various "mistakes" are discovered, the fertility centers may face both criminal and civil liability, with lawsuits brought by the government as well as by the former patients.

So Is It a Crime?

The criminal sanctions for mistakes can be quite severe under either federal or state laws. Take the infamous late-twentieth-century case of Dr. Cecil Jacobson, who egregiously abused the trust of his patients. For example, he used his own sperm to inseminate his patients rather than the donor sperm that he had promised to use, he lied to them about their pregnancies, and he deceived them about the need for an abortion. Although federal law does not explicitly prohibit these reproductive mistakes, prosecutors charged him with mail fraud, wire fraud, travel fraud, and perjury. He was ultimately convicted on fifty-two different charges in the early 1990s and faced a potential sentence of 280 years in prison, although he ultimately received a shorter prison term. Chief District Judge James Cacheris, who heard the testimony at the trial, observed that the court had "not seen a case the equal of this one in terms of the degree of emotional anguish, psychological trauma and, at times profound despair expressed by th[e] victims."[134]

In response to various reproductive scandals in California, including egg stealing (using one woman's eggs without consent in another woman), the state changed its criminal laws to respond explicitly to these situations. The California Penal Code now includes the crime of intentionally using or implanting sperm, eggs, and embryos contrary to the consent of the provider.[135] Anyone who engages in this crime can be placed in prison for up to five years and forced to pay a fine of up to fifty thousand dollars. Although California added this crime to its law in 1996, at the time of this writing, there are no reported cases in which it has been used.[136]

So Is It a Tort?

Along with potential criminal charges brought by the government, a physician may face lawsuits from patients and their children that are based in contract or tort, with claims such as medical malpractice and fraud. But when patients sue their treating physicians, it may be difficult to fit the types of damages that they have incurred into existing legal theories, which shows the disconnect between the mechanics of the donor industry and the operation of the legal system. And when children sue, often for "wrongful life," based on a claim that the child would not have been born without the clinic's wrongful actions, courts typically dismiss the suits on the basis that being born is better, under any circumstances, than not being born.[137]

To bring a tort suit against a medical practice, the plaintiff must show four elements. First, the medical practice must have owed a duty to the plaintiff. In the typical malpractice case, this is framed as owing a duty to exercise reasonable care. Second, the practice must have breached its obligation. Third, this breach of responsibility must have been the cause of the plaintiff's suffering an injury. And the plaintiff's actually having suffered an injury is the fourth element.

That fourth element is the hard part—what is the injury? It may be impossible to measure the damages. In a 1998 Utah case, for example, David and Stephanie Harnicher underwent IVF, using a mixture of donor sperm and the husband's sperm to fertilize the wife's egg, at the University of Utah Medical Center Fertility Clinic.[138] The Harnichers specifically selected Donor 183, a man who they thought looked like David and whose blood type matched David's, so that no one would know the identity of the biological father. Stephanie gave birth to triplets, two girls and one boy. When one of the babies became ill and underwent blood tests, it became clear that at least two of the children were not biologically related to either David *or* Donor 183. The Harnichers sued the medical center, claiming that it had negligently inflicted emotional distress on them. The appellate court refused to find that they had suffered severe emotional distress that rose to the requisite legal level of "illness or bodily harm." Somewhat caustically, the court noted,

> As a result of their fertility treatment, the Harnichers became the parents of three normal, healthy children whom [sic] the couple suggests do not look as much like David as different children might have and whose blood type could not be descended from his. This result thwarted the couple's intention to believe and represent that the triplets are David's biological children. Exposure to the truth about one's own situation cannot be considered an injury and has never been a tort. Therefore, destruction of a fiction cannot be grounds for either malpractice or negligent infliction of emotional distress. The Harnichers' assertion that David did not want children unless they were biologically his own is belied by the couple's knowing consent to the use of donor sperm.[139]

The court hinted that it might have reached a different result if the physician's action had resulted in children who did not match their parents racially or ethnically, or who were disabled.

A series of cases in New York has provided additional details about the types of potential tort claims against physicians. In 1998, Deborah Perry-Rogers and Robert Rogers contributed their gametic material to create embryos at the In Vitro Fertility Center of New York. Their embryos, however, were not transferred to Deborah but, instead, to Donna Fasano. The center notified both families of the mix-up. Donna gave birth in December to two boys, one of whom was biologically related to the Fasanos, while the other one was related to Deborah and Robert. Deborah and Robert sued the Fasanos as well as their physicians. The court allowed the claims against the physicians to go forward, emphatically denying that the claim was based on damages resulting from the creation of a child. Rather, they were seeking damages for the "emotional harm caused by their having been deprived of the opportunity of experiencing pregnancy, prenatal bonding and the birth of their child, and by their separation from the child for more than four months."[140]

Although emotional-distress damages are generally only available when there is also a physical injury, the court allowed this case to proceed even without the showing of a physical injury because it was the physicians' breach of duty that caused the emotional damages. Two years later, Josephine and Gerard Paretta sought damages from the Center for Human Reproduction for failing to screen the couple adequately for cystic fibrosis and to inform the Parettas that their donor egg had tested positive for the disease. Their daughter, Theresa, was born with cystic fibrosis, a genetic disease that requires that both parents be carriers. The court refused to allow the Parettas to proceed with a claim for emotional distress based on the birth of their child with a congenital disease. Indeed, the court snapped, "Theresa, however, like any other baby, does not have a protected right to be born free of genetic defects," but the court did allow the Parettas to claim damages for Theresa's medical treatment.[141]

In a 2007 case, Justice Sheila Abdu-Salaam similarly refused to recognize the claim of Nancy and Thomas Andrews for emotional distress based on the birth of their child, Jessica; although the Andrewses had intended for their physician to use sperm from Thomas for their IVF procedure, a stranger's sperm was used instead. Even before they performed a home DNA test, the Andrewses knew that something was wrong. Nancy Andrews was born in the Dominican Republic and Thomas is white, but Jessica's skin was darker than both of theirs. Justice Abdu-Salaam found, however, that even though Jessica was of a different race and color from her parents, the Andrewses could not recover for any emotional distress that this fact, by itself, might cause them. On the other hand, she did find that the Andrewses could recover for the emotional distress they experienced from not knowing whether their genetic material had been used by others and for their fear that the man whose sperm they actually used might claim paternal rights.[142]

As these cases show, the accidental use of one person's gametic material, which creates high levels of emotional distress, nonetheless is not necessarily sufficient to create a legally cognizable claim for damages. This reflects, to some extent, the wise public policy that parents cannot recover for actions that result in the birth of a child, healthy or not. Yet it utterly ignores the pain that parents experience from the negligent actions of their trusted physicians, giving them no recourse for seeking justice.

Of course, the law does not provide a right for every wrong. The history of recovering for emotional distress is complex; although every state now recognizes the ability to recover for some forms of emotional distress, there is enormous variation in what plaintiffs must prove to show the legal level of damages. As the American Law Institute explained in 1965, because of "the fear of fictitious or trivial claims, distrust of the proof offered, and the difficulty of setting up any satisfactory boundaries to liability, the law has been slow to afford independent protection to the interest in freedom from emotional distress standing alone."[143] Plaintiffs could recover for emotional distress if it resulted in physical harm—or for emotional distress that resulted from a physical harm. Today, the law recognizes the ability to recover for emotional distress regardless of the existence of physical injury.

There are two types of torts for the causation of emotional distress: intentional and negligent. The intentional tort requires outrageous conduct that produces the mental distress. The negligent tort of emotional distress, which is the one most likely to be used in the gamete cases, is based on the question of what the typically prudent person would do under the circumstances. The tort typically requires that the defendant's actions fall below the standard set by the actions of the reasonably prudent person and that the damages to the plaintiff were foreseeable. Although the physicians' actions clearly meet the standard of negligence and plaintiffs can document the emotional distress that they are suffering, courts founder on the question of whether the plaintiff has truly been damaged. When deciding on these claims, courts throughout the negligent-infliction field have been inclined to limit liability to the defendant.[144]

Given the depth of injury and the breach of responsibility to the patients/intending parents, these harms deserve legal remedies. Indeed, because of the legal difficulties in getting these claims recognized, the law may need to develop new torts. In law review articles, Fred Norton argues that the law should recognize a parent's interest in "genetic affinity" with a child as a basis of a tort suit if the interest is thwarted, and Joshua Klein-feld suggests that the law should recognize a new tort, that of "procreative injury."[145] The procreative-injury claim would require a showing that the "doctor has undertaken a duty to care for a patient's procreative interest, and negligently breaches that duty so as to cause the patient procreative injury [resulting in] a prima facie case for 'reprogenetic malpractice.'"[146]

As these proposals recognize, the facts of these cases truly are tragic and deserve a legal remedy. As Norton observes, although it may be "un-seemly" for parents who have undergone fertility treatments to claim that the birth of a child has caused them damages, such a claim "is premised, however, on a privileged view of reproduction in which the physical health of the baby is the only substantial variable."[147] He argues that conduct that interferes with the planned genetic relationship between the parent and the child is an injury. This notion—a tort recognizing interference with an attempt to have genetically related children—allows for relief in some circumstances but does not adequately capture the harm of the generic interference with an individual's reproductive liberty, even if the person has chosen to use donor gametes. Kleinfeld's concept of procreative injury starts to provide the appropriate framework because it captures the harm to an individual's procreative expectations, which may or may not involve creating children with genetic links to the parents. The goal is not just try-ing to make the intending parents "whole," an impossible concept given the nature of the injury, nor is it to recognize that they have been wronged (which they have); tort cases serve a policing nature for the profession, and awarding damages for putting the wrong material into the right per-son provides a cautionary lesson for other physicians.

So Is It Lost Property?

In contrast to the emotional-distress claims, intending parents have been able to sue clinics for loss of their gametic property. Belinda and William Jeter went to the Mayo Clinic of Arizona in 2001 for help in get-ting pregnant. They paid twenty-five thousand dollars to Mayo, which, after fertilizing Belinda's eggs with William's sperm, ultimately produced twenty-two fertilized eggs. When the couple's attempts at pregnancy were unsuccessful, they went to a second clinic with what they thought were the remaining ten fertilized eggs that Mayo had agreed to freeze and store;

it turned out that only five of the fertilized eggs remained. The Jeters sued the Mayo Clinic for negligently losing five of their preembryos. The court did not recognize a claim for wrongful death but did allow the Jeters to proceed against the clinic for the negligent-loss claim and to claim emotional-distress damages based on the loss of the fertilized eggs.[148] In a similar Rhode Island case, three women sued the fertility clinic that had lost their preembryos, claiming property loss as well as emotional distress.[149] Although a subsequent investigation by the state health department was reassuring in finding it unlikely that the embryos had been wrongfully implanted in other women, it did find serious flaws in the clinic's record-keeping.[150] One study, reported in 2007, of more than twelve thousand egg-retrieval cycles in a large IVF center, found about seventy-four mishaps, with approximately forty of these having an effect on patient care; the mishaps resulted from, among other reasons, labeling problems, clinical procedures, and equipment malfunctions.[151]

It is important to remember that there is a series of standard operating procedures that any good reproductive endocrinology practice should follow. These include quality-assurance programs, comprehensive personnel training, and meticulous and detailed procedures for labeling gametic material. If a mishap has occurred, the Ethics Committee of the American Society for Reproductive Medicine suggests that clinics are ethically required to disclose at least certain types of errors, such as those involving switched gametic material.[152] Even if the patient has not become pregnant, the Ethics Committee recommends disclosure based on a theory of patient autonomy.[153]

As this chapter has shown, there is limited regulation in the area of reproductive technology. This lack of regulation is partially due to the rapid changes in reproductive technology and the social controversies that surround the use of reproductive technology. Moreover, the industry prefers self-policing to other interventions. Although the federal government and some states have developed minimal regulations to test the safety of gametes and to guard against egregious deceptive practices, there is a dearth of laws controlling fertility clinics and gamete banks. Federal law is limited to regulations covering gamete transactions prior to their actual use. There is no regulatory agency that oversees individual donors or that monitors gamete banks on a routine basis. Banks and clinics are not required to verify the personal information or much of the medical information that donors provide them, nor are donors typically tested for most genetic diseases. There are no enforceable limits on the number of times that one individual can provide gametic material to another. Nor must banks monitor what happens to the gametic material once it leaves their offices, and there is no tracking of donors' or their offspring's genetic diseases or other problems. The occasional "mix-ups" that make their way into court remind consumers and the public of the lack of oversight, but the existing legal framework for remedying and preventing these mix-ups is entirely inadequate. Laws must mandate better practices, rather than relying on industry internal guidelines and voluntary compliance.

4

Parenting Regulation

IS A SPERM donor a father? An egg donor a mother? In 2003, the Maine Supreme Court struggled with whether to notify an anonymous sperm donor of a court action involving "his" child. A lesbian couple purchased sperm from California Cryobank (the bank also involved in the kidney-disease case discussed in chapter 1). One of the women became pregnant and gave birth to a boy (called only "I.H." by the court). The biological mother wanted to recognize her partner's relationship to I.H. by making the partner a guardian for her son. The two women went to court to guarantee that the partner could legally act like a parent. Under Maine law, however, "any parent" must be informed before the court can appoint a guardian, and Maine law does not specify the relationship between donor, recipient, and child. Consequently, there was an important issue to resolve concerning whether the sperm donor needed to know about the court action.

In its painstaking review of the relevant authorities, the court concluded that nothing in Maine law precluded an anonymous donor from being considered a parent who should have been informed about the guardianship. Nonetheless, the court found that it would be useless under these circumstances to try to notify "the child's father" if he was an anonymous donor.[1] The court conceded that, given the assurances of confidentiality to the donor, the mother's and child's names would be meaningless to the donor.

This chapter discusses the law's response to the families created through sperm, egg, and embryo donation. By tracing the history of how the law has responded to families formed through gamete provision, the chapter shows how judicial and legislative interpretations of the implications of these technologies have been cabined by the traditional significance of genetic and marital relationships. Early cases struggled with whether children born through gamete provision were "legitimate" or whether the mother had committed adultery; although later cases are no longer concerned with adultery, they similarly struggle with the status of the child and with the newer issues of the "rights" of the gamete provider. States have also enacted a bewildering array of laws that address these issues. They range from Oklahoma's prohibition on anyone but a married couple using artificial insemination, and related termination of any rights and obligations between provider and child, to the Uniform Parentage Act's provisions, which recognize the rights of single people to use artificial reproductive technology.[2] There are two sets of issues. First, what rights, if any, can a donor assert? Second, if ARTs are used in a relationship, then what are the rights of each partner? This chapter provides an introduction to parentage rights in the United States. The next chapter explores the issues of a donor versus intending parent(s), as well as the partnership rights that a couple may have against each other.

The treatment of adoptees serves, throughout this chapter and the rest of the book, as a comparison and contrast to the treatment of ART children. Outside of adoptions by relatives, adoptees are not biologically related to either parent, unlike donor children, who often have some biological relationship to one of their parents. On the other hand, in both legal contexts, the absence of a full-blooded relationship has meant different inquiries and different legal treatment from children who are biologically related to both their parents. Although the laws of adoption have a much longer history than those involving reproductive technology, advocates within both the donor and the adoption communities are just beginning to explore the connections. Earlier legal treatment of the donor relationships in reproductive technology drew on common-law reasoning concerning nonmarital children rather than adoption. Although adoption does not provide a complete model for reproductive technology laws, it does provide useful analogies.

A Family Affair?

Beginning in the colonial United States, children born to married women have been presumed to be children of the marriage, with the husband and wife as mother and father. Being declared a parent has enormous legal, social, and psychological significance. Married parents have had virtually absolute child-custody rights against anyone who sought to interfere with them, while unmarried parents have always—even today—had less determinate rights (as anyone knows who has read *The Scarlett Letter*). Until the early nineteenth century, in the rare event that married couples separated, the father was entitled to custody of the children because they were his "property"; by the late nineteenth century, the mother was seen as the proper custodian. Today, when married or unmarried parents separate, both parents have equal rights to custody under a best-interest-of-the-child standard, and third parties are subject to a different standard in order to receive custody.

Under the historical application of the marital presumption, once a couple married, the presumption has discouraged too close an inquiry into the actual paternity of the children born during the marriage. The rule, which originated in the 1777 British case of *Goodright v. Moss*, prohibited spouses from testifying against each other, protecting not just marital harmony but also the legitimacy of children.

As an example of how this worked, the Pennsylvania Supreme Court considered a case in 1874 involving the legitimacy of Francis Hoagland, who was born three months after Mary Ann Lyons married Amos Hoagland. Mary Ann wanted to testify that it was her employer, not her new husband, who was the father of her son. The Pennsylvania court refused to allow her testimony, explaining that the rule that a child "born in wedlock, though begotten before, is presumptively legitimate is an axiom of law so well established, that to cite authorities in support of it, would be a mere waste of time." For parents to testify in a manner that would "bastardize the child, is a proposition which shocks our sense of right and decency."[3]

In many states, the marital presumption has never been absolute, however, and did not apply to cases in which the mother's husband clearly could not have fathered the child—"cases in which a man was sterile, impotent, or, in Blackstone's words, 'extra quatuor maria,' [beyond the four seas] for above nine months."[4] Yet the courts did not permit either spouse to testify about the husband's nonaccess.[5] Nor were they receptive to testimony about the husband's impotence; a 1952 Louisiana statute, for example, prevented the husband from proving his impotence in order to rebut the marital presumption.[6] Consequently, the presumption was virtually impossible to counter.

Blood Tells: Adopting Presumptions

The historical record of adoption laws helps to show the complexity of children's relationships to their parents when they are not biologically related to both parents. In the donor context, children are typically related to only one of their legal parents, so the adoption laws provide the opportunity for both comparison and contrast. The early adoption laws attempted to secure to adopted children many, but not all, of the same rights as biological children. There remained, and remains today, a distinction between adoptive and biological children, with adoptive children still not granted the same set of rights accorded to biological children. The mid-nineteenth-century adoption statutes provided that the adopted child should be generally treated as though "he had been born to [his parents] in lawful wedlock; except that he shall not be capable of taking property expressly limited to the heirs of the body or bodies of the parents by adoption, nor property from the lineal or collateral kindred of such parents by right of representation."[7] Property rights as much as family law affected the rights of an adoptee.

Moreover, the best-interest standard was not a firmly entrenched benchmark in adoption cases. As the "property" of children became less valuable while children themselves became more "precious,"[8] custody law began to transfer the economically valueless children to their mothers. The best-interest standard itself, then, reflects these notions of property. Finally, in a land-based society, succession to property—the primary form of wealth—was a critically important legal concept that was closely tied to blood; any derogations from blood were to be construed strictly. When property was the primary source of wealth, adoption law focused on children's access to that property. When infertile parents wanted children, adoption law focused on facilitating that matching process. Although the discourse of adoption law uses the children's best interests, those interests have varied depending on broader cultural concerns.

Over the past fifty years, many social workers (and others) have reinforced the belief that a biological connection has no role to play once an adoption has occurred. Whether it be in the context of open adoptions, through which a biological parent retains some contact with the adoptee, or open records, such that an adoptee has access to his or her original birth certificate, this approach views adoption as a complete substitute for any blood ties and is thus generally against allowing any type of tie between adoptive and biological families.

In an effort to "overcome" biology, adoption experts have attempted to erase it completely. Accordingly, biological mothers were frequently told that they would be able to move on with their lives, as though they had never given birth to a child. The biological mother was told that she would not have any connection with her child, and doctors attempted to ensure that this occurred. For example, birth mothers were often blindfolded in the delivery room, so they would not see their children.[9] Adoption records were sealed so that the adoptive family served as a complete substitute for the biological family. The biological tie was considered erased for both the birth mother and the adoptee. The 1851 Massachusetts adoption statute, considered to be the first "modern" adoption statute, expressly provided that the adopted child would become the "legal child" of the adoptive parents.[10]

These attitudes are still reflected in contemporary adoption law, which presumes that biological ties can be severed in all cases without damaging impact. The adoptive family is considered to be a complete substitute for the biological family and, indeed, is often created to look like the biological family through various matching policies.[11] Under the proposed Uniform Adoption Act (UAA), the biological mother has eight days in which to change her mind about relinquishing a child for adoption. Although this period of time ensures stability for the adoptive family, its brevity indicates an assumption about the ease with which biological ties can be terminated. Adoption records are sealed for ninety-nine years, thereby firmly establishing the notion that the adoptive family is, for all adoptees, a full and complete replacement of the biological family. The UAA does include provisions for state mutual registries, so that adult adoptees and biological parents can contact each other if they so choose. The state mutual registry option is, however, considered to be the weakest possible support for facilitating reunions.

Blood Tells: The Analogy of Adoption

The notion that blood families trump adopted families remains deeply embedded in American culture. The cultural preference for blood ties explains some of the stigma that has accompanied adoption and the secrecy that has accompanied the use of donor gametes. During the mid-twentieth century, many parents did not tell their children that they were adopted, lest the family be seen as different from, and worse than, other families.[12] The cultural preference for biologically based families can be seen in the first survey of attitudes toward adoption. In the survey of more than fifteen hundred adults, 90 percent of the participants had a positive opinion of adoption, and 95 percent generally supported it. Nonetheless, when it came to an examination of the adoptive family, respondents were somewhat more cautious. Half the respondents believed that, although having an adopted child was better than infertility, it was not quite as good as having a biological child.[13] Only two-thirds of the respondents believed that it was highly likely that an adoptee would love his or her adoptive parents as much as biological parents. There is, then, continuing ambivalence with respect to families formed through adoption, rather than through biology, a belief that blood ties are stronger and more desirable than adoptive ties.

Within the law, the significance of blood relationships retains validity, such that the adopted child is still, in some circumstances, treated very differently from the biological child. When it comes to the death of a parent, an adopted child has different rights because of his or her status. This is clear in the legal approach to an adoptee's inheritance rights, as well as in other contexts. The historical record on the legal treatment of adoptees, which shows their ambiguous relationship to families to which they were biological "strangers," provides context for understanding the complexities in the legal status of donor children. Both adoptees and donor children are legal, but not necessarily biological, family members.

Adoption and Inheritance

Historically, under the "stranger-to-the-adoption" rule, an adopted child generally could not inherit through relatives who were not a party to the adoption. The adopted child could inherit from his or her parents, but not from relatives of the parents. Because they were "strangers" to the adoption process, these relatives were presumed not to have intended for their property to be inherited outside the bloodline. In 1915, the U.S. Supreme Court upheld Alabama law that specifically denied inheritance rights to adopted children.[14] Under the inheritance statute, children adopted in other states could not inherit land in Alabama.[15] Although the instrument of adoption vested the children with "all the rights and benefits of legitimate children in [the parents'] estate," this was insufficient under Alabama law to allow the children to inherit the land. The assumption underlying the disinheritance of adopted children was that decedents wanted their estates to go to blood relatives. As the South Dakota Supreme Court stated in 1978, inheritance follows blood.[16]

Today, in a few situations, an adopted child may have fewer rights to inherit from various relatives in the adoptive family than would a biological child. On the other hand, an adoptive child may have the same rights as a biological child of the adoptive family and may also be able to inherit from his or her biological family.

In Vermont, until 1996 an adopted child could not inherit from relatives of his or her adoptive parents.[17] In that year, the Vermont Supreme Court held that an adopted child could inherit from her uncle, her father's brother. In Mississippi, the rights of adoptees to inherit from collateral relatives is still unclear.[18] In some states, depending on the phrasing of the will, an adopted child may not be able to inherit through a "class gift,"[19] or a gift that is phrased as, for example, to my "descendants" or to my "grandchildren."

In Colorado, an adoptee may inherit from his or her biological parents if there are no other heirs.[20] In Pennsylvania, when the biological relatives—other than the parents—have maintained a relationship with the adoptee, then the adoptee may inherit from those relatives.[21] In other states, an adoption decree can protect the child's rights to inherit form his or her biological family.[22] Under the model statute that governs inheritance, a child adopted by the spouse of one of his or her biological parents can still inherit from the other biological parent, even though all legal ties have otherwise been severed between that parent and the child.[23] Although some of these statutes protect a child's relationship with biological kin, the assumption behind these provisions seems, nonetheless, to be based on blood: the decedent would prefer that his or her estate be left to a blood relative rather than to distant relatives.

Incest

The notion of blood telling is also evident in other contexts. The incest prohibition that prevents relatives from marrying each other is deeply rooted in American law.[24] Nonetheless, states vary as to whether they sanction people related by adoption, rather than blood, from marrying each other and as to whether adoptive relationships, or biological relationships, constitute grounds for criminal incest. Although brothers and sisters—adopted or not—generally cannot marry each other, in some states, a man and his brother's adopted daughter can marry each other, even though the man would be prohibited from marrying his biological niece.[25] The blood relationship is seemingly "stronger." In New York, a father was allowed to marry his adopted daughter on the theory that they were not related by blood; the daughter was not "descended" from her father.[26] Similarly, two first cousins related by adoption were allowed to marry each other, even though a blood, rather than an affinity, relationship would have precluded the marriage.[27]

With respect to criminal incest, states have taken inconsistent positions on whether adoptive relationships have any effect. It is unclear whether a man who has intercourse with his adopted daughter, or with his biological daughter who has been adopted by someone else, would be subject to penalties. In *State v. Fischer*, Indiana overturned the incest conviction of a man who had intercourse with his biological daughter who had been adopted by another family at the age of four.[28] The court reasoned that the adoption completely severed the biological relationship; the child's actual parents were her adoptive parents.[29] Similarly, several states have held that a father does not commit criminal incest when he has sexual intercourse with his adopted daughter.[30] In South Dakota, incest can only be perpetrated against someone in a blood relationship.[31] The court rejected the state's argument that adoption creates "legal consanguinity" and stated that the adoption laws could not create new bloodlines.

Other Contexts for Adoptees

Some judges reinforce the primacy of blood ties even outside of incest and inheritance. Scott Albrecht and his sister, Susie, had been adopted as infants and grew up as brother and sister. When Susie and her husband died, Scott sued to adopt their child.[32] Scott wanted to use a special legal process that would have allowed him to adopt the child quickly, and which is available to a "relative of the child by blood" wishing to adopt. A Wisconsin judge flatly stated that, because Scott and Susie had themselves been adopted, they were not blood kin, and thus the brother was not eligible for the special procedures applicable to family members seeking to adopt. As the grandmother said, "[The judge] told my son that he was not his sister's brother. . . . He essentially said our family didn't exist." On appeal, two judges disagreed with this interpretation of the statute and held that the uncle was eligible for the special procedures; one judge opined, however, that this decision contravened the plain language of the statute.[33]

In an ironic twist that serves to reinforce the primacy of biologically formed families, agencies have attempted to match the adoptive parents with their potential child. They have tried to match physical and intellectual attributes, religion, and race[34] between adoptees and adoptors. Such matching attempts to make adoptive families look just like biological families, in an effort to dissolve the perceived stigma of adoption.

The Legitimacy of Adultery: Artificial Families

Although artificial insemination by a husband has not presented controversial legal issues concerning parentage and legitimacy, inheritance, and incest, as has adoption, artificial insemination by donor has the potential to confuse the application of the marital presumption and the status of the child. Indeed, cases involving artificial insemination have reached conflicting conclusions on whether a child born to a married woman, who had been inseminated with a third party's sperm, albeit with the husband's consent, was legitimate or whether the wife had committed adultery and had thus made the child illegitimate because the marital presumption did not apply. For example, in the 1963 case involving Stanley and Annette Gursky, a New York judge held that, even if Stanley had consented, artificial insemination by a donor was indeed "adultery," and any resulting child was "illegitimate." Although the court acknowledged that the New York Sanitary Code regulated the practice of donor insemination, it held that this law was entirely separate from any parentage determination "and can in no wise be deemed to sanction the practice of artificial insemination or to render legitimate any issue thereof."[35] In a Canadian case, the court held that donor insemination of the wife without the consent of her husband is adultery, regardless of the fact that no act of sexual intercourse had occurred.[36] By contrast, in a 1945 Chicago case, the judge held that adultery did not include artificial insemination by donor.[37]

If artificial insemination by donor has presented various legal and visible issues for married couples, it has been virtually invisible when it comes to single women or gay and lesbian couples. As late as 1988, artificial insemination could be casually described as insemination of a "woman whose husband is infertile or at risk for a genetic disorder."[38]

What's Wrong with Nonmarital Children?

The consequences of being labeled a nonmarital child have been dire. Up until the late 1960s, a nonmarital child born was deemed by many states to be illegitimate and, as a result, was denied the same legal protection given to children of married parents. State laws descended from the old English doctrine of "filius nullius." William Blackstone, the preeminent chronicler of British law in the eighteenth century, explained that the child born outside of marriage was literally "the son of nobody":

> The incapacity of a bastard consists principally of this, that he cannot be heir to any one, neither can he have heirs, but of his own body; for, being nullius filius, he is therefore of kin to nobody, and has no ancestor from whom any inheritable blood can be derived.[39]

Such a sanction, in a society that privileged land ownership and inheritance by the first son, was harsh.

State discrimination between legitimate and illegitimate children affected numerous areas of the law, ranging from eligibility for wrongful-death tort claims to insurance benefits, inheritance without a will (intestacy provisions), custody, parental visitation, and adoption. In 1968, the U.S. Supreme Court began the process of dissolving the distinctions between marital and nonmarital children in a pair of cases challenging the limitations of Louisiana's wrongful-death statute. Louisiana's law precluded nonmarital family members from bringing various claims. In *Levy v. Louisiana*,[40] the Court held the Louisiana statute unconstitutional because it did not allow an illegitimate child to recover for his mother's wrongful death. In *Glona v. American Guarantee & Liability Insurance*,[41] the Court overturned another part of the statute, which prohibited a nonmarital mother from recovering for the wrongful death of her child. Justice Black, writing for the majority in *Levy*, rebuked advocates of differentiation for their failure to focus on the child's interests, declaring, "it is invidious to discriminate against [illegitimate children] when no action, conduct, or demeanor of theirs is possibly relevant to the harm that was done the mother."[42]

Following the Supreme Court decisions in *Levy* and *Glona*, state and lower federal courts began to address the relationship between parents and their nonmarital children in other areas of the law.[43] Portions of the multiple pieces of federal legislation, including the Copyright Act, were questioned for their constitutionality.[44] Even though courts repeatedly struck down existing statutes, state legislatures were not quick to fill in the gaps with new laws. Many statutes remained silent on the procedures to establish links between unmarried parents and their children, leaving these relationships, albeit temporarily, without legal certainty.[45]

Uniformity and Legitimacy—at Last?

Even before *Levy*, in April 1966, professor Harry D. Krause published a cry for reform in the *Texas Law Review* with an article titled "Bringing the Bastard into the Great Society: A Proposed Uniform Act on Legitimacy."[46] In his article, Krause cited statistics showing that illegitimacy was a growing problem and related the rise in illegitimacy to the "poverty problem." He urged broad legal reform of parental support as a solution, arguing that legislation, not incremental judicial decision-making, was appropriate. Krause used his article to set out a comprehensive—yet straightforward—model for state regulation. His Proposed Uniform Act, which was not focused on reproductive technology, nonetheless included provisions concerning the status of a child born through artificial insemination. He proposed that, if a husband had consented to artificial insemination of his wife, then the resulting child would conclusively be deemed legitimate, with the right to share the same name as the father.[47]

The National Conference of Commissioners on Uniform State Laws (NCCUSL) heard the cry for reform and in 1969 appointed a committee to study the law relating to a child born out of wedlock.[48] The NCCUSL is an organization made up of commissioners appointed from each state who study laws among the states and draft proposals for uniform legislation. Commissioners are not paid for their work. To help develop the new law, NCCUSL asked Harry Krause if he would serve as the official reporter, or drafter. He accepted. Countless hours were indeed put into the Uniform Parentage Act between the time the first committee was formed and when the act was approved by the National Conference on Uniform Laws in 1973.

Not surprisingly, the Uniform Parentage Act of 1973 (UPA) closely followed the model published by Krause (early drafts even had a familiar title: "The Uniform Legitimacy Act").[49] The first two sections expressed the substance of the act, including the proclamation that "the parent and child relationship extends equally to every child and to every parent, regardless of the marital status of the parents,"[50] and the following twenty-seven sections provided for the procedures to establish paternity and support. Because biological testing had not yet been made widely available, the act instead relied on a network of rebuttable presumptions to determine paternity. For example, a man was presumed to be the biological father of a child if the man had been married to the child's mother at the time of the child's birth, if the marriage ended less than three hundred days after the child's birth, or if he had received the child into his home and "openly [held] out the child as his natural child."[51]

Ensuring equality in an era when nonmarital children otherwise faced discrimination meant a mother and a father for every child. Indeed, one proposed section provided that if the child had no presumed father within one year, then an action to determine the identity of a father would be brought by the appropriate state agency in order to ensure that every child would have a known father. However, this provision never made it into the commission's final draft. In Krause's description of the demise of this provision, he lamented, "in the press of the afternoon's business, the conference failed to see the Committee's argument that substantive equality is an empty promise so long as the father remains unknown."[52] Contemporary child-support laws echo the original presumption that every child needs two parents, even though society has become far more accepting of nonmarital children, and the law has moved toward the substantive equality that Krause sought.

Like Krause's 1966 article, the Uniform Parentage Act also recognized status issues involving children born through artificial insemination. These provisions applied only to married couples and stated that if (1) the husband's consent was given in writing and (2) the insemination was done under the supervision of a licensed physician, then the husband would be the father, with the same rights as any other legal father. The actual language stated,

> If, under the supervision of a licensed physician and with the consent of her husband, a wife is inseminated artificially with semen donated by a man not her husband, the husband is treated in law as if he were the natural father of a child thereby conceived. The husband's consent must be in writing and signed by him and his wife. The physician shall certify their signatures and the date of the insemination, and file the husband's consent with the [state department of health], where it shall be kept confidential and in a sealed file. However, the physician's failure to do so does not affect the father and child relationship. All papers and records pertaining to the insemination, whether part of the permanent record of a court or of a file held by the supervising

physician or elsewhere, are subject to inspection only upon an order of the court for good cause shown.[53]

Ultimately, the UPA determined parentage only for children conceived through donor insemination by married women. It specified that the donor had no parental rights and was not the father and that the husband was the legal father, so long as he had consented in writing. The UPA said nothing about the parentage of children conceived through artificial insemination when the woman was not married. As the act conceded, it covered only "one fact situation that occurs frequently," rather than all the difficult situations presented by artificial insemination.[54] Consequently, although the UPA did not prohibit the nonmarital use of artificial insemination, it left the parental status of the sperm provider unclear when either the woman was not married or, if she was married, had not used a physician for the insemination process. The UPA did, however, set the stage for addressing the more complicated issues of parentage through its attention to artificial insemination. By turning Krause's initial "legitimacy" act into a parentage act, the UPA became a comprehensive framework for establishing the parents of any child, marital, nonmarital, or produced through reproductive technology, setting the stage for "normalizing" children not born through traditional, marital intercourse.

The Uniform Parentage Act was adopted by eighteen states[55] between 1975 and 1985, while other states adopted their own approaches to this issue. Moreover, over the next several decades, there were enormous changes in the reproductive technology field, in government regulation, and in the construction of families (approximately one out of every three children born today is born to a nonmarital mother, a rate that has been increasing, with, for example, 28 percent of children born to unmarried mothers in 1990 and 33 percent in 1999).[56] Consequently, during this time period, NCCUSL developed several other piecemeal statutes before finally beginning to draft a new uniform parentage act. In 2000, it proposed a replacement Uniform Parentage Act, officially withdrawing all provisions of the 1973 version. The new UPA also incorporated most of the Uniform Status of Children of Assisted Conception Act, a 1989 proposal that had been enacted by only two states, North Dakota and Virginia,[57] and an expansive section on genetic testing (Article 5).[58] Although the 1973 act had dealt only with artificial insemination using donated sperm, in recognition of the changes in technology, the new act addressed a variety of legal parentage problems that might result from egg or sperm donation as well as from the freezing of embryos.[59] Nonetheless, the 2000 revision was limited in scope to determining paternity and donor status only for married couples. Although early drafts had continued the earlier requirements of physician involvement in order to terminate the parental rights of a donor,[60] the 2000 act did abandon the requirement that a physician must be involved in artificial insemination. It did require, however, that the married couple sign a consent form when donor sperm (although not eggs) were used in order to ensure that the husband was the legal father of any resulting child.[61] The final sections dealing with artificial insemination covered the effect of the dissolution of marriage or the death of a spouse before the placement of eggs, sperm, or embryos. In the event of divorce or death, the absent spouse would not be the legal parent of the resulting child unless he or she consented to parentage in record before the placement of egg, sperm, or embryos.[62]

Although the purpose of the Uniform Parentage Act of 2000 remained the same as the 1973 version—to bring equality to children regardless of their parents' marital status[63]—several groups believed that the 2000 act did not adequately protect the children of unmarried parents compared to the rights of children of married parents.[64] Both the American Bar Association (ABA) Section on Individual Rights and Responsibilities and the ABA Committee on the Unmet Legal Needs of Children lodged objections with the NCCUSL concerning the differential treatment of children of unmarried couples and children of married couples and the act's failure to include parentage issues concerning same-sex couples.[65] The objections led to reconsideration of specific provisions, extended discussions with all entities involved, and a vote on amendments by a mailed ballot. In November 2002, the amendments were unanimously approved.[66]

The 2002 amendments broadened the scope of the UPA in various ways, including through the substitution of "man" or "woman" where the 2000 act had said "husband" or "wife" and a provision allowing a man to establish his paternity if for the first two years he resided with the child. Although the changes seem small, they broadened the act's application to unmarried couples, although the act still does not address issues concerning same-sex couples and the new reproductive technologies.[67] Nonetheless, the changes may have a substantial effect on a family, such as allowing an unmarried man to back out of an artificial insemination agreement before the placement of the sperm. The UPA now provides that a donor is not a father unless he signs a consent to paternity or, during the child's first two years of life, lives with the child and holds out the child as his offspring.[68] Almost thirty years after the original uniform act, the Uniform Parentage Act finally addressed the relational rights established outside marriage. According to the act, an egg or sperm donor is not a parent when a child is conceived through "assisted reproduction," or reproduction not involving sexual intercourse.[69] As the comments to the revised UPA explain,

> it governs the parentage issues in all cases in which the birth mother is also the woman who intends to parent the child. . . . this section shields all donors, whether of sperm or eggs, (§ 102 (8), supra), from parenthood in all situations in which either a married woman or a single woman conceives a child through ART with the intent to be the child's parent, either by herself or with a man.[70] The UPA is now law in 7 states.[71]

The drafters of the act candidly admit, however, that the UPA does not deal with many of the other contentious issues involved in regulating the new reproductive technologies, including the status of embryos or oversight of fertility clinics.[72] And the act still contains vestiges of the earlier stigma of illegitimacy when a child was conceived with artificial insemination, allowing the husband to contest a finding of legitimacy within two years.[73]

This chapter's discussion of the history of the legal response to families formed outside of sexual intercourse within marriage provides the context for the multiple approaches taken to these families under existing laws. Tracing the history of how the law has responded to families formed through adoption and gamete provision shows the impact of genetic and marital relationships on family formation. Whereas early cases and laws struggled with whether children born through gamete provision were "legitimate," later cases struggle with the status of the child and with the newer issues of the "rights" of the gamete provider. The next two chapters examine issues raised by parentage determinations and reproductive technologies, exploring, first, the rights of a donor versus intending parent(s) and, then, the partnership rights that a couple may have against each other.

5

Donating to Parenthood

GAMETE PROVIDERS ARE not the legal parents of any resulting child—or are they? Most states have laws providing that a sperm donor has no rights to any resulting child and that the intending parents are the legal parents, but very few have comparable laws concerning egg or embryo donation. Even the statutes that do exist are often limited in scope; although many of those covering sperm provision address insemination of married women, like the 1973 Uniform Parentage Act, some do not address parenthood issues outside the marriage context. Given the legal history of parentage determinations, in which concerns about adultery initially affected decision-making concerning the legitimacy of children born through donor sperm, the focus in these statutes on the insemination of married women is not surprising. Moreover, the legacy of the 1973 UPA with respect to nonmarital children was equality, not parentage or reproductive technology.[1] The twin concerns of adultery and equality, combined with the novelty of egg and embryo donation, explain the limits of existing laws that focus on the parenthood of children born through reproductive technology to married couples. Among the states, there is no uniformity concerning gamete donation or surrogacy and the applicability of parentage statutes to define familial relationships established through collaborative reproduction.[2] Under our federalist system of government, each state zealously protects its rights to develop family law, and there is no one federal law that determines legal parentage. Moreover, each state's family laws are profoundly influenced by moral values.

States have essentially taken three different approaches to these issues: first, they have adopted statutes comparable to the 1973 UPA, providing that donors whose sperm is given to a physician for inseminating a married woman are not parents; second, some state laws are similar to the

2002 UPA and provide a gender-neutral approach by specifying that no donors will be considered a parent, regardless of whether a physician is involved and regardless of the marital status of the parties; third, a group of states has simply not addressed the issues.[3] Some statutes explicitly recognize that the parties may agree on certain rights for the donor, whereas others do not address this issue at all.

Underlying the jumbled, incomplete existing laws are two sets of profound issues concerning the identity of the parents: Are the recipients the parents? and, Can the egg, embryo, or sperm provider be considered a parent? The answers to these two questions determine the legal parameters of families formed through reproductive technology. This chapter discusses the varying approaches to the rights of donors and intending parents.

Because the technologies for sperm, egg, and embryo donation as well as the related issue of surrogacy have developed at different times, and because donor families may be formed by married couples, nonmarital couples (including gay and lesbian partners), and single individuals, the laws addressing each situation differ. This chapter summarizes the laws applicable to each of these various circumstances. It first analyzes the laws on families formed through sperm, eggs, embryos, and surrogacy, focusing on marital and nonmarital families. It then turns to particular issues of parentage when same-sex couples form families through any of the reproductive technologies.

Sperm-Formed Families

For sperm, the law typically facilitates transactions by allocating parental rights to the intending parents, rather than to the gamete provider. There are three different situations in which women use donated sperm: (1) married women may be artificially inseminated by a known or unknown donor because their husbands have experienced fertility impairments; (2) single women or lesbian couples use an unknown donor; or (3) single women or lesbian couples use a known donor. Virtually all states address the first situation. But there are gaps when it comes to the use of sperm donation outside of marriage, and not all states address the relationship between donors and unmarried parents. Even when the parties agree on parenthood, explicit contracts precluding rights for gamete donors are not necessarily enforceable because courts may invalidate these agreements based on such public policy concerns as the best interests of the child.[4]

Sperm Used by a Married Woman

Most states address paternity when a married woman uses sperm that has been provided by a man who is not her husband, and many states have adopted the 1973 uniform law on parentage. In order for the husband to become the father when the woman becomes pregnant through donor sperm, a doctor must supervise the insemination, the husband must consent in writing to the insemination, and the physician must file the husband's consent with the state health department. Only once these requirements have been satisfied can the husband become the legal father and the donor's legal rights be terminated.[5]

If the couple fails to follow the law's requirements, then the results may be disastrous. Consider what happened in California to three-year-old Alexandria, when her parents, Lorraine and Gordon, divorced.[6] Gordon had a vasectomy before he married Lorraine, so they discussed using a donor in order to have children. Both parents looked at a donor catalogue from the Pacific Fertility Medical Center before choosing a man who looked like Gordon. They then signed a consent form that required both of them to treat any resulting child as their child. But California law mandates that a doctor certify the signatures on the consent form; there was no physician certification on their form (Lorraine and Alexandria claimed that this was due to the negligence and contract breach of the medical center). As part of the divorce proceedings, Lorraine requested child support from Gordon. But the court decided that Gordon did not have to support Alexandria because no one had followed the law on how to establish parenthood after artificial insemination. The story is even more complicated: Gordon claimed that he had signed the consent form so that Lorraine could have a child but that he never wanted to be a father, and the divorce court seemed sympathetic to that claim. For Alexandria, the story is simple: she has no legal father. The applicable parentage laws are designed to effectuate the wishes of the intending parents, but their results can have harsh consequences.

Unknown Sperm Used by a Single Woman or Lesbian Couple

States generally address the parentage issues surrounding *married* women who become pregnant through donor sperm, but when it comes to *single* women, states vary considerably in their approach to the donor's status as a father. Some states simply do not recognize the possibility that artificial insemination might occur outside of marriage. For example, in Oklahoma, only doctors can perform artificial insemination, and their patients are limited to married couples; the child is considered the same as a "naturally conceived legitimate child of the husband and wife."[7] Similarly, Connecticut resolves these issues by restricting the application of its artificial insemination laws to married couples. Under Connecticut law, a physician cannot perform artificial insemination by donor (AID) unless "the physician receives in writing the request and consent of the husband and wife desiring the utilization of A.I.D.," and the permission must be filed in the local court.[8] Numerous states have adopted the 1973 UPA or a slightly revised version of it that similarly addresses only artificial insemination by married couples.

Finally, other states have clearly addressed the donor's status, providing that a donor has no potential rights regardless of the marital status of the woman. For example, the New Jersey law uses the UPA language and states, "Unless the donor of semen and the woman have entered into a written contract to the contrary, the donor of semen provided to a licensed physician for use in artificial insemination of a woman other than the donor's wife is treated in law as if he were not the father of a child."[9]

Known Sperm Used by a Single Woman or Lesbian Couple

Artificial insemination typically involves unknown donors, but recipients sometimes turn to a man they already know for his sperm. When single women or lesbians search for a known donor, they may—or may not—want the man to continue to be involved in the child's life. In the first situation, the parents may enter into an agreement that sets out exactly what rights each participant has. These agreements can entirely preclude the donor from any rights or might establish a different status that allows for contact between the donor and the child. Indeed, some men consider themselves "co-parents" and may move to be closer to "their" children, while others arrange for visits throughout the year.[10] One of my single lesbian friends became friendly with Walter, a gay man, in graduate school; once she found herself unable to conceive through anonymously provided sperm, she asked Walter if he had any interest in becoming a part-time parent. He said yes, they agreed to an informal parenting arrangement, she became pregnant through alternative insemination, and Walter, who lives half a continent away, attended the birth. She now has a room set aside in her house for Walter's frequent visits, and she takes the child on visits to him and his family.

In other situations, women may want to preclude entirely the donor's involvement in their lives and may sign agreements to that effect. The enforceability of these agreements varies, however, depending on state laws concerning how artificial insemination must be performed and whether there is explicit statutory recognition of these contracts.

A few states explicitly recognize that a sperm donor's rights can be established through an agreement between the parties. In Kansas, the law provides that a sperm donor who provides sperm to a doctor for the insemination of a woman to whom the donor is not married does not have any parental rights, unless he and the mother have agreed otherwise. In other words, the default rule is that a sperm donor has no rights, even if he is known to the mother. This rule did not prevent a man from claiming that he was the father of his former girlfriend's twins, even though they did not have a formal agreement establishing his rights.[11] Daryl Hendrix and Samantha Harrington were friends, and Hendrix provided sperm to a doctor so that Harrington could have children. After Harrington gave birth, Hendrix filed a paternity action, asking the Kansas courts to make him the father. He claimed that his biological connection was sufficient for him to be the legal father. The case raised questions concerning the state's authority to define parental rights and the circumstances under which gamete donors have the choice to become involved in children's lives. It also flatly posed the question of whether every child should have two parents. Ultimately, the court upheld the state statute that precluded paternity for donors when their sperm was provided to a physician.

Unlike Kansas, Texas law provides that sperm donors are not fathers but says nothing about how an agreement might affect parental rights. So, what happens when the sperm donor signs an agreement stating that he will be the parent of any child? In 2003, Sharon Sullivan, a lesbian, and Brian Russell, a gay man, signed a "co-parenting" agreement in which Brian agreed to provide his sperm to Sharon. Their agreement also said that if Sharon became pregnant, the baby would be "the child of BRIAN KEITH RUSSELL as if he and SHARON SULLIVAN were married at the time of conception, and that BRIAN KEITH RUSSELL will be named as the father on the child's birth certificate."[12] Although Brian did provide the sperm, other parts of the agreement began to fall apart. Brian asked to attend the birth of the child but did not. Less than a month after the birth, he sued Sharon, requesting that he be named the father of her daughter.[13] Faced with a conflict between a law stating that sperm donors have no parental rights and an agreement that explicitly gave

Brian paternal rights, the Texas courts allowed him to try to establish his paternity.

Although courts often defer to the parties' stated intentions, men have sometimes successfully claimed paternity and visitation rights even with an agreement providing otherwise. These cases typically involve women who have used known donors and inseminated themselves outside of a doctor's office.[14] By contrast, courts will typically preclude a man from asserting paternity if state law terminates a donor's rights when a physician is involved in the insemination process, and the parties have complied with this provision. Consider what happened to Steven S., who was married to another woman when he provided sperm so that his girlfriend, Deborah, could get pregnant. Because Deborah followed the letter of the law and used a physician for the insemination, Steven S., who wanted to establish a relationship with his children, was out of luck.[15]

The stories in these cases are fascinating human-interest narratives, but they are also extremely sad—whether it be for the woman, the man, or the child. Agreements, intent, and the law can be tricky.

The laws that currently exist are simply not clear about the paternal rights of sperm donors, particularly when a single woman or lesbian gives birth. When the mother knows the sperm donor, the issues are even more complex. Courts will generally defer to a woman who has complied with a state's artificial insemination statute, even when the donor is known. This prevents a sperm donor from changing his mind and allows the woman to control the determination of paternity. If the woman does not use the state statute—which may require the use of a doctor or may recognize agreements or may not apply to in vitro fertilization—then courts are more likely to defer to what the donor wants, often reasoning that every child deserves a mother and a father.

Egg-Formed Families

Because of the possibility that a woman can use someone else's eggs to create a child, there are three possible mothers for any child: a genetic mother (who contributes the egg), a gestational mother (the woman who carries the baby), and an intending mother (the woman who wants to take the baby home). In most families, the same woman combines all three roles. Generally, where an egg is donated—just as when sperm is donated—as in the E.G. case discussed in chapter 1, donors sign an agreement waiving all parental rights and responsibilities with respect to any child conceived from their eggs.[16] In *E.G.*, the egg donor was living with her partner and ultimately succeeded in voiding the agreement, obtaining status as a parent.

Only a few states have enacted specific legislation assigning parental status after egg donation. These laws delineate the relationships and responsibilities between egg donors and their offspring, and similarly provide, albeit applying different language, that an egg donor relinquishes all maternal rights and obligations with respect to the donation itself and the resulting child. Although few states have such legislation, courts in other states have adjudicated the parenthood status of an egg donor and some have simply analogized egg donors to sperm donors. Nonetheless, the rights of egg providers, recipients, and children are not clear in most states.

Even where there are laws, they generally address only a married recipient and her husband, labeling them the parents of a child from egg donation. As in the sperm context, however, these laws fail to deal with legal parentage of children conceived by single women using egg donation.[17] Fewer than ten states, including Colorado, Florida, North Dakota, Oklahoma, Texas, and Virginia, have specific legislation with respect to egg donation, and these laws have never been challenged.[18] A few other states— California, Ohio, Pennsylvania, and Tennessee—do have court decisions on the parenthood status of an egg donor.

State statutes vary considerably. Florida law, like that of many other states, addresses only the parenting rights of married recipients. If a child is born "within wedlock" as the result of donated eggs, then the husband-and-wife couple are the parents;[19] Florida law says nothing, however, about whether a recipient who is single is the parent. Florida's domestic-relations law permits only reasonable compensation directly related to the donation of eggs, and it releases egg donors from all maternal rights and obligations with respect to the donation itself or the resulting children.[20] Texas and North Dakota laws, which explicitly include egg providers as "donors," preclude a donor from serving as a parent.[21]

North Dakota has adopted the new version of the UPA in which an egg "donor" is defined as an individual who produces eggs used for assisted reproduction, not including a married woman who provides eggs to be used for her own assisted reproduction,[22] a woman who gives birth to a child by means of assisted reproduction,[23] or a woman whose body produces an egg used for the purposes of conceiving a child for herself.[24] Correspondingly, North Dakota law explicitly states that a donor is not a parent of a child conceived by means of assisted reproduction.[25]

Under North Dakota's UPA, the mother-child relationship is established between a woman and a child by the following criteria: the woman's having given birth to the child; a court adjudication of maternity; or the legal adoption of the child by the woman.[26] Contrarily, the father-child relationship is established under state law by, inter alia, the man's having consented to assisted reproduction by a woman that resulted in the birth of the child.[27]

Oklahoma, which has also adopted the updated UPA, has a slightly different twist.[28] Any child born as the result of "heterologous oocyte donation" or "human embryo transfer" shall be legally considered the same as a naturally conceived legitimate child of the husband and wife.[29] Similarly, an oocyte or embryo donor shall have no right, obligation, or interest with respect to a child born as a result of the donation and shall be relieved of all parental responsibilities for any child resulting from embryo transfer; a child born as a result of a heterologous oocyte donation shall also have no right, obligation, or interest with respect to the person who donated the oocyte that resulted in the birth of the child.[30] Oklahoma law also explicitly requires physician-obtained written consent of the husband and wife donating the human embryo and receiving the embryo transfer.[31] Texas, another 2002 UPA adopter, similarly provides that a donor is not a parent of a child conceived by means of assisted reproduction,[32] defined as a method of causing pregnancy other than sexual intercourse and including the donation of eggs or embryos.[33] If a husband provides sperm for or consents to assisted reproduction by his wife, then he is, under Texas law, the father of any resulting child.[34] However, the requisite that consent by a married woman to assisted reproduction be in a record signed by both the woman and her husband does not apply to the donation of eggs by a married woman for assisted reproduction by another woman.[35] Similar to the statutory provisions in North Dakota's adopted UPA, Texas law defines a "donor" as "an individual who produces eggs or sperm used for assisted reproduction, regardless of whether the production is for consideration."[36] A husband who provides sperm or a wife who provides eggs to be used in an ART procedure, as well as a woman who gives birth to a child by means of assisted reproduction, is categorically excluded as a "donor" under state law.[37] Texas law also provides for the effect of dissolution of marriage or death on parental status.[38]

Virginia, which has not adopted the 2002 UPA, makes the intended mother the legal mother of a child conceived through the assistance of an egg donation and relieves the egg donor of all parental rights and obligations.[39] Under the chapter pertaining to the "status of children of assisted conception,"[40] which is based in part on another uniform act (the Uniform Status of Children of Assisted Conception Act), Virginia's domestic-relations law determines parentage generally when resulting from the performance of ART, stating that the mother is the gestational mother[41] and the husband of the gestational mother is the father.[42] Only if the donor, defined as "an individual, other than a surrogate, who contributes the sperm or egg used in assisted conception,"[43] is the husband of the gestational mother will a donor be the legal parent of a child conceived through ART.[44]

Several states have explicitly stated that they will apply laws concerning the establishment of paternity to the establishment of maternity. For example, Wyoming changed its law in 2003 to provide, simply, that anything in the parentage act that relates to determining paternity will similarly apply to determining maternity.[45] This gender-neutral approach supplies a relatively straightforward template for handling the developing legal issues concerning egg donation.

Embryos and Parentage

Like egg donation, embryo donation is a comparatively new technology that is slowly affecting the law. Many states have not yet addressed issues involving embryo donation. For those that have, as with other areas of donation, states vary in how they approach the determination of parentage for embryos transferred to a recipient. They may treat embryo donation like other forms of assisted reproduction, or they may have developed entirely new statutes reflecting the popular belief that there is something different about embryos compared to eggs and sperm alone. Again, the same issues concerning marital versus nonmarital couples appear.

In states that have adopted the new UPA, embryo donation is included as one of the means of "assisted reproduction." In those states, the participants in embryo donation are treated like participants in any other reproductive technology. Consequently, the man must indicate, in a "record" signed by both him and the woman bearing the child that he intends to become the parent. Moreover, the UPA contains a specific provision establishing that the donor is not a legal parent, thereby preventing the donor from later claiming parentage. Although the statute is silent about whether embryo donation is also available to lesbian couples and single women, it was drafted broadly enough to include these potential recipients.

No state explicitly bars gay and lesbian access to assisted reproductive techniques, including embryo donation,[46] but language may refer to donation to "married couples" or it may be clear through other language that gays and lesbians are not allowed. For example, Utah's statute is somewhat restrictive in that it refers to the "husband's" and "married woman's" consent to embryo donation.[47] By contrast, because it adopted the 2002 UPA, North Dakota's law refers only to the consents required from the "man" and "woman."[48] Utah's statute uses the phrases "husband's paternity" and "child born to his wife," and Wyoming's law refers only to "paternity" and "resulting child," without any explicit language about marriage.[49] Given that the statutory language in Utah, Texas, and Washington only addresses and expressly allows for embryo donation to married couples, the assumption that gay/lesbian couples and single women are ineligible for embryo donation seems quite plausible. (If any of these states enacts a law that accords the same rights to couples joined by civil union as to married couples, then gay and lesbian partners would be covered by the "married couples" language.)

Oklahoma's law is quite different from those in other states because it explicitly addresses the rights not just of recipients and donors but also of children. As in other states, embryo transfer is seemingly restricted to married couples on both sides of the transaction; the parents are referred to as the husband and the wife. Moreover, written consent must be obtained from both the husband and wife *donating* the embryo and the husband and wife *receiving* the embryo. Finally, Oklahoma's statute, like that of several other states, explicitly takes away any rights that the donor might want. The law notes that the child is the "natural child" of the receiving couple and removes any obligation that the "donating couple" or their children might otherwise have with respect to the donor child.[50] Similarly, in Delaware, the law recognizes that the donating couple are not the parents.[51]

Although Florida does not allow adoption by gays and lesbians, it does not explicitly prohibit gamete donation to single women or lesbian couples. On the other hand, states such as Connecticut allow embryo donation to a "person," implying that the recipient need not be married.[52] Moreover, the California courts have analogized paternity establishment to maternity establishment for egg donors, perhaps setting a precedent for maternity establishment with respect to embryos. Moreover, in California, as in other states that have broad domestic-partnership or civil-union statutes, provisions applicable to married couples would also apply to those in comparable, legally recognized relationships.

In many ways, Louisiana is a complete outlier because it treats an embryo as a person, rather than as gametic material. As a result, it has passed laws prohibiting the use of embryos for research purposes and bans the destruction of human embryos.[53] Under Louisiana law, if in vitro fertilization patients renounce their parental rights in writing, then the resulting embryo is available for "adoptive" implantation.[54] "As with traditional adoption, embryo adoption may be open, [where] the parties are aware of each other's identity, or closed, [where] the parties' identities remain confidential. [Still], either form requires a home study to determine whether the adoptive parents can provide a proper home for the child they will bear."[55] One remarkable difference from conventional adoption, however, is that the law contemplates only that another married couple can receive the embryo. Opponents of adoptive implantation argue that Louisiana treats embryos like people, effectively asserting that life begins at conception.[56] Supporters of Louisiana's approach argue, however, that adoptive implantation offers significant benefits, such as allowing infertile women to become pregnant at a lower cost than in vitro.[57] In light of such controversies over the legal status of an embryo (discussed further in chapter 9), it is not hard to see why Louisiana is the only state that has granted such extensive rights to embryos.

As embryo donation becomes more common, the variations in laws reflect states developing their own distinct approaches to the new technology. Yet, as discussed in chapter 9, embryo donation has become tied up in the politics of stem-cell research, prompting laws that protect donor "choice" when it comes to disposition of their embryos. A few states have recognized that embryo transfers raise parentage issues and have chosen to expand current laws covering donor gametes to donor embryos, including the same restrictions on donors' rights and on the identity of the recipients. Some states have enacted entirely new provisions, and only Louisiana precludes donor "choice" based on the status of the embryos. Most states have not yet addressed the issue at all, illustrating how the law must play catch-up to stay in place with technological changes.

Cases of Eggs: Surrogacy

Although there are very few cases involving confused parentage and embryo or egg donors, courts are frequently called on to decide comparable

issues involving gestational carriers in alleged breach of surrogacy contracts. Surrogacy comes in two forms: genetic and gestational. In the traditional, or genetic, surrogacy cases, the woman contributes her egg and carries the baby. More-recent surrogacy cases involve gestational surrogacy,
with one woman carrying an embryo created by using the eggs of another
woman, either from one of the intending parents or from a stranger. People turn to surrogacy for a variety of reasons: a heterosexual couple may
be infertile, with the woman unable to produce eggs or carry a pregnancy;
a gay couple or a single man may want to find a woman who can produce
eggs and carry a baby.

As in other areas of reproductive technology, the laws throughout the
United States are entirely conflicting when it comes to the rights of the
surrogates, the egg and sperm donors, and the "intending parents" (the
people who initially arranged for the child's birth). Some states ban surrogacy entirely, finding it contrary to the state's public policy. In states
where surrogacy is allowed, everyone involved typically signs a contract
that sets out their understanding that the intending parents are the ones
who should be receiving custody. And in the overwhelming number
of cases, the intending parents are the ones who walk away with a baby.
When these contracts fall apart, however, courts may not uphold the
agreement. Instead, courts can use a variety of bases for deciding on the
parenting outcomes: biological connection, contract, intent, marriage, or
some other legal construct.

In the surrogacy cases, courts generally assign parental status to two individuals rather than recognizing the interests of all members of the potential
sets of parents. In the traditional surrogacy cases in which the same woman
is the genetic and gestational mother, courts apply a best-interest analysis to
choose the two parents, although the intent of the parties is highly relevant.
In the genetic surrogacy cases, disputes are between two biological parents.
What is different from the typical child-custody case, of course, is the context: instead of two biological parents who have had an intimate relationship with each other, the biological parents have entered into a contractual
arrangement to create the child. The contract between the two biological
parents purchases them potential rights to the child. In the nontraditional
surrogacy cases in which one woman contributes the genetic material and
another gestates that material, courts find only two "natural" parents, typically the individuals who contributed egg and sperm, not the carrier.

The 1988 case of *Baby M.* is the classic surrogacy case. At the time
that *Baby M.* was decided, surrogacy was still relatively new, and no state

had laws on how to handle the situation. Since then, of course, numerous states have reacted by passing laws concerning surrogacy, and the 2002 UPA explicitly addresses the various relationships.

In *Baby M.,* the dispute was between Mary Beth Whitehead, the woman who had agreed to become pregnant through artificial insemination, carry the baby to term, and then relinquish the baby along with her parental rights, and William and Elizabeth Stern, the man whose sperm was used and his wife. The Sterns had engaged in surrogacy because they believed that pregnancy would endanger Mrs. Stern's health, and the couple wanted a child who could carry on Mr. Stern's blood line. The contract provided that Mr. Stern would pay Whitehead ten thousand dollars after the child's birth, when the child was delivered to him. In a separate contract, Mr. Stern agreed to pay seventy-five hundred dollars to the Infertility Center of New York (ICNY), which had facilitated the entire surrogacy process.

When the child, Melissa, was born, Whitehead changed her mind and decided to keep her. Mr. Stern, who lived in New Jersey, went to court, trying to enforce the surrogacy contract so that Melissa would live with him and his wife. The lower court, also appealing to the child's best interests, enforced the surrogacy agreement and terminated the biological mother's parental rights. By contrast, the New Jersey Supreme Court found that the surrogacy contract was unenforceable. First, analogizing the surrogacy contract to an adoption, the court held that Whitehead could not irrevocably relinquish her maternal rights to the Sterns but could only relinquish them to a state-approved agency. Correspondingly, state law did not recognize a voluntary surrender of parental rights via private contract. Next, the court held that parents could not determine child custody in advance of the child's birth, given the state's public policy that all child-custody decisions must be made by a court based on the child's best interests. The court virtually thundered, "This is the sale of a child, or, at the very least, the sale of a mother's right to her child, the only mitigating factor being that one of the purchasers is the father. Almost every evil that prompted the prohibition on the payment of money in connection with adoptions exists here."[58] Mr. Stern and Whitehead, as Melissa's biological progenitors, became the legal parents. The court thus was faced with a more traditional custody dispute between the two biological parents, to which it applied the perennial standard of the best interests of the child. Ultimately, the court awarded custody of Melissa to the Sterns (technically to Mr. Stern), and Whitehead received liberal visitation. The two opinions thus provide useful examples of how the definition of parent interacts with intent, contract, and the marital presumption.

The trial court judge began his opinion by articulating the court's role to protect the best interest of the child over the parents' rights. He then upheld the surrogacy agreement against various challenges, primarily based in contract law, such as claims that it was unfair or gave no choice to Whitehead, before turning to the issue of the appropriate remedy. The critical determination was whether "an order for specific performance [enforcement of the terms of the contract] would be in the child's best interest." After considering the extensive evidence proffered as to the best custodial arrangement, the court held that it was appropriate to enforce the contract against Whitehead. And since an order of specific performance pursuant to the contract would terminate the biological mother's parental rights, the court held that it had the power to do so.[59]

The contract gave the judge the discretion to treat Whitehead—the biological mother under any test that depends on genetics or gestation—as a nonparent. Similarly, the contract deprived her husband of any benefit of the marital presumption of paternity. Instead, Mr. Whitehead's parental rights (which are rarely addressed in discussion of the case) became nonexistent based on the agreement. Although New Jersey has a rebuttable presumption that the husband is the biological father, the surrogacy agreement required Mr. Whitehead to take all appropriate actions to relinquish his rights. Unlike the lower court, which used the best-interest-of-the-child standard essentially to rubber stamp its decisions on parental rights, the appellate court applied the same standard in the most conventional way possible: to a dispute between the two biological parents.

The New Jersey Supreme Court declared that paid surrogacy arrangements were void, contrary to statute and the public policy that only the child's best interests, not the parents' prior agreement, could be considered in deciding custody. Under New Jersey law, each biological parent has an equal right to custody, and thus the court was faced with a dispute between the biological father and mother, to which the best-interest standard is applicable. The child's best interests, the court held, would be served by a custody award to the biological father with the possibility of visitation to the biological mother.

The case was thus transformed, appropriately in many ways, from a contract dispute into a custody proceeding. Rather than an analysis of the rights of all the potential parents (the Whiteheads and the Sterns) pursuant to the surrogacy contract, *In re Baby M.* becomes an examination of what custodial arrangement will best serve the child's interests. The focus is seemingly deflected from the parents to the child. Nonetheless, regardless of the validity of the surrogacy contract, both the trial and appellate courts in *In re Baby M.* found that the child's best interests dictated a custody award to the biological father. Each court was able to use the best-interest standard to support its conclusions, although their determinations differed as to whether the standard required complete termination of the mother's rights or the opportunity for visitation.

Questions surrounding the desirability of surrogacy agreements have continued to swirl around the procedure, becoming even more contentious after the *Baby M.* case. Some states, such as Arizona, ban surrogacy contracts entirely, and others ban only payment for surrogacy; and some states have enforced surrogacy contracts as an explicit exemption to their baby-selling laws. Many entities advertise surrogacy, and it is a growth industry, especially in the gay community.

Given this chapter's focus on parentage, however, it is not the agreement itself that is so interesting, but, instead, it is the bases on which courts have declared various individuals to be parents or nonparents. Mary Beth Whitehead won parental rights only after protracted, high-visibility litigation when the state supreme court held the surrogacy agreement unenforceable. Other carriers have not been so successful, and courts in some states have enforced surrogacy agreements over the objections of the gestational mother, using a variety of legal grounds for deciding on parentage. Some states have achieved results similar to those in *Baby M.,* in which the intending parents receive custody by enforcing, rather than voiding, surrogacy contracts. These courts rely on the intent to become a parent that is inherent in the agreement. Intent is a traditional basis for enforcing contracts, but it is highly problematic in surrogacy cases. Under contract law, the agreement becomes enforceable at the time that it is signed; in surrogacy, however, a woman's emotions attending pregnancy and childbirth may not be readily apparent to her when the parties sign the surrogacy contract and may change by the time she must relinquish the child. Also, in the comparable context of adoption, these proceedings are rooted in the best interests of the child, not the intent of private contracting parties. Moreover, the mother who has decided prior to birth that she will give up her child for adoption always has some period of time after the birth in which to change her mind, ranging from twelve hours to longer than a month.[60]

Professor Katharine K. Baker explains that when courts enforce surrogacy agreements, the law honors the traditional surrogate's intent not to be a mother, despite her genetic connection to the child. The law finds the traditional surrogate's intent in the surrogacy contract. When it honors gestational surrogacy contracts . . . the law allows the gestational surrogate to sign away whatever parental rights she might acquire by virtue of her gestational labor. It also allows the contract to bestow parental rights on the male and female genetic contributors.[61]

The 2002 UPA refers to surrogates as gestational mothers and recognizes the enforceability of surrogacy agreements so long as they have been validated by a court. Validating gestational agreements is somewhat comparable to completing an adoption, because the court must verify the intending parents' qualifications as parents and the gestational mother's qualifications to carry the child.

In the traditional surrogacy situation, there are only two potential biological parents (the sperm provider and the woman who provides the egg and gestates the child), and, as in *Baby M.,* courts often turn to the best-interest standard to decide on the appropriate custody award between the two biological parents. In nontraditional surrogacy cases, the situation is more complicated, as there may be multiple biological parents and there are several potential bases beyond the child's best interests for deciding on parenthood, including contract, intent, marriage, or biology. But what actually happens is that courts rule on parenthood, and the custody decision flows inexorably from that determination. Of course, in a harmonious relationship in which the genetic and gestational parent are different but they both agree on who should be deemed the mother, it is sensible simply to designate the two intending parents.

The situation becomes more complicated when there is a disagreement between the gestational and genetic mothers. In *Johnson v. Calvert,* the California Supreme Court held that the woman who contributed the egg, and not the woman who gestated the fertilized egg and gave birth to the child, would be considered the legal mother. Crispina and Mark Calvert had signed an agreement with Anna Johnson, pursuant to which Johnson agreed to gestate an embryo created from the Calverts' genetic material. Subsequently, Johnson became pregnant with such an embryo. During her pregnancy, the agreement broke down, and the Calverts and Johnson filed lawsuits seeking to be declared the legal parents.

Both Johnson and Crispina Calvert could have been defined as the mother pursuant to California's Uniform Parentage Act, which provides that a mother-child relationship "may be established by proof of her having given birth to the child."[62] The different California courts that heard the case acknowledged that both women had legitimate claims to being the mother but emphasized that California law "recognizes only one natural mother,"[63] so only one woman could hold that title. Even though California law declared that the woman who gave birth could be recognized as the biological mother, the court created another biological basis for motherhood: it decided that, as in paternity, maternity could be shown by establishing a genetic connection to the child. Even though Johnson had given birth to the child, Mrs. Calvert was genetically related to the baby. To break the tie between the two women, the court looked to intent as the touchstone of parenthood. Accordingly, "she who intended to bring about the birth of a child that she intended to raise as her own" is the biological mother.[64] The combination of Mrs. Calvert's genetic connection to the child along with her intent to raise a child resulted in her being deemed the "natural" mother under California law. This seems analogous to what the trial court did in *In re Baby M.*, when it used intent not just to create parental status but also to deprive a "nonintending" party of that status. By contrast, the dissent in *Johnson v. Calvert* would have relied on the best-interest-of-the-child standard—the touchstone of all child-custody decisions— not intent or biology, to determine parentage.

In *Johnson*, the intending mother was the genetic mother, and biology was instrumental in establishing parentage. What happens when neither the intending mother nor the carrier provides the egg? Such was the case in a 2006 Pennsylvania case, in which James Flynn and Eileen Donich, who actually lived in Ohio, signed an agreement with a company called Surrogate Mothers, Inc., so that they could have children.[65] In the agreement, Flynn was listed as the "Biological Father or Adoptive Father," and Donich was listed as the "Biological Mother, Adoptive Mother, or Partner." The company then found Jennifer Rice, who agreed to serve as the egg donor, and Danielle Bimber, who lived in Pennsylvania and agreed to serve as the gestational carrier. Flynn promised to pay up to twenty thousand dollars for multiple births, as well as medical and travel expenses for Bimber. According to the agreement—which she subsequently violated— Bimber agreed that she would not try to act as a parent to any resulting child but would instead give up any parental rights that she might have.[66]

Flynn provided the sperm, Rice provided the egg, and Bimber became pregnant.[67] In November 2003, Bimber gave birth to triplets, Matthew, Mark, and Micah, all of whom were then placed in the hospital's neonatal intensive-care unit. Donich called the hospital frequently to find out how the boys were doing, but Bimber brought them to her house in Pennsylvania when the boys were eight days old. Bimber, Flynn, and Rice each went to court, trying to establish their rights to the boys. The first Pennsylvania court gave custody to Bimber because she was the "legal mother" and also found that the surrogacy agreement was not valid. A second court, in Ohio, decided that Flynn and Rice, who were biologically related to the triplets, were the parents.[68] Ultimately, an appeals court in Pennsylvania decided that Bimber had no legal relationship to the triplets and that Flynn was the father; only he could allow Bimber to take custody of the children.

At the same time, one of the Ohio judges explained that the legal issues were enormously complicated and novel and risked neglecting the child, who was the central player:

> there are only a few states that have even begun to address the issue of determining who the parents of a surrogate child may be. Even the few states that have begun to address the issues involved have approached the issues from four different directions. Unless the state legislators begin to address the multiple issues involved, it will be the children that will be caught in a continual tug of war between the egg donor or donors, the sperm donor or donors, the surrogate parent or parents, and those that simply want to adopt a child from what they perceive as the ideal parents.[69]

If the courts were confused, so was the media coverage, which misidentified the outcome and mislabeled the parties. One newspaper reported, "Surrogate mother gets custody of 3; Judge Criticizes Sperm Donor," and another concluded, "Surrogate awarded custody of triplets; [man] who fathered babies gets visitation."[70] Is the surrogate the mother? Is the "sperm donor" the father? How should the law determine these issues? These questions, at the core of this book, have not yet received uniform answers in the law.

As one possible solution to preventing these postbirth disputes, parents in some states may go to court for a prenatal birth certificate establishing the legal parents. In another Ohio case, this one involving a gestational carrier, the sperm and egg providers filed a complaint seeking a judgment declaring them to be the parents of an unborn child and seeking an order that the child's birth certificate should correspondingly reflect their status as the parents of a child to be born to a surrogate mother.[71] However, the court held that it could not determine the parentage of an unborn child or issue an order directing the hospital to designate the child as the biological child of the donors. In reaching its decision to dismiss the action, the court used Ohio's Parentage Act, which states that a legal relationship exists between a child and the child's natural or adoptive parents. By contrast, courts in California have been willing to issue such prebirth declarations.

Even when the relationship between the biological progenitors of a child is not disputed, the identity of the parents can still be confusing. Roberto d.B. had arranged for a woman to serve as a gestational surrogate for an embryo created using his sperm. When the woman gave birth to twins at Holy Cross Hospital in Silver Spring, Maryland, in 2001, the hospital listed her as the mother and Roberto d.B. as the father. The problem was that the gestational carrier never intended to serve as the mother, so both she and Roberto d.B. asked a court to issue an accurate birth certificate that listed Roberto d.B. as the only parent. The court refused to do so, claiming that it did not have the power to remove the mother's name from the birth certificate and that, anyway, doing so would be inconsistent with the child's best interests. Maryland's highest court first heard the case in 2002 but did not issue its opinion until five years later in 2007, an unusually long time for a court to consider a case. The court acknowledged that technological developments were challenging the law before turning to the question of whether the "genetically unrelated gestational host of a fetus" must, nonetheless, be deemed the "legal" mother. No, the court decided; just as a "genetically unlinked" man can challenge his paternity, so too should a "genetically unlinked" woman, such as a gestational surrogate, be able to challenge her maternity.[72]

This case is fascinating in its illustration of how reproductive technology tests conventional conceptions of the family. First, the gestational surrogate was treated like a stranger with respect to the child because she had no genetic connection—the court used words like "carrier" and "host." Second, laws drafted to cover male paternity may now, as a result of gender equality, apply to female maternity; the court explained that the paternity statute had been enacted in 1984 and simply did not contemplate parents who were unmarried or who had used assisted reproductive technologies. It is this second point that is potentially revolutionary. If all sperm-donor statutes are simply made gender-neutral and equally applied to the marital and nonmarital situation, then states do not need to enact new laws specifically applicable to egg or embryo donation. Indeed, the court denied that it was using a test based on the intent of the parties, claiming that it was relying solely on the language of the paternity statute as applied to maternity.[73]

The surrogacy cases provide no clear lessons on parentage for embryo or egg donation. Claims to motherhood based on biology have been recognized when the mother provides the egg (*Johnson*). When a gestational/genetic carrier has not wanted to claim motherhood, courts generally defer to her wishes. When a gestational mother does want to claim maternity rights, however, courts are not necessarily hospitable to her. As professor Jennifer Hendricks explains, when courts allow an intending mother to prevail over a gestational mother, "Intent theory elevates the abstract desire of the contracting couple above the concrete connection between the child and the gestational mother. . . . It disregards both the biology and the caretaking relationship of pregnancy."[74]

It Takes Two: Gay and Lesbian Parents

Janet Jenkins and Lisa Miller were romantically involved from 1998 until 2003. For most of their relationship, the couple lived in Hamilton, Virginia, although in December 2000, they traveled to Vermont to cement their bond with a civil union. When they decided to have a child, Jenkins said that they worked together to choose a sperm donor who would resemble her, so that their child would look like the two of them. When Miller gave birth to Isabella in April 2002, Jenkins was in the delivery room.

Jenkins did not adopt Isabella, because she thought she was protected by the Vermont civil-union law. Under that law, the "rights of parties to a civil union, with respect to a child of whom either becomes the natural parent during the term of the civil union, shall be the same as those of a married couple, with respect to a child of whom either spouse becomes the natural parent during the marriage."[75] Consequently, so long as they stayed in Vermont, both Miller and Jenkins were the parents.

A few months after Isabella's birth, the family moved to Fair Haven, Vermont. Miller and Jenkins's relationship ended in mid-2003, and Miller returned to Virginia with Isabella. She explained that she "left the homosexual lifestyle and drew closer to God."[76] In November 2003, Miller sued Jenkins in Vermont to dissolve their civil union. As part of her lawsuit, Miller asked the Vermont courts to grant her custody over Isabella and to require Jenkins to pay child support. In June 2004, the Vermont family court issued an order that awarded Jenkins visitation rights in both Vermont and Virginia.

Notwithstanding the Vermont order, on July 1, 2004, the date that Virginia's Affirmation of Marriage Act took effect, Miller filed a second suit concerning Isabella, but this time in a Virginia court. Frederick County judge John Prosser held that he had jurisdiction to hear the case, and in October, he granted full custody to Miller, reasoning that, legally, Jenkins was no more than a friend to Isabella.

With this Virginia ruling in her favor, Miller returned to Vermont and asked family court judge William Cohen "to grant 'full faith and credit' to the judgments reached by the case in Virginia."[77] Judge Cohen rejected the request and denied Miller's bid for permission to appeal.

Miller refused to comply with the ordered visitation for Jenkins, so the Vermont court held her in contempt. In November, Judge Cohen ruled that Jenkins had all the same rights over Isabella as any other legal parent, reasoning that couples joined in a civil union should be treated no differently than married couples who choose to conceive a child through artificial insemination.[78] Cohen explicitly ruled that it was in Isabella's best interest for her to have "two mommies." But the Virginia courts did not want to give Jenkins any rights. For three years, poor Isabella was stuck in the middle of the fight between her parents.

Not until 2006 did Virginia concede that it was the Vermont court that could decide the issues, not because of the civil union but because the case involved a custody dispute that was governed by federal law and not state law, as is true in most custody cases. Miller and Jenkins were fighting each other in different states. What happens when people who are parents in one state try to get another state to give them the same status? Under the Constitution's Full Faith and Credit Clause, one state is supposed to recognize the laws of a second state. Generally, then, people who are parents in one state will be the legal parents in another state. Yet here again, however, federal law requiring this recognition may conflict with state laws that prevent gay and lesbian couples from being identified as the parents. Such a conflict became a federal case in Oklahoma, when several couples asked the Oklahoma health department to respect the adoptions that they had done in another state. Heather Finstuen adopted Sarah and Katherine Finstuen-Magro, twin daughters born to her partner, Ann Magro, through artificial insemination when the family lived in New Jersey. They moved to Oklahoma, and Finstuen's status as a legal mother became uncertain when Oklahoma enacted a law stating that it would not recognize same-sex adoptions from other states. After several years of legal battles, in August 2007, the Tenth Circuit applied the Full Faith and Credit Clause of the U.S. Constitution to adoptions by same-sex couples and found the law unconstitutional in its failure to recognize out-of-state same-sex adoptions.[79]

These relationships illustrate two problems: first, as discussed in chapter 5, what rights to parenthood does one partner have against another? and, second, what happens when people who are defined as parents in one state move into another state that may not recognize their rights? Janet Jenkins won visitation rights, but only because Lisa Miller filed the first lawsuit in Vermont, not Virginia. Heather Finstuen and Ann Magro faced uncertainty concerning what would happen to the children if Magro, the biological mother, died. Although the courts reached the right results in both cases, it was only after a time-consuming, emotionally draining process.

Determining parenthood for marital couples is typically quite easy, as chapter 4 shows. When two people are married, a child born to one spouse is presumed to be the child of the other spouse. And in the increasing number of states that have enacted civil-union or domestic-partnership statutes that grant registered couples substantially the same rights as if they were married, a child born during the relationship to one partner is the other partner's child as well. But what if the parents are not married? If both parents' names are on the birth certificate, then the child has two legal parents in the state that issued the birth certificate. Some states, such as California, allow two parents of the same sex to be on a birth certificate, but other states do not. So, when one partner has a child through reproductive technology, the parenthood status of the other parent is uncertain in these other states. One option is second-parent adoptions, whereby a child born to one parent is adopted by the nonbiological or nonlegal other parent. This legal parent, who does not lose any of his or her rights and responsibilities, must give consent. It is not certain, however, that other states will recognize such adoptions.[80]

Florida is the only state that expressly prohibits individuals who are gay or lesbian from becoming adoptive parents. The statute has been challenged as unconstitutional, but the U.S. Supreme Court refused to review the Eleventh Circuit ruling upholding the statute. In addition, Utah prohibits anyone who is cohabiting in a relationship outside marriage from adopting, and Mississippi prohibits "adoption by couples of the same gender."[81]

In all other states, lesbian and gay individuals are statutorily eligible to adopt. There have been gay and lesbian second-parent adoptions in Maryland and the District of Columbia. In California, gay and lesbian partners can both be named on the child's birth certificate through a prebirth judicial declaration. In theory, such adoptions or parental designations should be recognized in other states. In practice, however, judicial reaction in other states to openly lesbian, gay, and bisexual adoptive parents ranges from supportive acceptance to overt hostility.

Indeed, on the opposing side of the spectrum, courts in Colorado, Nebraska, Ohio, and Wisconsin have held that second-parent same-sex adoptions are not permissible under their state adoption statutes. In jurisdictions where second-parent or joint adoption is not available, the only alternative that lesbian, gay, and bisexual parents have to attempt to protect their relationship with their children is through privately executed documents such as parenting agreements, wills, guardianship agreements, authorizations to consent to emergency medical treatments, and similar documents.

Other planning issues arise if one parent is incapacitated and the other parent has no legal rights to the child, or if both parents are incapacitated. To guard against these contingencies, each parent can take advantage of medical-consent authorizations or other state mechanisms permitting a parent to appoint an agent to make medical decisions on behalf of a minor in the event of the parent's incapacity. In states with a standby-guardianship statute or other provisions relating to the guardianship of minors, each parent can provide that the other is responsible for the child, or they can choose a third party. Finally, each parent can appoint the other as the testamentary guardian of the minor's person in the event of death.

Despite these legal arrangements, if the couple dissolves their relationship, as in the case of Lisa Miller and Janet Jenkins, the rights of the non-biological mother could still be in jeopardy, depending on whether the state where the couple lives will validate the agreements. A number of states have shown a willingness to do so. In some states, gay and lesbian partners have been recognized as de facto or equitable parents by virtue of their involvement with their children and have been able to sue for visitation rights.

The influential American Law Institute's (ALI) Principles of Family Dissolution recognize the status of a "parent by estoppel."[82] Individuals who have entered into a co-parenting agreement with the legal parent and have acted as a parent since the child's birth can be recognized as parents by estoppel, when such designation is in the child's best interests. A parent by estoppel has the same rights to custody and visitation as a legal parent. But contracts and ALI recommendations go only so far. Ultimately, states will need to address this legal problem.

What if the parents are in a civil union, domestic partnership, or Massachusetts same-sex marriage, and acquire parental rights there, but move to a state that does not recognize the legal status of their relationship? Approximately forty states have statutes or constitutional amendments banning gay marriage. And in some states, including Virginia, there is legislation that extends beyond gay marriage, refusing to recognize civil unions or domestic partnerships that have been entered into in other states. Moreover, the federal Defense of Marriage Act provides that "[n]o State . . . shall be required to give effect to any public act, record, or judicial proceeding of any other State respecting a relationship between persons of the same sex that is treated as a marriage under the laws of such other State[s] or a right or claim arising from such relationship."[83]

The intersection between these statutes and the reality of gay parents creates complicated legal issues. The problem arises most acutely when a couple, joined in a legal relationship through one state's law, asks a second state to intercede in a custody dispute. Not only are the first state's laws frequently pitted against the laws of the second state, but also the constitutionality of federal and state defense-of-marriage statutes are called into question under the Full Faith and Credit Clause of the federal Constitution.

There are three different, albeit interrelated, legal issues involved in custody disputes between same-sex partners. First, is the partner of the biological mother a "legal parent" or parent by estoppel who is entitled to seek custody and visitation under the laws of either state? Custody disputes typically occur between the two legal parents, and the general standard that courts apply is "the best interest of the child." If there is a dispute over a child between a parent and a third party, then the parent must typically be proved unfit before custody can be awarded to a nonparent, although this distinction is starting to blur as lesbian and gay partners seek to establish parental rights even without legal parenting status.

The extent to which parental status in one state will protect same-sex parents in other states turns on the interstate recognition not just of gay marriages, civil unions, or domestic partnerships but also of same-sex adoption decrees and other means of conferring status. The second issue is, Can state and federal defense-of-marriage statutes overcome the presumption of full faith and credit to the status of legal parent? This is a constitutional question that the federal courts have not yet resolved.

Finally, the third issue concerns cases in which there is litigation both in the state where the partners entered into their relationship and in a second state. In such cases, which state should have jurisdiction? Under the Uniform Child Custody Jurisdiction and Enforcement Act, currently in effect in forty jurisdictions (including Utah and Virginia), only the child's "home state" has jurisdiction to decide custody. The home state is defined as "the State in which a child lived with a parent or a person acting as a parent for at least six consecutive months immediately before the commencement of a child-custody proceeding."[84] And the federal Parental Kidnapping Prevention Act supports the home-state jurisdiction, requiring that there be full faith and credit given in other states to a home state's decree.

Ideally, the parenthood status of couples in civil unions, domestic partnerships, or same-sex marriages should be respected in all states, pursuant to doctrines of full faith and credit or comity. Yet as the Virginia case shows, this respect is not inevitable. Once parenthood is resolved for opposite-sex parents who use ART, then the parents can move anywhere, confident that their rights will be respected. Parenthood for same-sex couples is more uncertain, both in establishing the initial set of rights and then in interstate recognition.

Ultimately, there is no uniformity on parentage or on identity issues when it comes to families formed through ART. Even the model legislation in this area, the Uniform Parentage Act, which provides a gender-neutral approach to donor eggs, sperm, and embryos and which applies to both marital and nonmarital parents, does not address gay and lesbian parenting issues. More troubling, however, is that the laws and cases consider parenting in isolation from technology and identity. The UPA does not try to cover market issues, nor does it cover issues involving anonymity of donors. The private nature of these transactions, as well as the fast pace of the technology, has allowed them to escape much regulation.

Yet the reluctance to provide consistency and coherence also stems from the highly controversial nature of the new reproductive technologies. Because they involve sex, reproduction, nature, parenting, technology, and money, they touch on many contemporary social debates: the technologies allow children to have only one legal parent, they are contrary to the moral beliefs of many people, and they have become confused with political conflicts on cloning and stem-cell research. Clarifying the varying interests involved in reproductive technology—including the gamete providers, the children, the family members who raise the child, the market participants, and the state—provides the basis for deciding on the systems for acknowledging, and regulating, those interests.

6

Donor Identity

Hello, I'm Your Sister. Our Father Is Donor 150

Family Vacation; Why Would Raechel McGhee fly her two beloved children across the country to stay with a man they had never met?

The Legacy of Donor 1047

Are You my Sperm Donor? Few Clinics Will Say

Sperm Donor Father Ends His Anonymity

Bill Would Forbid Anonymous Sperm and Egg Donors[1]

THESE NEWSPAPER HEADLINES tell compelling stories about the contemporary nature of anonymity and disclosure in gamete provision. They portray the differing and often converging interests that gamete-provided children, their parents, their providers, the clinics, and the state may have. Should there ever be disclosure of the donor's identity? If so, under what circumstances? Will donors still provide gametes if there is the possibility (or certainty) of disclosure? Is it the children's right to know who provided their genes? Does this smack of privileging biology? Is it the parents' right not to know? To know? Must parents tell their children of their origins?

Each participant has differing interests in the disclosure issue, and, as a society, we may have altogether different preferences. Clinics are concerned that requiring disclosure would dry up the supply of donors; donors vary as to their willingness to disclose; recipients may reveal nothing, may struggle with how to disclose, or may be open from the start; and the resulting children—who will someday be adults—may or may not ever want to know their genetic progenitors. The secrecy surrounding these de-cisions stems, once again, from efforts of individuals to create their "what-if" families, from fears by donors that they will be "outed" and perhaps forced into unwanted relationships or unwanted child-support obligations, and from the very origins of ART with donor gametes at a time when not being able to have your "own" child was a stigma.

There is little legal guidance in this area concerning disclosure. Sperm donation, the oldest of the reproductive technologies, is rooted in secrecy, and the newer technologies have borrowed this legacy. Families have wanted to keep their donor origins private, physicians and gamete banks may not have complete records, and there is no state involvement in the creation of donor families. Although states are slowly moving toward more openness in adoption records, this is not true in the donor area. Fewer than twenty states address disclosure for sperm donation, allowing for access to records upon a showing of "good cause,"[2] a highly ambiguous term that, in the context of gamete donation, is virtually untested in the courts. For egg and embryo donation, there is virtually no law concerning disclosure except by analogy to the sperm situation. Instead, the more-restrictive anonymity protections are contained in the private contracts between clinics, gamete providers, and the intended recipients, which generally do not have a "good cause" exception. It is only when these ar-rangements break down that the law must decide between the differing interests. When courts are called on to deal with these issues, they have to draw from contract law, from constitutional law concerning privacy and familial rights, and from bioethics. So far, there have been few direct chal-lenges to the promised anonymity because donors and recipients have had few reasons to try to breach these promises. Indeed, there are no pub-lished court cases involving children who have sought the identity of a donor parent.

Instead, the primary challenges to anonymity come from outside the law. Recipient parents may want to find others who have used the same donor, children may want to find the identity of the donor, and the donors themselves may seek information. But rather than using clinic records to track down information—clinics will not disclose the identity of donors protected by contract—they can use Oprah and the Donor Sibling Reg-istry to allow them to bypass the often carefully worded agreements on confidentiality. Journalist David Plotz explains in his 2005 book about the sperm bank for Nobel Prize winners that he was able to track down nu-merous donors and children simply by advertising on the Internet.[3]

As the Internet and other nonlegal measures have brought together families that have used the same donor, questions have been raised as to whether these children really are half "siblings" of the same "father." Policies and practices within the gamete community for the past several decades have attempted to make these families "the same as" biological families. In the past, one of the principal strategies was an attempt to replicate the family that the couple and the child otherwise would have had by choosing a "matching" donor. The philosophy underlying this attempt to create a new family has begun to disintegrate as gamete children, recipients, and the donors themselves question this model. As single individuals and gays and lesbians form families through the gamete-provision process, they inherently expose their need for, and use of, donor gametes.

As a policy matter, is this type of transaction entitled to secrecy? Perhaps the answer is yes, except to all those involved in the transaction itself: the bank, the intending parents, and the child. Just as the initial move to secrecy in adoption records was not designed to protect against disclosure within the relationship, the protection accorded to gamete donors should not extend to disclosure to anyone not directly involved in the "transaction." The information could remain private, a secret shared only by the child, the parents, and the provider. Identifying information could be released, upon request, once the gamete offspring reach eighteen or through a confidential intermediary system that would allow for national searches and that would require all donors to register. States or the federal government should guarantee the release of such information to mature adults through laws that would preempt private agreements (such as between the gamete provider and the intending parents or between the gamete provider and a gamete bank) to the contrary. Although all states have addressed this issue in various ways for adoptees,[4] few states have considered legislation on disclosure of the identity of gamete providers.

If the United States begins to consider legislation on disclosure, then it would be following the lead of other countries. Sweden was the first country to end donor anonymity in 1984, and many other countries have done so. In Switzerland, the constitution requires that children have access to identifying donor information.[5] In the United Kingdom, as of April 1, 2005, donor anonymity ended, and all children born after that date will be able to find out the identity of their donor once they turn eighteen. To facilitate this, the British Human Fertilisation and Embryology Authority has established a national registry that keeps track of all assisted reproductive technology treatments and their outcomes and also collects

information about donors; when a child turns eighteen, he or she can receive the donor's name and last-known address.[6] In Canada, federal law
makes it illegal to disclose a donor's identity unless the donor consents,
and there is no requirement that clinics save information about a donor.
Yet, as more critics have pressured the government to open up records,
the Canadian Parliament passed a law that sets up a registry so that at least
information about the donor's medical history will be available.[7]

This chapter explores cultural anxieties about disclosure and examines
the status of promises of anonymity in an era of increasingly sophisticated
genetic testing and Internet searches. Because there is so little law in the
United States in this area, any discussion of anonymity must include a discussion of this issue outside the law, from sociological, psychological, and
practical perspectives. This examination provides the basis for the book's
argument that, notwithstanding the legacy of secrecy and the potentially
conflicting interests of those involved, participants must have access to
identifying information about one another. The argument for disclosure is
ultimately based on public policy considerations that focus on the child's
interest, but it also brings in constitutionally recognized interests.

Why Anonymity?

The history of secrecy surrounding gamete provision is complicated:
sperm providers are often promised anonymity in their contracts with
sperm banks[8] and may have relied on that promise in agreeing to donate
sperm. Even though recipients may have studied detailed profiles of their
unknown donors, they use numbers rather than names to procure the
gametes they want. Because of the shame attached to infertility, recipients
of donor sperm have typically been counseled not to reveal, to anyone,
their use of another person's gametes. Similarly, although the identity of
egg providers was often well-known in early cases when recipients solicited family members and friends, the growth of the egg industry also
means that there is now more anonymity and secrecy attached to this
process as well.

The intending parents may have relied on these guarantees of anonymity and, consequently, never revealed their children's donor origins to
them. Indeed, gamete recipients have generally been subject to much less
pressure to disclose the biological background of their children than have
adoptive parents, who have been counseled to tell their children that they

are adopted. Families have been able to hide their use of donor gametes because only their doctor knows for sure. On the other hand, intermediary banks are, increasingly frequently, offering the option of "known" donors, or providers who agree to disclose their identity at some point in the child's life. Beginning in 1983 in the United States, recipients could select donors who were willing to have various identifying details released once the child turned eighteen, including their name, address, and driver's license number. Moreover, Internet registries are helping to facilitate contact between gamete providers and gamete-formed families. The remainder of this section provides further details on the conventional story of anonymity and the changing approaches to the issue.

Donors

As chapter 2 shows, the first sperm donors were utterly anonymous, and, in the first contemporary recorded cases, the first recipients may not have realized that they became pregnant with sperm from a legal stranger. As the use of donor sperm increased, physicians were entrusted with choosing the donors, and recipients were given no information about that choice. The use of donor sperm remained a secret among the recipient, her husband, and their physician, an exclusive group that did not include the children. It was not until the 1970s that recipients became more involved in choosing their donors, but as late as 1979, 92 percent of physicians selected the donor themselves, and almost two-thirds used medical students.[9] David Plotz traces the development of increasing recipient involvement to the origins of the Nobel Prize sperm bank, when its founder began providing details to "consumers" about their potential donors.[10]

Today, donors can choose at the time of providing the sperm whether to remain anonymous. At the Sperm Bank of California, which was a "pioneer" in the donor-disclosure area, participants in the Identity-Release Program sign a contract that strictly limits the authority of the bank to disclose information only to the child who is at least eighteen and has written requesting this information.[11] In a study of why donors participate in this program, the bank found that almost half felt that any children should have the right to know the identity of the donor, approximately one-third indicated that they would be curious to see any resulting children, and 20 percent agreed to release their identity because if they were donor children, they would want access to the donor's identity.[12] Increasing numbers of men are choosing the option of identity release at banks that offer those services.[13]

Even those who have provided sperm pursuant to guarantees of anonymity may be able to connect with the families that they have helped to create. Consider Mike Rubino, Donor 929 at California Cryobank. Nine years after Donor 929 began providing sperm, Oprah Winfrey aired an episode about donor-conceived families. Rubino logged on to the Donor Sibling Registry website and began to browse. Rubino ultimately discovered that Raechel McGhee had written a thank-you message to Donor 929. He responded, and later that day, the two of them talked; she and the two children that resulted from his sperm spent a week in California with him. He admitted that if given the choice, he would "love it if the kids called [him] 'Dad.'" They even visited California Cryobank together.[14] Similarly, Jeffrey Harrison, Donor 150 at California Cryobank, responded to a *New York Times* article about two children born through his sperm and is in touch with several of the children he has helped produce.[15]

Notwithstanding the publicity that ensues when donors find their "children," such cases have been rare. Dr. Cappy Rothman, who co-founded and is the medical director of California Cryobank (one of the largest sperm banks in the world), believes that most sperm providers do not want their identities known: "I can't think of one that said, 'Boy, I just look forward to meeting my child when they reach the age of 18,' not one."[16]

The issue has received much less attention when it comes to egg donors. The recipients typically do meet with donors in advance, although egg donors themselves generally sign contracts protecting their anonymity from any resulting children. And because egg donation is a far newer technology, the children are younger and far fewer. But the same policy issues of disclosure for sperm donors apply in the egg-donation context, with respect to whether parents should disclose their children's donor origins, whether donors want to disclose their identities, and whether the children will ultimately want contact.

Promises of anonymity are contained in private contracts between physicians and patients. There are virtually no laws that address these contracts by guaranteeing their validity. Nonetheless, the legal system has typically supported the confidentiality of sperm providers, unlike surrogacy agreements, for which courts or lawmakers have overridden the contractual arrangements between the parties. In one of the first cases to deal with the disclosure of the identity of a sperm donor, discussed at the beginning of the book, the court crafted a compromise.[17] As we saw in chapter 1, in *Johnson v. Calvert*, the court sought to balance the interests of the parents of a girl with a rare kidney disorder, of California Cryobank, which had provided the sperm, and of the donors' claims of anonymity.[18] The donor's privacy claims were grounded in the contract between the Johnsons and Cryobank, which states that the donor's identity will not be disclosed, as well as in the California and federal constitutions.[19] By contrast, the contract between the donor and the bank recognized that his identity would not be disclosed "unless a court orders disclosure for good cause."[20] The court held that the absolute prohibition in the contract was contrary to California law, which, like that in a minority of other states, allowed for disclosure based on "good cause." Although the court recognized a limited constitutional right to privacy under the California constitution, it held that a donor's identity could be disclosed when this would serve the child's best interests, just not in this case; instead, it might be possible to depose the donor without ever revealing his identity.

Clinics

Although the ASRM has taken the position that donor-conceived children should know they are donor-conceived, many clinics do not offer the option of voluntary identity disclosure. At the beginning of the twenty-first century, there were only two open-identity programs in the United States,[21] although that number has since increased. But most clinics still do not offer this option. As a nursing supervisor at one clinic explained, "Donors remain anonymous, . . . and [I've] never heard of couples requesting information about the donor other than non-identifying characteristics, such as hair and eye color, height, level of intelligence and educational background."[22]

Although clinics may facilitate open-identity gamete provision, they typically argue against mandatory disclosure. Their concern is less with children's interests than with the effect on the supply of donor gametes. Stephen Feldschuh, who operates one of the oldest sperm banks in the country, explained on a 2006 PBS television show that if there is mandatory disclosure, then "[y]ou're going to lose the really smart, the really wonderful people who I think are now going to question, . . . 'Do I really want to be in a situation where, down the road, someone may contact me?'"[23]

Open-disclosure programs remain a minority, and banks' disclosure programs may differ substantially as to the circumstances under which they will release information. The SpermCenter.com, which was established to facilitate recipients' finding the right donor, warns consumers that banks may label disclosure programs "'ID-release' or 'open' donors; however, the exact meaning of these terms is different at each sperm bank!"[24] Banks are free to choose any type of identity-release programs that they want, and there are no legally defined obligations imposed on them, outside of the individual contracts they sign with each donor and recipient. The Sperm Bank of California, which offers both anonymous and identity-release programs, releases information upon request of the child, but only after asking the donor for updated information and the preferred means of being contacted.[25] Anonymous donors have the option of subsequently deciding whether they may wish to be contacted, but identity-release donors have made an irrevocable choice.

Whereas some identity-release programs are political statements concerning the rights of those involved in the donation process to know one another, others are responding to a demand from potential recipients for donor-disclosure programs. Explaining why one bank began offering an identity-release program, the chief operating officer of Fairfax Cryobank observed, "There is a group [of] women out there who wanted to be able to tell their offspring who the donor was. . . . The market demanded it."[26] And they were even willing to pay more for this privilege. Outside of contract law, there are no other laws upholding the legitimacy of identity-release programs, no requirements that donors provide their actual names to the banks, and no legal mandate that donors provide updated information to the banks.

Recipients

For recipients of gametes, there has always been a set of special issues that implicate secrecy. Do they tell anyone—families, friends, or others—that they have used donor gametes? How do they explain it to their child? Should they ever disclose to their child? Should they choose a known or unknown donor? Today, there are actually three categories of donors: unknown; unknown but with the option, typically when the child turns eighteen, of identification; and known, or directed, donors, who are specifically chosen as providers. One woman wrote to the "Since You Asked" column at Salon.com for advice on choosing between a known and unknown donor, worried by an internal "nagging voice [that] keeps asking me whether it would be more beneficial for the child to know its father." Cary Tennis, the columnist, responded, "I would not want to know that I came from an anonymous sperm donor."[27] This woman's dilemma of trying to decide, prepregnancy, whether a child should know the anonymous donor reflects the concern of many donor-recipient parents with the child's interests.

Various studies of disclosure have shown that most heterosexual parents do not disclose to their children that they have been conceived with third-party gametes.[28] It is, of course, far easier to hide the use of third-party sperm or eggs when there is both a mother and a father. Recipients must decide whether to tell their children of their genetic origins and, given the various identity options concerning donors, what kind of relationship (if any) they want with their donors. Notwithstanding the paucity of legislation on this issue in the United States, parents' decisions on donor disclosure receives both scholarly and practical attention. Although the law does not yet address the enforceability of anonymity agreements, it is an issue that appears extensively in the research and popular literature. Given the public focus on identity release, this section explores parents' approaches to disclosure.

Who chooses donor release? In one Dutch study, virtually all the lesbian couples and almost two-thirds of the heterosexual couples chose identified, rather than anonymous, donors; the heterosexual couples choosing disclosure were likely to be of a higher socioeconomic status, to have fewer difficulties dealing with male infertility, and never to have considered not disclosing the information to their child.[29] Similarly, in a Canadian study, about one-fifth of the sperm vials ordered through one clinic were open identity, but 95 percent of the women who did not have male partners chose open-identity donors.[30]

In contrast to gamete donation, openness has become a key word in the adoption context. Most private infant adoptions are now "open" from the outset, meaning that the biological and adoptive parents "choose" each other, often after a face-to-face meeting. In many cases, biological and adoptive parents also agree to ongoing postadoption contact, which can range from an annual exchange of photographs to regular visitation or telephone communication. Many of these changes result from pressures exerted by the biological parents who relinquish their children only upon an agreement for some type of openness; accordingly, there has been a significant increase in the number of agencies offering adoptions with contact.

Nonetheless, the overwhelming majority of parents who have used either donor sperm or donor eggs do not disclose to their children that they were created through donor gametes.[31] They may want to protect the child from the knowledge that he or she is not biologically related to a parent, to protect the parent from the stigma of infertility or rejection by the child, or they may be uncertain of how to disclose.[32] On the other hand, the rate of disclosure varies by family form. In 2004, the American Society for Reproductive

Medicine advocated that the fact of donor conception, if not the actual identity, be disclosed to children.[33] This recommendation is not, however, binding on the numerous fertility clinics that are members of the ASRM.

When does disclosure occur? Not surprisingly, disclosure that a child is biologically not related to one parent appears much more common in families that choose open-identity donation than in the traditional anonymous-donation families. In one study of these two different kinds of families, only about 5 percent of parents who had chosen anonymous donation had informed their children of their origins.[34] The experiences of families with identity-release donors differ, depending on the structure of the family. Interestingly, in one study of seventy open-identity donor-created families that included single women, lesbian couples, and heterosexual couples, about one out of seven families called the donor "father" or "dad." But it was only the families headed by a single woman or a lesbian couple that did so; the sperm donor was never called "father" or "dad" by anyone in the families headed by a heterosexual couple.[35] And in families headed by single women, children were far more likely to call the donor "father" or "dad" than in families headed by couples—either lesbian or heterosexual.[36] All the families headed by a lesbian couple or a single woman had told their adolescent children that they were donor children, and 70 percent of the heterosexual couples had told their children.[37] Of course, in heterosexual couples, it is much easier not to tell children of their donor origins because the children will assume that they know who their father is.

When parents do disclose, they may be uncertain of how to approach the issue. On its website, the Donor Sibling Registry provides a series of frequently asked questions concerning disclosure:

> *When is the best time to tell my child that she is donor-conceived?*
> It is never too early to begin telling your child the circumstances of her conception and birth. Small children love to hear the story of their beginnings and often ask to have it repeated. Don't worry about having the right language or perfect terminology. The way you tell this story should reflect the way you always speak in your house, with the same tone, length and level of seriousness. When the story of the donor-conception is told from the beginning of your child's life, the information becomes embedded in the relationship between your child and you. It is shared and it is a non-event, compared to the experience of disclosing the information for the first time at a later date. . . .

• • •

Why should I tell my child he is donor conceived?
Some parents are reluctant to tell their children that they were conceived with the aid of donor gametes (eggs or sperm). . . .
Parents who believe their children deserve to know their genetic origins tend to frame the issue in terms of "honesty" versus "secrecy."
They value openness in the family and believe that secrets are dangerous and uncontrollable. For example, in cases where there are some
other people who do know the circumstances of a child's conception,
there is always the risk of unplanned disclosure by someone besides
the parent.[38]

In one of the first studies to explore how parents actually disclosed, a
team of researchers identified two strategies: the "seed planting" method,
which ensured that the child knew from an early age about donor conception, and the "right time" method, through which parents sought to
disclose donor-conception issues when the child was best able to understand his or her origins.[39] Many parents were frustrated with the paucity
of vocabulary for helping them convey this information to their children,
as well as with the lack of resources.[40] Although there are numerous books
that help adoptive parents explain their relationship to their children, such
as Jamie Lee Curtis's *Tell Me Again about the Night I Was Born,* there are
few comparable books dealing with donor children.

Once parents decided to disclose, in discussing donor sperm they
tended to use stories focused on the need for "spare parts" to replace a
broken piece; according to one story, "daddy's sperm was broken, so we
got sperm from a doctor."[41] Donor-egg recipients were more likely to use
a narrative with the idea of a "helper," in which "the donor was often described as having provided a 'gift' to the parents."[42] Indeed, in their book
Having Your Baby through Egg Donation, authors Ellen Glazer and Evelina
Sterling recommend openness throughout a child's life, suggesting that
parents begin discussing these issues with their young children by using
a version of the "helper" story.[43] Although parents may worry about their
children's reaction to this information, studies have repeatedly shown
that when young children learn that they have third-party gametes, it has
no effect on their relationship with their parents or adjustments to their
environments.[44]

Parents also must decide whether they will disclose their use of donor
gametes to other family members and to friends. Given a cultural emphasis on identifying similarities between parents and children, it may

be particularly difficult to disclose the use of gametes. "Does your child look like you or your husband?"—which for many people is an innocuous and common question—becomes fraught with difficulties when the children are not biologically related to at least one of the parents. When medical anthropologist Gay Becker and two colleagues interviewed 148 couples who had used donor gametes to create a child, they found that everyone was concerned about the challenges posed by "resemblance talk." The concern was equally shared by couples who intended to disclose and those who did not intend to disclose their use of gametes. Resemblance talk, or discussion of how a child looked like its parents, reminded couples of the loss of genetic connection that they experienced with their child, caused couples to worry about their children's identity within their family unit, and caused worry about potential stigma for children who look different from other family members. Becker and her colleagues concluded,

> Because resemblance talk and discourse decisions are frequently tied to each other, it is likely that if the public were more accepting of difference, parents would likely feel more comfortable with disclosure. Yet resemblance talk may make it more difficult for parents to disclose, not easier, as long as attitudes about the implicit primacy of genetic connectedness prevail.[45]

Resemblance talk is generally taken for granted, but I see its significance in my own life when my husband, who is adopted, is almost constantly amazed and delighted (sometimes chagrined) by our children's physical similarities to him, similarities that many of us assume without further thought when we look at our children and other family members.

Revealing to children that they have no biological connection to one parent but that they do have a biological connection to the other parent can be emotionally difficult, making one parent feel left out of a "club." For some people, however, it can be liberating. One participant in the resemblance-talk study reported that she was "kind of proud" that she had used an egg donor and that telling people was almost a teaching moment in which she could let people know about infertility procedures.[46]

The Children

Although there are estimates of approximately one million donor-sperm children and several thousand donor-egg children in the United States, no one knows for sure whether this number is accurate—including the children themselves. Fertility clinics are legally required to report the use of donor eggs in their practices, but not the use of donor sperm. Regardless of clinic reporting requirements, however, parents are not required to tell their children of their donor origins. Indeed, because parents rarely tell their children that they are the result of donated gametes, many children will never know that they are biologically unrelated to one of their social parents.

A law that required parents to tell their children of their donor origins and that permitted children to contact their donors could be justified on a showing that, without this information, children experience grave psychological, social, mental, and emotional difficulties. These data do not, however, exist. Children born through the new technologies appear to be as well adjusted as other children.[47]

Nonetheless, several studies have examined whether donor offspring experience identity problems that are similar to those of adopted children, and although the studies often conflict, they do indicate that at least some donor children experience a sense of loss for not having information about their biological pasts or being able to establish a relationship with their gamete providers.[48] Like adoptees, children of donated gametes may feel a sense of "genealogical bewilderment," a feeling that they are confused about their identity and different from other children. In fact, a number of groups are forming to work on the issues that the children and their parents confront.[49] In one study of children who were not told until they were adults that they were born through donor insemination, the (now adult) children explained that they were experiencing problems of personal identity in conjunction with some hostility toward their families for not disclosing their origins.[50]

For some children, the hostility and anger become quite bitter. Tom Ellis is a Cambridge University graduate who found out, when he was in his early twenties, that the man married to his biological mother is not his biological father and that, instead, he and his brother had been conceived through different anonymous donors. As a result of this revelation, he stopped seeing the man he had always thought of as his father and felt betrayed by his mother. Ellis flatly stated in a British newspaper, "It is torture to go on living without knowing half of who you are. . . . I don't think I should have been born."[51] Such a perspective, though not universal among donor children, represents one extreme in a continuum of the anguish that other children may feel.

When donor children do know of their status and are interested in contact, they generally do not want a new father or mother.[52] On the other hand, they believe that finding the donor will help them to learn more about who they are.[53] The desire of some of them to find out about their biological past does not indicate psychological imbalance, nor does it threaten their existing relationships with their parents. Katrina Clark, a student at Gallaudet College, explored her reactions to not knowing the identity of her sperm donor "father":

> I'm 18, and for most of my life, I haven't known half my origins. I didn't know where my nose or jaw came from. . . . I was angry at the idea that where donor conception is concerned, everyone focuses on the "parents"—the adults who can make choices about their own lives. The recipient gets sympathy for wanting to have a child. The donor gets a guarantee of anonymity and absolution from any responsibility for the offspring of his "donation." . . . Those of us created with donated sperm won't stay bubbly babies forever. We're all going to grow into adults and form opinions about the decision to bring us into the world in a way that deprives us of the basic right to know where we came from, what our history is and who both our parents are.[54]

There is substantial evidence that, for some gamete children, access to information about their biological origins may be important to their own construction of identity.[55] Not only are they curious, but they often feel a need to understand their "heritage" and to integrate the circumstances surrounding their birth into their overall sense of self. Social workers who counsel donor-assisted children report that these children often do have strong curiosity about their origins, similarly, in many ways, to the feelings of adopted children.[56] Children want to know why they have a certain eye color, where their musical talent comes from, whose sense of humor they have,[57] and they want to know their medical histories.

In the comparable context of adoption, adoptees have become increasingly vocal about their desires for access to their original birth records.[58] Some of them explain that there are medical reasons, such as the need to know of hereditary diseases, such as cancer or a family history of heart disease. Additionally, adoptees sometimes longingly express the need simply to find out where their hereditary characteristics, including their physical appearance, come from. Adoptees' desire to search develops from a variety sources, possibly including both physical and psychological reasons.

Although donor children may face easier psychological issues surrounding their origins, and knowing the identity of their genetic parents may be less central to their sense of self than for adopted children, they may still express strong interest in meeting their biological relatives. They may also wonder why their biological progenitors provided the gametes for their creation.

In the first study of adolescents' experiences with an open-identity sperm-donor program, published in 2005, the participants were generally interested in knowing what the donor was like, and they felt that contacting the donor could help them understand themselves better.[59] In fact, the number of groups formed to work on helping with disclosure indicates the dimensions of concern about this issue.[60] At the website for the group People Conceived via Donor Insemination, non-DI children cannot join because, as moderators Bill Cordray and Shelley Kreutz explain, opening up the group could compromise the trust required for honest discussion.[61]

Regardless of the laws, some donor-conceived children are taking actions to find their allegedly anonymous sperm donors. In November 2005, newspapers reported that a fifteen-year-old boy had swabbed the inside of his cheek, sent his saliva to a company that traces family trees, and found his father.[62] Or consider the 1993 movie *Made in America*. Zora is a highly intelligent, extremely race-conscious young African American woman who discovers in a biology class that her late "father" was not really her biological father. When she confronts her mother, Sarah (played by Whoopi Goldberg), with this information, Sarah confesses that she was artificially inseminated. Sarah had requested "the best they have, smart, black, not too tall." Because Zora is curious about her biological roots, she hacks into the computer files of her mother's sperm bank to uncover the true identity of her biological father. It turns out that the alleged father (played by Ted Danson) is white, appears to be something of a redneck, and is a used-car salesman. Zora tracks him down, and, in fantasy fulfillment for many donor children (and perhaps their parents), it appears that Danson's and Goldberg's characters will live happily ever after—together.

The Donor Sibling Registry was started in 2000 by Wendy Kramer and Ryan Kramer, Wendy's donor-conceived son, to provide an Internet meeting place for mutually desired contact between donor-created offspring and their biological relatives. In 2007, almost ninety thousand people visited the site, and it has been successful in facilitating genetically related contacts among more than four thousand people.[63]

So far, disclosure issues have focused on donor-sperm children. As donor-egg children become adults, they will undoubtedly experience the same identity issues and come across the same types of contracts guaranteeing anonymity and the same mechanisms for attempting to circumvent these contracts. The lack of legal mandates concerning anonymity or disclosure has resulted in a cottage industry of websites—which, like the Donor Sibling Registry, have been highly successful—and informal contacts in which donor children try to discover their biological origins. While the law is silent on anonymity, others entities, including Internet registries, are beginning to allow donor children to find their genetic relatives. Just as adoptees have used the judicial and legislative systems to gain access to their birth records, it is likely that gamete-conceived children will follow suit. Although secrecy and nondisclosure are easier in the donor context than in the adoption context—because there is no court involvement or home visits to determine suitability or the like—as increasing numbers of donor-conceived children become adults, they will undoubtedly raise similar issues. In our era of ever more sophisticated genetic tests, it will also be harder for the donor-recipient parents to keep their secret.

PART III

Race, Class, and Gender: Who Benefits?

7

Barriers to Conception

Guadalupe Benitez is a medical assistant who lives in San Diego, California. She tried to get pregnant for two years but was unsuccessful. Her doctor referred her to North Coast Women's Care so that she could receive fertility treatments to help her conceive. North Coast is the only fertility clinic that was covered by Benitez's insurance plan.

At her first meeting at North Coast with Dr. Christine Brody, Benitez informed Brody that she was gay. At that point, Brody explained that she would not inseminate Benitez because the procedure would be contrary to her religious beliefs, either because Benitez was single or because she was a lesbian. But, Brody said, other doctors at the fertility clinic would perform the insemination. A year later, without having performed any inseminations, North Coast referred Benitez to another doctor so that she could receive care that "was not discriminatory." Unfortunately, her insurance plan did not include this second doctor, so she paid for the procedures herself (although her insurance plan did ultimately make an exception for her). Benitez, who now has a son and twin daughters, sued North Coast, claiming that it had discriminated against her as a lesbian based on the physicians' religious beliefs.[1]

Q. What is Fertility4Life.com?
A. For years Lesbian and Single Women have been discriminated against and denied the opportunity to use clinics for artificial insemination, they have resorted to locating a donor or even advertising. The company and this unique service evolved out of this to assist as a conduit for both parties and ensuring the donor is genuine, fully screened and tested and as safe as possible.[2]

A recently published survey of fertility clinics found that 50% were likely to turn away a man who does not have a wife or partner, 20% would not offer their services to a single woman, 17% would not provide services to a lesbian couple, and 5% would not give services to a biracial couple.[3]

Scroll through the Medicaid coverage of most states, and, among the list of prescriptions excluded from coverage are those for fertility, alongside those for weight loss.[4]

As these vignettes show, infertility crosses class and race. Indeed, poor and African American women are more likely to be infertile than wealthier, white women, reproductive services generally are not available across class, and black families are less likely, even within the same class, to use these services.

This chapter explores these barriers to conception. There are numerous barriers to fertility, including financial difficulties, even for heterosexual couples. Some European countries provide routine funding for IVF, while American health care does not tend to cover IVF costs. Reasons for infertility may also differ by race. Cultural factors may be a determinant of who will seek infertility treatments. For example, embarrassment stemming from negative cultural pressures may discourage blacks to seek infertility treatments.

The question largely becomes, Should there be a right to use reproductive technologies to have a child? More specifically, does the state have a right to interfere with an individual's reproductive interests?

In evaluating potential answers to this question, it is important to recognize that even if the Constitution does not require the government to facilitate equal access to the right to procreate, the government may be precluded from imposing limitations on the ability to procreate. Thus, for example, government regulation limiting access to any type of infertility services to people of a certain race, or certain gender, would be unconstitutional. Another question then arises—regardless of whether the Constitution might allow the government to prohibit reproductive technologies in general—is, How should access to infertility services be regulated? Courts have held that a denial of infertility-related health services is not a violation of the Americans with Disabilities Act (ADA) because it does not treat one class of people—the fertile—any differently from the infertile; that is, it does not cover infertility services for either fertile or infertile employees. There are, however, federal laws that prohibit discrimination in programs that receive federal funding, which would apply to fertility clinics that receive federal funding, but it appears that private clinics are free to discriminate.

Whittier Law School professor Judith Daar usefully distinguishes between medical and structural infertility. Medical infertility is the kind that is diagnosable through medical testing, and structural infertility refers to an inability to bear children because the individual is not involved in a heterosexual relationship. To these two types, I would add a third type, cultural infertility, which refers to an inability to become pregnant because of cost or discrimination or social attitudes. This chapter examines the practical meanings of structural and cultural infertility, paying close attention to the paucity of laws that, because of their silence, allow the continuation of these forms of infertility.

Clinics screen patients based on a variety of criteria, some related to medical treatment, some not. This "clinical gatekeeping" may examine patients' fitness or even attempt to determine their appropriateness for parenthood based on a best-interest-of-the-child standard,[5] and, as in the case of Benitez, parental fitness may exclude nontraditional families. Clinics explain that they engage in this screening to protect a child's welfare as well as the mother's health; under current criteria, this means that some clinics will prevent single men and women and gay couples from using their services.[6]

Some people have proposed additional screening to ensure that patients exceed a basic threshold of minimal care, similar to state standards for terminating parental rights based on abuse and neglect.[7] The focus of this test would not be on the parents' lifestyle but on their ability to care for their children.

The question of whether fertility clinics should screen for anything but medical factors—quality and motility of sperm, depth of endometrial lining, age of the patients—implicates, of course, our perspectives on access to health services. But it is also related to views of the family, to the changing dimensions of family form as well as to the interests of children. Given that adoption requires parental screening and a court order determining that the adoption is in the best interest of the child, it may seem logical to argue that patients who seek the intervention of third parties should similarly be required to undergo screening. Yet, of course, home-based reproduction itself requires no screening and occurs regardless of the marital status or income of the participants.

In the past, prenatal screening was a form of eugenics that meant sterilizing women and men who were believed to be "feeble-minded" so that they could not reproduce at all. In 1907, Indiana enacted the first sterilization law justified by a theory of eugenics, and a majority of states enacted similar laws over the next thirty years.[8] The Supreme Court validated this practice as constitutional in the 1927 opinion of *Buck v. Bell,* with eight Justices permitting states to sterilize those "who are manifestly unfit from continuing their kind"[9] (and with only one dissent). Carrie Buck, in the words of the Virginia Supreme Court, "was committed to the State Colony for Epileptics and Feeble-Minded, . . . was seventeen years old and the mother of an illegitimate child of defective mentality. She had the mind of a child nine years old, and her mother had theretofore been committed to the same Colony as a feeble-minded person."[10] In the words of Stephen Jay Gould, the late great Harvard evolutionary biologist, "Carrie Buck was a woman of obviously normal intelligence. She was apparently raped by a relative of her foster parents, then blamed for her resultant pregnancy. Her case never was about mental deficiency; it was always a matter of sexual morality and social deviance."[11]

Buck was not successfully challenged until fifteen years later, in *Skinner v. Oklahoma*, a case involving a man jailed for stealing chickens and sentenced to sterilization. The Supreme Court struck down a law allowing for sterilization of repeat criminal offenders but did not entirely repudiate the holding of *Buck*: sterilization of "imbeciles" continued for the next several decades.[12] Indeed, notwithstanding potentially broad language in the opinion concerning procreation as a basic civil right, and the impact of sterilization on "a basic liberty," the ultimate holding was based on equal protection because the punishment of sterilization was inconsistently inflicted on only some of the people who had committed crimes of comparable severity.[13] The eugenics movement stands as a frightening example of the dangers of reproductive screening, of trying to determine who is appropriate to bear children. As discussed in the remainder of this chapter, and as the controversies over preimplantation genetic diagnosis (PGD) that are discussed in chapter 9 illustrate, issues of genetic screening are still ongoing sites for cultural battles.

Screened Out

Even medically infertile people in two-parent heterosexual families may not have access to reproductive technologies—because they cannot afford it. One in six Americans, or forty-six million people, have no health insurance. Almost three-quarters of the people who are uninsured live in working families, but they do not have access to health insurance because their employer does not provide it or they cannot afford the premiums. And infertility may serve as a preexisting condition to preclude an employee's eligibility.[14] Even for workers with health insurance, infertility services will probably not be covered. Few states require that health-insurance plans cover—or even offer the option of coverage—for infertility services.[15] In only three states—Illinois, Maryland, and Massachusetts—employees' health-care plans must cover most aspects of the diagnosis and treatment of infertility and reproductive services.[16] Another twelve states have a variety of approaches to insurance coverage.

Among states that have a "mandate to cover" are Massachusetts, Rhode Island, and New Jersey.[17] Texas and California are examples of states that mandate certain insurers to offer coverage for infertility diagnosis and treatment.[18] Although the difference between "mandate to cover" and "mandate to offer" coverage for infertility treatment seems insignificant at first glance, in practice the difference is much greater. Whereas a "mandate to cover" requires health-insurance companies to cover certain types of infertility treatment in every policy, a "mandate to offer" ensures only that health-insurance companies make available for purchase a policy that offers such coverage.[19] Consequently, in the states that require only that insurance policies offer, rather than cover, infertility services, policies that include coverage of infertility diagnosis and treatment are likely to be more expensive and, as a result, less accessible to lower-income populations. Five states limit infertility coverage to married couples, and others limit coverage based on the age of the patients.[20] The final limit on insurance coverage is that it is ultimately available only to those people who have jobs with insurance. And no state provides infertility coverage to those who receive public benefits.[21]

By contrast, some European countries provide routine funding for IVF. In Denmark, the government will cover up to six cycles of IVF, and almost 4 percent of children born there in 2003 were the product of IVF. In Britain, the government provides coverage for up to three cycles of IVF treatment. Several researchers have even argued that a solution to the shrinking population of many European countries is increased funding for patients to use reproductive technology.[22]

Although the limitations on access to infertility services in the United States may appear to be only about money, they express a variety of policy judgments concerning who should be able to reproduce. First, by excluding people on public benefits, states add diagnosis of cultural infertility to the medical diagnosis. Although not the same as sterilizing the "mentally unfit," this decision about how to allocate state funding deprives a group of people of the means of reproduction. Second, by not requiring employers' insurance plans to cover a range of infertility services, states are deciding that even people who are medically infertile should not be treated in the same way as those who are eligible for pregnancy and other health-care-related services. Finally, by limiting coverage to married couples, some states are reinforcing the exclusion from parenthood of people who are single and of gays and lesbians.[23] Even given scarce resources, there are questions about the structure of funding decisions on health-care coverage.

Screened In

These restrictions lead to the question of whether there should be a right to use reproductive technologies to have a child. It is useful to distinguish between two sets of rights: positive entitlements to obtain certain types of

Table 7.1
State Infertility Coverage at a Glance (October 2005)

State	Date enacted	Mandate to cover	Mandate to offer	Includes IVF coverage	Excludes IVF coverage	Only IVF coverage
Arkansas	1987	X[a]				X
California	1989		X		X[b]	
Connecticut	1989	X		X		
Hawaii	1987	X				X[c]
Illinois	1991	X		X[d]		
Maryland	1985	X[e]				X
Massachusetts	1987	X		X		
Montana	1987	X[f]				
New Jersey	2001	X		X		
New York	1990				X[g]	
Ohio	1991	X[h]				
Rhode Island	1989	X		X		
Texas	1987		X			X
West Virginia	1977	X[h]				

[a] Includes a lifetime maximum benefit of not less than fifteen thousand dollars.
[b] Excludes IVF but covers gamete intrafallopian transfer (GIFT).
[c] Provides a one-time-only benefit covering all outpatient expenses arising from IVF.
[d] Limits first-time attempts to four oocyte retrievals. If a child is born, two complete oocyte retrievals for a second birth are covered. Businesses with twenty-five or fewer employees are exempt from having to provide the coverage specified by the law.
[e] Businesses with fifty or fewer employees do not have to provide the coverage specified by the law.
[f] Applies to HMOs only; other insurers specifically are exempt from having to provide the coverage.
[g] Provides coverage for the "diagnosis and treatment of correctable medial [sic] conditions." Does not consider IVF a corrective treatment.
[h] Applies to HMOs only.

Source: American Society for Reproductive Medicine, "State Infertility Insurance Laws," http://www.asrm.org/Patients/insur.html. Courtesy of the American Society for Reproductive Medicine.

services and negative rights, or the liberty to make personal choices without interference from the state. The Constitution's Due Process Clause protects against government overreaching and undue state interference with fundamental personal decisions and beliefs. When a right is deemed to be "fundamental," such as the right for married couples to have access to contraceptives, then the government can only interfere if it has a compelling interest, and only then with means that are narrowly tailored to achieve that interest. If a right is not fundamental, then governmental regulation must satisfy a rational basis test.

In the context of children and parents, the Supreme Court's jurisprudence—outside the contraception and abortion context—has largely reinforced the notion that the traditional family unit provides adequate constitutional protection for children, rather than focusing on how these children came to be. To the extent that the Court has focused on the right to procreate, aside from the opinions on compulsory sterilization, the cases have involved challenges to limits on the right not to procreate, both with respect to compulsory sterilization and access to contraceptives. Within the parameters of a right not to procreate, the Court has never decided that the government must facilitate procreation. Moreover, the Due Process Clause has not generally been interpreted to require that the government act affirmatively,[24] such as by facilitating (as opposed to not interfering with) the opportunity to have a child.

Although the constitutional issue may seem clear with respect to whether the government must ensure access for all to the technologies, there are two additional issues: first, even if the government is not required to provide equal access to the technologies, there may be constitutional limits on whether the technology can be regulated in any manner; and second, constitutional issues aside, the policy options with respect to which technologies to regulate and how to protect access are quite complex, particularly because race is correlated both with access to infertility services and with causes of infertility.

Even if the Constitution does not require the government to facilitate equal access to the right to procreate, the government may be precluded from imposing limitations on the ability to procreate. Thus, for example, government regulation limiting access to any type of infertility services to people of a certain race, or certain gender, would be unconstitutional. By contrast, it is unclear whether it would be constitutional for the government to preclude access to specific types of reproductive technologies, such as the use of donor embryos, while permitting access to donor sperm

and eggs. Some scholars take the "strong" position and argue that the government cannot limit use of the technologies, absent a significant governmental interest.[25] Others take a more nuanced approach, arguing that the
government may limit access to various technologies that might otherwise
help infertile people.[26] Both perspectives agree, however, that the government cannot discriminate when it comes to potential users of the technology. A third approach argues that the government is entirely free to make
whatever choices it wants concerning the technologies.[27]

At this point in our history of regulation of the new reproductive technologies, this debate is almost entirely theoretical at the federal level. Federal regulation provides a system for collecting accurate information concerning the effectiveness of infertility services, for monitoring the safety
of gametes, and for denying funding for stem-cell research. Some states
provide additional regulation, or none at all. Given the advocacy strength
of the members of the infertility market, it seems unlikely that most types
of reproductive technology will be banned, with the exception of such
controversial techniques as reproductive cloning.

Instead, the focus of the law is more appropriately on the question of
how to regulate, regardless of whether the Constitution might allow the
government to prohibit reproductive technologies in general. And in this
context, the constitutional guarantees of equal treatment, regardless of sex
or race, provide a baseline from which to engage in policy issues concerning access. Accordingly, the debate among reproductive-rights scholars has
instead turned to questions of whether there is a right to use reproductive technologies or whether the government is precluded from regulating
them.

Overall, there is widespread belief that the majority of people suffering
from infertility are white, upper middle class, educated couples.[28] Interestingly, the few studies that have been conducted regarding this topic demonstrate just the opposite. For instance, comprehensive data collected in
1995 indicate that while 6.4 percent of white married women are infertile,
an estimated 7 and 10.5 percent of their Hispanic and Black counterparts
are faced with the same problem, respectively.[29] Further, the same study
showed that 5.6 percent of married women with a college degree or higher
are infertile, while 8.5 percent of women without a high-school diploma
or its equivalent confront the same problem.[30] When analyzing these data,
it is tempting to conclude that education levels per se are directly associated with infertility rates. However, such a correlation is unlikely. The
more reasonable conclusion is that sociocultural factors may have a strong

impact on educational levels and health-care usage. Correlation is not equivalent to causation.

Moreover, the reasons for infertility differ by race. The primary cause of infertility in women appears to be tubal-factor problems, and studies have repeatedly shown that this condition may affect black women at double— or more—the rate of white women.[31]

As a general matter, black patients do not access health care at the same rates as white women. Almost 20 percent of blacks (19.5 percent), and almost a third of Hispanics do not have health-care coverage, while the comparable rate for whites is 11.3 perecnt.[32] This lack of access appears to be the case also when it comes to infertility, with blacks significantly less likely to access artificial reproductive technology than whites are. Although whites are 75 percent of the population, they constitute 85 percent of those who use the technology; blacks, by contrast, who are 12.3 percent of the population, make up only 4.3 percent of the reproductive technology population; Hispanics, at 12.6 percent of the population, are 5.5 percent of the ART population; and Asians, at 3.7 percent of the population, constitute 4.5 percent of the ART population.[33] Class also affects usage, with high-school dropouts, who are typically clustered in a low income range, 25 percent less likely than college graduates to have received services.[34]

When infertility services are low cost and easily available, however, this disparity may decrease. In an extensive study of the use of infertility services in the military health-care system, where health care is easily accessible, black patients accessed infertility services at a rate roughly proportionate to their percentage of the military population.[35] The authors of that study speculated that economics, not cultural factors, was the significant factor in blacks' access to infertility services, and they suggested that broader insurance coverage in the general population might increase blacks' use of infertility services. In a study of whether state insurance mandates make a difference for infertility access by blacks, however, the authors found no correlation.[36]

Indeed, financial obstacles and income disparities prove to affect directly a couple's choice of whether to seek fertility treatments. Furthermore, the high cost of ART may result in prejudiced selection, with couples with higher educational levels and financial means more likely to use ART, and may create an invisible, albeit clearly delineated, ART hierarchy. Since higher educational levels and greater financial means are more common among white women than among Hispanic and black women, seeking infertility services has also been more common among whites.[37] A study published in 2000 found that although the city of Cincinnati's population was 18.3 percent black, only 6.2 percent of infertility patients were black; 40 percent of the black population, as opposed to 5 percent of the white population, did not have insurance.[38] In the absence of legal mandates to fund access to infertility services for the poor, this demographic split will continue.

Even in states that do offer coverage for ART, legal access may be irrelevant; instead, cultural factors can be a strong determinant of who will seek such treatments. Although people may want to use reproductive technology, their access may be impeded by cultural factors and other issues, including social stigma and stereotyping, lack of specialists for minority populations, and language barriers.[39]

Social stereotyping and stigma affects certain populations. Northwestern law professor Dorothy Roberts found that African Americans tend to feel ashamed when they are unable to conceive.[40] This may help explain why studies show that only one-third of African Americans who face infertility seek treatment.[41] Although financial difficulties and lack of insurance coverage may partially account for such a low percentage, social factors may have greater impact than was once believed. Embarrassment stemming from negative cultural pressures may discourage blacks to seek infertility treatment, while white culture's willingness to promote and support such technologies may explain whites' tendency to be more open to different treatment options.

Although there has not yet been a comprehensive study regarding the ethnicity of doctors who specialize in reproductive endocrinology, independent research seems to suggest that there are many more white, as opposed to black or Hispanic, specialists.[42] These differences in race, ethnicity, or class may be important because a client may feel particularly vulnerable, "especially given the history of social control over the reproduction of low income and minority women."[43] When dealing with a sensitive issue such as infertility, even perceived power differences may discourage and negatively affect minorities and economically disadvantaged individuals in seeking treatment. Moreover, differences in language and culture between doctors and patients may be detrimental to their communication and understanding of one another, causing patients to feel uncomfortable and even affecting the quality of care they receive.[44]

There is no simple solution to these problems, as they are deeply engrained in these various cultures. As society evolves and minorities continue to become more prevalent in professional fields, however, the gap between education and financial status among different cultures continues to grow smaller, and hopefully inequality in the utilization of ART will diminish as well.

The access issues to infertility services operate on two different levels: first, as discussed in the constitutional context, whether infertility services must be provided, regardless of income, race, sex, or other classification, and second, whether fertility clinics must treat all patients, regardless of the race, sex, or sexual orientation of the patients. Existing discrimination laws generally require that the fertile and infertile be treated similarly and that physicians not discriminate on the basis of race, sex, or national origin, and sometimes, sexual orientation.[45] The federal Americans with Disabilities Act (ADA), the Pregnancy Discrimination Act (PDA), and Title VII (the broad civil rights act that proscribes employment discrimination based on race, sex, or national origin) can each be a source for nondiscrimination between the fertile and infertile. The ADA prevents employers from discriminating against employees with a disability, which is defined as an impairment that significantly limits a "major life activity." In 1998, the Supreme Court held that reproduction qualified as a major life activity, albeit in a case involving HIV rather than infertility.[46] In subsequent cases, however, courts have held that a denial of infertility-related health services is not an ADA violation because it does not treat one class of people—the fertile—any differently from the infertility: that is, it does not cover infertility services for either fertile or infertile employees.[47] The Pregnancy Discrimination Act prohibits employers from discriminating on the basis of pregnancy or related medical conditions. So far, women have been unsuccessful in arguing that infertility is a medical condition related to pregnancy; for example, a 1996 appellate federal court held that the PDA referred to conditions related to pregnancy and childbirth, which occur postconception.[48] And in its 2003 opinion in *Saks v. Franklin Covey*, a federal court decided that a PDA claim must be based on conditions that are sex-specific to women but that infertility affects both sexes.[49] Courts have used similar reasoning in deciding that the broader protections of Title VII against sex discrimination do not apply to infertility-related services.

When it comes to disparities in treatment, there are federal laws that prohibit discrimination in programs that receive federal funding, some states preclude health-care providers from discriminating, and some states have broad antidiscrimination requirements that include not just race, sex, and national origin but also sexual orientation.[50] Fertility clinics that do not receive federal funding can, however, discriminate in patient selection, at least without fear of federal liability; and in states without broad protections against discrimination based on marital status or sexual orientation, clinics are free to choose patients on that basis. Although such discrimination is contrary to the ethical principles of professional associations such as the ASRM, clinics are not legally bound by these principles.[51]

As this chapter has shown, there are three barriers to conception: medical infertility, structural infertility, and cultural infertility. Structural and cultural infertility are facilitated by laws that remain unevaluated and unchanged. Nonheterosexual couples, as well as single women, may be discriminated against by fertility clinics through a screening process. Clinics explain that they engage in this screening to protect a child's welfare as well as the mother's health. Given that adoption requires parental screening and a court order determining that the adoption is in the best interest of the child, it may seem logical to argue that patients who seek the intervention of third parties should similarly be required to undergo screening. Home-based reproduction itself, however, requires no screening and occurs regardless of the marital status or income of the participants. This screening process bears some resemblance to widely criticized sterilization theories and attempts in the past.

8

Expensive Dreams

THE FOLLOWING AD appeared on the San Francisco Bay Area Craigslist in August 2007:

> Are you a female age 21–30? Nation Wide Egg Donation is looking for egg donors IMMEDIATLY for clients we are working with. . . .
> Donors should be 5ft 4in or taller, college educated (in college ok), height and weight proportionate, not taking or have taken any anti-depressant drugs for severe depression or ADD (Zoloft etc), non-smokers, very reliable and responsible, able to go to a few early morning doctor appointments with notice (will reimburse lost wages, mileage, babysitter reimbursement etc up to $800 per cycle), possibly travel for 5–7 days with all expenses paid for (will have advance notice and you can bring a friend) and have a good family (including self) health history. To earn $6,500 (for first time donors) and up to $10,000 (for successful proven donors) plus up to a $800 reimbursement for lost wages for time taken off work as well as help our clients start their families, please go to our website . . .[1]

The thesis of this chapter is that issues involving commodification—such as market access, price, safety of gametes, exploitation of providers, and sale of children—are intertwined with regulation of the resulting relationships, such as whether sperm donors can assert parental rights or whether children will be able to learn the identity of their donors. If, for example, single women, gays, and lesbians are unable to purchase gametes, then the laws governing parenthood will undoubtedly reflect similarly discriminatory attitudes. If the two-heterosexual-parent presumption controls the gamete market, then that same presumption will, as was true when similar presumptions dominated the adoption world, affect the rights of gametic children to discover their biological progenitors, and the rights of those biological providers to learn about their gametic children.

The chapter first discusses the market in gametes, before examining commodification anxiety, the concern about placing economic values on activities as a means of removing all associated emotion values. Putting a price on something does not necessarily destroy its intrinsic value or indicate that it is measured only by its economic price. Commodification anxiety actually hinders the need to regulate the gamete-transfer process by focusing on the sale of gametes rather then the financial and social relationships that result. The chapter discusses various options for controlling the commodification of gametes.

There are three policy options for regulating commodification of gametes: (1) apply a uniform fee schedule to all sales of egg, sperm, and embryos, providing a standard rate for providers and recipients, (2) set a tax on provider fees, with higher fees subject to higher rates, or (3) regulate the context of the market rather then the prices.

The chapter concludes that regulations should protect (1) the donor, ensuring complete information about the donor process and potential impact on them, (2) the recipients, by ensuring that the information provided about the donors is accurate and that they are paying a "reasonable price," (3) the children, by ensuring they have access to information about their origins, and (4) the intermediaries, by ensuring immunities from market-based lawsuits.

Moreover, regulations should recognize both the financial and social relationships that result from ART and prevent exploitation, rather than just banning financial transactions altogether.

Limits on Sales?

Federal law does not regulate the price of human eggs or sperm. No state prohibits banks from charging what they want for their services, and only a few states limit the amount of compensation that providers can receive. There are simply no laws concerning payment for sperm, although some states have adopted legislation concerning the sale of eggs and embryos.[2] Unlike transactions in blood or organ donations, the sale of eggs and sperm are not regulated. While federal law prohibits payment to organ donors, reproductive commodities are not covered.

State laws are typically based on the Uniform Anatomical Gift Act (UAGA), which was originally written in 1968 and provides a procedure for individuals to donate organs, eyes, and tissue after their death. The law also prevents anyone—either the potential donor or a family member—from selling body parts if removal of the body part will occur after the death of the donor, although these laws do allow a recipient to receive compensation for the costs of removal.[3] The law is quite clear on what can and cannot be sold. In states' enactments, they have often expanded on the UAGA and included provisions relating to the sale of other body parts. For example, in Virginia (which has adopted the Uniform Anatomical Gift Act), the sale of body parts is illegal, except for "hair, ova, blood, and other self-replicating body fluids."[4]

Florida law provides the most explicit regulation of gamete sales by allowing for "reasonable compensation directly related to the donation of eggs, sperm, and preembryos," thereby sanctioning the sale of eggs but limiting the amount that can be paid.[5] The law does not, however, define when payments are "unreasonable." Some clinics have taken it upon themselves to regulate the market price in their area, but these controls have not lasted long.[6] In 2000, the American Society for Reproductive Medicine suggested the following analysis: if sperm donors are paid sixty to seventy-five dollars per donation, and egg donors spend about fifty-six hours in medical clinics for activities such as undergoing interviews, counseling, and medical procedures, then egg donors should be paid approximately four thousand dollars per cycle. It concluded,

> Although there is no consensus on the precise payment that oocyte donors should receive, at this time sums of $5,000 or more require justification and sums above $10,000 go beyond what is appropriate. Programs recruiting oocyte donors ... should establish a level of compensation that minimizes the possibility of undue inducement of donors and the suggestion that payment is for the oocytes themselves.[7]

Even those agencies that have agreed to follow voluntary guidelines are not necessarily in conformity with them, according to a study of egg-compensation practices. They may, for example pay bonuses to women with highly competitive qualifications, such as higher IQs or particularly desirable physical characteristics. And there is regional variation in payment to donors and to agencies, with egg-donor compensation lower in the South than in other parts of the United States.[8] By contrast, agency fees for donor eggs were lowest in the Midwest and highest in the West. As the researchers—one of whom is the chief physician at the Massachusetts General Hospital Fertility Center—concluded, "The donor egg [industry is] still unregulated with significant regional differences in operational fees and compensation to donors and surrogates. Many of these centers, although having signed an agreement with ASRM, do not follow their guidelines."[9]

Not only are eggs, sperm, and embryos sold, but they are generally sold to the highest bidder. The sales practices reveal the blatant, unregulated market that characterizes the ART industry; gamete prices are the result of supply and demand. Aside from the minimal federal testing requirements, there is no further market regulation. The price of a desirable egg may be more than fifty thousand dollars, although eggs are available for less. X and Y Consulting, which claims to be the "longest operating donor recruiting agency in the U.S.," explains that its donor fee is based on the cost of living and wage rates in the state where the donor lives, so the fee can be quite variable; and, in addition to the actual cost of the egg, the consumer also pays various expenses associated with the donation process, including medical fees as well as transportation.[10] Egg producers can earn sizeable fees. The George Washington University Medical Center pays egg donors a standard four thousand dollars and earnestly explains that the money is earned income, so it must be reported on the recipient's tax return.[11] Across the Potomac River, donor compensation begins at six thousand dollars for those women fortunate enough to provide eggs to the Genetics and IVF Institute—the women must have a body-mass index less than 27 percent.[12] Choices Donations explains that providing eggs will only "take about 10–20 hours of your time over a 4–12 week period" and that providers "will receive a generous donation for your time and effort."[13] The Ethics Committee of the American Society for Reproductive Medicine has even defended payment for eggs, explaining that payment does not discourage the provider's altruistic motivations and also promotes fairness to the providers.[14] On the other hand, the President's Council on Bioethics, although unwilling to recommend against the sale of eggs and sperm, has set out options for limiting or restricting the sale of gametes, including embryos.[15]

Sperm sales are a transnational market with highly variable costs for different components in the process. The price of a sperm vial ranges, but it may cost hundreds of dollars. As one search engine for the right sperm donor explains, a vial of sperm—enough for one insemination—can cost between $200 and $600, although sperm from donors with advanced degrees or who agree to release their identity may cost more.[16] In 2006, the cheapest vial of sperm available from the Sperm Bank of California, a non-profit organization, cost $295, and shipping charges added at least another $190.[17] The Virginia-based Fairfax Cryobank charges $400 for a donor who is either pursuing or has already obtained a doctorate, while the cost of sperm from less-educated donors ranges from $170 to $310—although donors who agree to be identified command a premium.[18] A British service, Fertility4Life.com, offers several different options for sperm purchase, ranging from the "Diamond Plan" to the "Beat the Clock" plan to single-donation sales.[19] In Denmark, sperm is more expensive than gold.[20] Although California Cryobank provides its donor catalogue for free, a baby photo of the donor costs $21, and a longer profile of the donor costs $16.[21] And the different freezing options command different fees; dry ice preserves the sperm for a few days, and liquid nitrogen, which requires a special tank, preserves sperm for up to a week. Sperm producers themselves are typically paid less than $100 per "deposit," and sperm banks pocket the mark-up from there.

Embryo sales represent a new, potentially lucrative market that has not yet reached its price point. Embryos are available through several different options, including through contributions that are truly uncompensated for the donors,[22] embryo-selling banks, and embryo "adoption" agencies. Consider the efforts of Jennalee Ryan to establish her new business, the euphonious Abraham Center for Life. At the Abraham Center, "donor-created embryos" are made available for infertile couples.[23] Ryan assembles embryos, and then she sells them for $2,500 per embryo. She provides donor profiles to prospective parents, allowing them to select their embryo of choice from those that she has already manufactured.[24] As an alternative to the explicit sale of embryos, the pro-life Nightlight Christian Adoptions allows potential parents to adopt an embryo.[25] Only parents who are committed to offering "a constructive, wholesome, and spiritual home environment" to their child, as verified by a home study, are eligible to participate. As the Snowflakes Embryo Adoption fact sheet explains, for a program fee of $8,000, parents can help embryos "achieve their ultimate purpose—life."[26]

Should Gametes Be Sold?

The mere existence of this extensive, international market in gametes, however, obscures a variety of broader legal and social tensions. One of the primary issues concerns access, as discussed in the previous chapter, because gamete providers do not offer their services to all who would like to choose them (and, as some people would argue, should not do so); a second issue involves potential consumer preferences for certain (bordering on the eugenic) characteristics of their gamete providers, characteristics that go beyond basic gamete safety and the desire to become a parent but turn on the nature of identity. The third issue is the nature of what is sold: sperm banks sell sperm, egg donors sell eggs, the Abraham Center of Life sells embryos,[27] surrogacy centers sell the services of gestational carriers. Each of these market participants and each of these items for sale could, and perhaps should, be an appropriate subject of legal regulation. Regulations might—but do not currently—provide a series of interrelated protections including (1) for the donor, ensuring complete information about the donor process and its potential impact on them; (2) for the recipients, by ensuring that the information provided by donors is accurate and that they are paying a "reasonable price"; (3) for the children, by ensuring that they have access to information about their origins; and (4) for the intermediaries, by ensuring immunities from market-based lawsuits.

For many people, the initial and critical question is whether gametes should be sold at all. For some people, eggs and sperm should never be sold. They argue that the sale of eggs and sperm results in a series of quantifiable harms, ranging from exploiting the gamete providers to encouraging eugenics, as consumers choose the "best possible" genes, to leading down the slippery slope that ends in buying children, to discrimination based on class because of who is able to buy gametes.[28] Others argue that, because it interferes with "natural" reproduction, gamete sales result in unnatural families with two moms or two dads or only one parent. And political philosophers argue that allowing the sale of human gametes offends human dignity. Indeed, Vassar political scientist Mary Shanley observes that a market-based system in gametes "perpetuates an overly individualistic understanding of human society and distorts the liberal commitment to human freedom," suggesting that, if we cannot achieve the "ideal" of making "gamete transfer a real 'gift' by forbidding all payment, the main harm of a market system would be avoided if a uniform fee for donating and for receiving gametes was put into effect" along with abolishing anonymity.[29]

On the other hand, marketization—the creation of a free economy—facilitates access by marginalized groups, such as single women and gay and lesbian partners, fosters new family forms through allowing the creation of families outside the heterosexual nuclear and biologically related family, and does not objectify women—at least in the context of sperm sales.[30] The law so far has been relatively silent on the marketing of gametes, outside of attempts to prevent deceptive advertising and consumer fraud and to establish minimal safety standards.

Can This Market Be Saved? Should This Market Be Saved?

There is a continuum of options when it comes to markets in gametes ranging from prohibiting sales completely to allowing an unfettered market that extends—perhaps—through the sale of embryos. As part of this focus, it may be useful to distinguish the different markets involving eggs, sperm, and embryos. Although the consumers and sellers may be the same, the producers of egg and sperm face quite different experiences. Rather than focusing single-mindedly on regulating the sale of gametes, we should discuss regulating different actors—and acts—within the transactions, whether regulations should differ depending on the type of gamete, and the impact of each kind of regulation. Coherent discussions of commodification should begin with parsing out the stakes and interests of each market participant and examining why regulation might be appropriate.[31]

An examination of the rhetoric of commodification shows that suspicions about marketization are tangled up with fears about eugenics, slavery, and personhood. It seems to me that the marketization obsession brings together the most important issues in this debate—identity, parenthood, and the impact of technology—but that any discussion of the sale of gametes must be concerned with the equity of the market for those who are involved in it and want to be involved in it, as well as the implications of any sale for the provider, recipient, and child. Banning the sale of gametes will result in the inequities and inefficiencies that Minnesota law professor Michele Goodwin identifies in the body-part sale.[32] It might possibly result, as legal scholar Martha Ertman fears, in a majoritarian rule that precludes access for single women and lesbians.[33] Nonetheless, allowing an unfettered market, though perhaps efficient, is inequitable. Because of the nature of what is being sold—reproduction dreams—this is the type of transaction that we, as a culture, want to regulate and for which we might want to redefine efficiency to include access and equity. With appropriate regulation concerning gamete safety, nonexploitation of providers, and equal access, then, the actual market transactions should pose little danger to human flourishing. Nonetheless, by focusing primarily on the particular set of issues involved in market sales, we obscure the human relationships at the core of these sales: the relationships among gamete providers, children, and ultimate parent(s).

Such sales should continue, but the market needs to fundamentally change in order to recognize the interrelationship of the technology of gamete provision to identity and parenthood. Indeed, these sales might best be subject to a hybrid model that draws on both private ordering and altruistic donation.[34] Jennalee Ryan's Abraham Center can coexist with Snowflake Embryo Adoptions; egg and sperm donations from relatives does not preclude sale of these gametes by unrelated providers. A market economy can simultaneously include both the monetary transactions inherent in buying and selling gametes as well as the nonmonetary transactions inherent in gifts.

The gamete market mixes money and identity. Suggesting that the use of money taints otherwise pure relationships ignores the myriad situations in which intimacy and economic transactions already occur. The mere ascription of financial value to these items, including the use of commodification discourse, does not necessarily destroy all other values that they may contain.[35] As Princeton sociology professor Viviana Zelizer points out, "people invest a great deal of effort in creating monies designed to manage complex social relations that express intimacy but also inequality. . . . the point is not that these areas of social life valiantly resisted commodification. On the contrary, they readily absorbed monies, transforming them to fit a variety of values and social relations."[36] Zelizer's key insight, that social relationships may be entirely independent of a market exchange, is critical to understanding that the market in gametes may create social, familial relationships and may include both altruistically and financially motivated participants. Money does not—necessarily—cheapen intimacy.

There are multiple situations in which people are paid for work that benefits other people, ranging from nannies to clergy to medical professionals.[37] The problems result from determining whether there is a distinction between selling the "factors or services" that may result in a baby and selling the baby itself.[38] Texas law professor John Robertson, a long-term scholar of this field, argues that even if the exchange of money is involved in some part of the process of using the reproductive technologies to have a baby, this is not the equivalent of baby buying and that nonpayment raises significant issues of both efficiency and equity.[39]

Assuming that the market continues, the question is how to structure it to recognize both the financial and social relationships that result[40] and to prevent exploitation, rather than banning financial transactions altogether. In some ways, commodification is beside the point because, even if it were banned, underground markets would develop.[41] Instead, we should more profitably focus on the relationship between "human flourishing" and gamete sale.[42]

Neither a complete lack of regulation nor a complete banning of gamete sales is viable, for different reasons. Instead, we need to expand the purpose of regulation by focusing on economic and social interactions and then design interventions that will achieve those purposes. At the least, for example, we need market regulation to ensure the enforceability of contracts relating to sperm provision and physician/clinic services, but we also need to ensure that contracts relinquishing parental rights are enforceable. Moreover, regulations should seek to ensure that providers (particularly egg providers) are not exploited. Laws must clearly identify the parents of any child produced through gamete provision, specifying that the recipients are, indeed, those entitled to assert parental rights. Regulations must ensure equality of access, regardless of race, income, sex, sexual orientation, or other criteria. Finally, market regulation must ensure that a gamete-provided child has access to identifying information once the child is eighteen. Although a few of these regulations exist in piecemeal fashion in a few states, there is no comprehensive scheme that ensures that all these strands—identity, parenthood, access, and freedom from exploitation—are bundled together. This bundling might occur through federal law that binds all states or through the development of model legislation that each state could then enact.

Regardless of the pricing system applicable to sperm, eggs, and embryos, the anticommodification arguments are entirely accurate when it comes to the critical issue of what is being sold. Gametes can create people and familial relationships, unlike the sale of kidneys—or potatoes. It is the regulations concerning those resulting relationships that should assume critical importance. These issues are significant, of course, for market purposes (they may, for example, contribute to market efficiency) but also because, even if gamete sales are regulated like potato sales, the underlying products differ. Recognizing these differences does not mean that there should be no market but, instead, requires market adjustments. There is a patchwork of state regulation concerning the relinquishment of rights by donors, the establishment of rights for parents, and the need for identity disclosure, each of which inherently affects the existence and operation of a market in gametes. Any discussion of market structure must also examine the need to enforce contracts that both set the terms of a sperm sale and establish the parental role, if any, for gamete providers.[43]

The remainder of this chapter explores the rhetoric of market regulation, beginning with concepts of baby selling before moving to gamete sales. The existence of baby selling helps in understanding the "yuk" response that some people articulate when they contemplate a market in gametes.

Babies have literally been sold throughout American history. "Baby farmers" were paid to take in children, and then they tried to sell the children to families that would take them.[44] Most families wanted older children who could work and saw babies as a burden, not a wanted blessing, so sales were difficult. Today, of course, babies cannot be sold, and adoption is framed as a gift that centers on the noncommodified transfer of a child from a biological family to an adoptive family. All states have laws that prohibit baby selling. Contemporary questions about the sale of baby-making parts are framed by the concept of a nonmarket in babies.

Notwithstanding the rhetoric, however, even adoption involves a transfer of money. Adoptive parents may pay pregnancy and birth-related costs for the biological mother, so long as they are "reasonable and customary," as well as agency fees, which can range from fifteen thousand to thirty thousand dollars.[45] As an example of the market, consider that states explicitly regulate adoption-related advertising, with nine states allowing either agencies or adoptive or biological parents to advertise, two states banning any form of advertising altogether, and another twelve states permitting advertising only by a state agency or other licensed agency.[46] Even when children are adopted from foster care or have special needs, money is involved; for example, the adoptive parents may receive special subsidies in recognition of the additional financial strain imposed on them. Children may also be valued differently based on their race. As Michele Goodwin observes, it may cost parents who want to adopt a healthy, white baby more than fifty thousand dollars, while a black baby may be available for four thousand dollars; Goodwin concludes that "fee structures based on race give evidence that adoption is subject to the free-market forces of supply, demand, and preference."[47] International adoption practices, it is frequently alleged, provide additional support for the existence of an adoption market. The line between the crime of baby selling and the permitted payment of fees is difficult to draft.

The other analogy for selling gametic body parts involves the transfer of organs and blood. Organ donation is heavily regulated by the federal government under the National Organ Transplant Act of 1984 (NOTA), which prohibits the use of "valuable consideration" to pay for organs, and by the states' Uniform Anatomical Gift Acts. NOTA also established a national Organ Procurement and Transplantation Network (OPTN), requiring that hospitals engaging in organ transplantation comply with OPTN rules in order to be eligible for continued Medicare funding. Because the number of people waiting for an organ far exceeds the number of organs donated, there is an extensive waiting list (according to the OPTN's annual report, in 2005, there were almost ninety thousand people on the waiting list for donors, and fewer than thirty thousand organs were transplanted that year).[48] This situation, in turn, has prompted the development of an underground domestic and international market in body parts[49] and numerous proposals for revising the altruistic system of donation in favor of at least a limited market.

As is clear from the operation of the processes for both adoption and organ transplant, banning sales does not eliminate the exchange of money or even the development of a market. Instead, we might think of a continuum with money and complete marketization on one end and personhood and inalienability on the other. This continuum recognizes the possibility that there may be market transactions that involve no social relationships or social relationships that should be outside the market. Virtually all human transactions fall somewhere between these two theoretical points. In this regard, we can constructively use the formulation of Viviana Zelizer, who suggests three competing approaches to the question of intimacy and economic relationships:

1. Hostile Worlds. Such a profound contradiction exists between intimate social relations and monetary transfers that any contact between the two spheres inevitably leads to moral contamination and degradation.
2. Nothing But. Intimate relations involving monetary transfers are (a) nothing but another rationally conducted exchange, indistinguishable from equivalent price-making markets; (b) nothing but another expression of prevailing cultural values; or (c) nothing but coercion.
3. Differentiated Ties. Intimate relations involving monetary transfers include a variety of social relations, each marked by a distinctive pattern of payment.[50]

As an example of the Hostile Worlds approach, Mary Shanley argues that we should think of transferring eggs and sperm not as a market activity but "as a way to collaborate in others' efforts to conceive a child. . . . Subsuming collaborative procreation into other kinds of buying and selling commodifies either human gametes or the use of the body, or both."[51] She urges instead that, with a focus on the child and the child's relationship to the gamete provider, rather than on anyone else involved in the transaction, gametes should not be allowed to be sold.[52] Gametes are not simply things that can be detached from the body but objects of moral, emotional, and psychological significance. The title of one journal article suggests a conclusion that fits well within the Hostile Worlds approach: "Boutique Egg Donations: A New Form of Racism and Patriarchy"; the author argues that "[t]he glaring reality is that there are some legitimate restrictions that can and should be placed on a woman's right to make decisions about her body."[53] Margaret Radin argues that we devalue human life if we are able to place a price on various attributes of personhood, such as an individual's ethical commitments.[54] Although Radin does not directly address the sale of gametic material, she discusses the practice of surrogacy, suggesting that women should not be allowed to sell their capacity for procreation and that the effect of such sales on third parties (children, for example) supports the prohibition.[55]

Where Does This Fear of Commodification Come From?

If we prohibit the sale of gametes, it must be because of their significance to the person created, a fear of economic exploitation of people who need money and are willing to sell *anything*, fear of a stratified market in which some people can buy the "best" gametes. Gametes are tangible objects, but they have the capacity to create persons, whereas blood transfusions and organ donations do not. On the other hand, we can manage their significance to the resulting children by requiring identity disclosure. Facilitating the creation of both a child and a parent, which gamete sales do, justifies the continuation of this practice; presumably, the child who learns of the identity of the gamete provider would prefer to have been born than not to exist at all.

Indeed, it is important to appreciate the utility of the economic approach to intimate relationships, an example of what Zelizer labels Differentiated Ties. Commodification exists as background even in realms such as the family that are typically thought of as noncommodifiable. It is evident in mechanisms ranging from prenuptial contracts to childcare providers, from take-out food to equitable distribution upon divorce. For example, prenuptial contracts may have pay-out provisions that vary depending on the years of marriage, with more money for greater duration, or they may provide for waivers of property rights and the maintenance of separate property. It is a given that the family cannot be, and has never been, completely separated from money.

Money has been an integral part of marriage law in our country, including issues such as who owns property acquired during the marriage and who is obligated to support whom. The importance of breadwinning underlies the dependent nature of wives. Throughout the nineteenth century, aside from the limited property that women were allowed to own pursuant to the Married Women's Property Acts, husbands maintained financial control over all property during the marriage. Although men were supposed to provide the necessaries for their wives, this obligation was extremely difficult to enforce if men failed to do so. In order for a creditor to receive reimbursement for a woman's purchase of necessaries, the creditor was required to prove that the item purchased actually was necessary, that the husband had not already provided the item, and that the wife could not pay for it herself.

Because the labor contributed by women to the family has historically had economic value, the woman's rights movement fought to give women control over the money realized from that labor. Beginning in the nineteenth century, women fought for payment for their work within the home. Consider the 1915 plea of a farmer's wife, who wrote to the secretary of agriculture explaining that "the first need of the rural wife is a state income . . . thereby saving her the humiliation of asking for the money we have earned but don't get."[56]

The prominent economist Oliver Williamson has argued that, if calculating a monetary value "is inimical to personal trust, in that a deep and abiding trust relation cannot be created in the face of calculativeness, and if preexisting personal trust is devalued by calculativeness, then the question is how to segregate and sever relations of personal trust."[57] According housework economic value might lead to its recognition, but it would also challenge the dichotomy between personal caring relationships and financial value.

In addition, perhaps somewhat paradoxically, to quote legal scholar Lawrence Mitchell, "self-interest is a thin theory on which to build a social order."[58] Engaging in caretaking work is, regardless of financial remuneration, partially self-interested. The cleanliness of a person's house seems to say something about the person, and the success of one's children often affects one's own self-concept. Valuing this work in money merely provides one further way to recognize this self-interested action. To admit that one is motivated in part by money does not at all explain caretaking behavior. Children are probably worth more, economically, once they are dead, through life insurance or tort recoveries, but I do not think this suggests anything at all about why people have children and nurture them.

Nonetheless, and simultaneously with this understanding of the interrelationship between the market and the family, there has developed something identified as commodification anxiety,[59] or concern about placing economic value on activities as a means of removing all the emotional value associated with those activities, or what, as discussed earlier, Zelizer identifies as the Hostile Worlds model. In a critique often associated with Karl Marx, commodification leads to a flattening out of social relationship and a reduction of everything to money. Fertility clinics conceptualize egg donation as a gift and may condemn women who make repeated donations. Sociologist Rene Almeling found that "women who attempt to make a 'career' of selling eggs provoke disgust among staff, in part because they violate the altruistic framing of donation," and she found that clinics may even perpetuate this framing by requesting that recipients write thank-you notes to their donors.[60] Many women explain that they donate eggs because of a desire to help someone, although money is also a strong motivator. The process of egg donation, though not identical to the process of private adoption, has some parallels to it, although, of course, in adoption, the biological mother cannot be paid for relinquishing her child. In each process, recipients are seeking the means to become parents. In private adoptions, the adoptive parents may advertise and call on intermediaries to help them find a biological mother willing to give up her child; in egg donation, the intending parents may advertise and call on intermediaries such as clinics or recruiters to help them find a woman willing to give up her eggs. Here is the screening process that Jessica went through to become an egg donor to a couple through an agency called Creative Family Connections:

> The couple sent Jessica a letter about their quest to have a child. They'd tried everything; egg donation was their last resort. Their last egg donor had dropped out midcycle. They were desperate.

Jessica thought of her mother. She and her stepfather had struggled with infertility for years—and her mom never again got pregnant. Imagine that someone like me could have helped them, Jessica thought.

Jessica filled out a 15-page application and began the donor "screening" process, which includes the collection of a medical history and personality test. The clinic drew blood and checked her hormone levels and her ovaries.

Then officials sent her to a social worker to gauge how attached she was to her eggs. If she seemed too emotionally vested, clinics say, she'd be disqualified. The social worker asked whether her family was supportive. Many agencies strongly recommend that younger donors talk the decision over with their families. . . .

The social worker asked Jessica how she viewed her role in the donation. It was a way to help someone, she said. Jessica was asked about her circle of friends and her job—there's fear that loner or depressed women might focus too much on the resulting child.

"Are you going to feel resentful if you can't have your own children several years from now?" a therapist asked.

Jessica shook her head: "It would give me hope because I'd know that this process was out there."[61]

Payments for doing something that egg donors "want" to do may seem counterintuitive, and it may seem that money "cheapens" the act, decreasing the altruism and raising the greed factor. And Swarthmore professor Barry Schwartz argues that when you give people money for doing things they like, they will enjoy these same activities less and will require money to continue their participation.[62] Schwartz uses various studies to illustrate his point, including one in which Swiss citizens were asked about where to put nuclear-waste dumps. If there was only one reason to approve of locating a dump in their community, because they were good citizens, people were more likely to agree to it than if they were offered a second incentive as well, being paid lots of money. When researchers asked people if they were willing to accept a dump in their community, even though people knew that the dump might affect property values and be dangerous, 50 percent of those asked said they would allow one. But when people were asked if they would accept a dump if they were also given a significant amount of money, then only 25 percent said yes. Newspapers are filled with stories of conflicting motives.[63] Some egg donors explain that they are doing it to help other women, whereas others candidly acknowledge that they want the money. In *Confessions of a Serial Egg Donor*, Julia Derek, a Swedish journalism student who was living in New York, recounts how she saw an ad soliciting egg donors at a particularly vulnerable time in her life, when she was running out of money and would be forced to return home. "A woman might actually be able to get $3500 for one of her eggs?" she incredulously asked herself. "This just sounded too good to be true."[64] She questioned whether she would then become a "mother" of any children born, ultimately concluding that the baby would have only a minimal part of her genetic pool, that it was like giving away one of her "hairs."[65] When it came time for her to fill out the egg-donation application, she explains, "I was not going to put down that the prospect of making a few grand was my main motivation, as, clearly, nobody wanted to hear the bitter truth. . . . So I had to pretend that I was more of a saint than I really was."[66]

Like many other egg donors, Derek felt that she did not adequately understand the health risks involved in undergoing the medical procedures. There are, in fact, no disclosure requirements imposed on agencies, recruiters, or recipients, although federal regulations, discussed in chapter 2, do require a minimal health history of the donors.

Indeed, there are numerous difficult issues when it comes to money transfers between donors and recipients in the egg-donation industry. Lorna Marshall, a physician at Pacific Northwest Fertility and IVF Specialists, has documented a series of problems in reproductive technology transactions with third parties.[67] The list includes donors deceiving purchasers about the number of times they have previously donated or withholding other information that would make them less desirable, donors not wanting to donate to specific populations, recipients lying about how old they are or secretly paying additional money to the donors, and agencies skimming money from egg-donation fees.

The question, on this perspective, is not whether to commodify but what to commodify and how to commodify it. Introducing economic concerns into the family does not necessarily corrupt it with cold cash. We can distinguish between the payment that gamete providers receive and the resulting social needs of a child for information about that gamete provider. Money is already present in the family; to deny this fact buys into assumptions that, because caretaking is a labor of love, it is not labor at all. Nonetheless, many people are worried that paying money for reproduction will negate the richness and interdependence of a relationship that is inherent in our cultural concept of family. Accordingly, some people still wonder about the impact of commodification on baby markets. Professor Margaret Radin asks, "If a free-market baby industry were to come into being, with all of its accompanying paraphernalia, how could any of us, even those who did not produce infants for sale, avoid measuring the dollar value of our children? How could our children avoid being preoccupied with measuring their own dollar value?"[68] The answer to that is simple: I buy life insurance, valuing my life (at the time of my death) in a certain way that has relatively little to do with how I think of myself on a day-to-day basis. That is, putting a price on something does not necessarily destroy its intrinsic (nonmonetary) value or indicate that it is measured only by its economic price. For those who buy gametes, the value of their purchase cannot be quantified in monetary terms. Even many of those who sell gametes recognize that they are helping to create life, not merely selling excess gametic material. As Radin also points out, it is possible for both market and nonmarket understandings to coexist.[69] Consider the literature on tort remedies as well as domestic-relations concepts of equitable distribution and community property: these constructs show how economic valuation of household services can exist simultaneously with noneconomic understandings of caretaking and intimacy.[70] Commodification anxiety actually covers up the need to regulate the gamete-transfer process by focusing on sales rather than on the multifaceted financial and social relationships that result.

Indeed, as the Differentiated Ties model suggests, money has different meanings depending on the context. Payments to an egg donor allow the recipient to start a family; for the egg donor, it may mean the opportunity to finish her education as well as to help someone else. Suggesting that people sell gametes only for the money (though certainly true in some cases) overlooks the other values that influence people's choice to do so.

When we leave out money, when we refuse to value the work that is done, or when we reduce all work to money, we essentialize the complex transactions that characterize the gamete-provision process. We fail to value appropriately the work that is performed by the gamete providers. Arguing that paying people for their gametes would necessarily and completely commodify children by leading to baby sales overlooks the reasons why people pay: they need this commodity in order to create an intimate relationship. We should move past the debate on whether to apply market norms to gamete provision and instead recognize the value of this labor.

Interestingly enough, allowing payment for services and making the services quantifiable revisits the distinction between goods and services established by Article 2 of the Uniform Commercial Code, the state law that regulates transactions in goods. Article 2 covers goods but not services. In the domestic context, perhaps this distinction is backward. We may be unable to value appropriately a "good" child or a "clean" house, and we probably should not, but we can attempt to value the services involved in producing these "goods."

When it comes to policies, there is a range of options between banning gamete sales completely, as advocates of the Hostile Worlds model would like, and allowing them to continue without regulation, as advocates of the Nothing But model would prefer. One option would set a uniform fee schedule to apply to all sales of eggs, sperm, and embryos, providing a standard rate for providers and recipients. This model has the benefit of ensuring that Ivy League credentials, race, height, and other personal qualifications are financially irrelevant; it helps insurance companies set a fee structure; and, depending on the price, it may make these gametes more affordable. The fee would be established based on the reasonable expenses incurred by the donor and the clinic's recruitment efforts. Such a proposal is, however, unrealistic in a culture that values individual choice and market freedom.[71]

A second alternative is to set a tax on provider fees, with higher fees subject to higher rates[72] and with the tax used, perhaps, to subsidize gametes for people who otherwise could not pay. If the tax is simply added to existing prices, however, then gamete prices would increase, posing a burden on recipients, although it would not deter people who could afford to pay premium prices. Moreover, such a tax would be difficult to monitor as it would require full disclosure of all gamete-based transactions.

A third alternative is to regulate the context of the market, rather than the prices themselves. This would involve structuring procedural rules to create a more equitable market, albeit without controlling payments within particular transactions. For example, such regulation could include an improved system for informed consent for all gamete providers concerning not just the physical risks (which vary for sperm and egg donation) but also the consequences of providing gametes: the creation of a child. It might include informed consent from recipients and providers concerning mandatory disclosure for children. It might require improved monitoring of gamete-provided information, clinic safety procedures, and limits on the number of embryos transferred. It might also include a national registry, similar to the British system, keeping track of donors. With a registry, the law could impose limits on the number of times one person could provide gametes.

At the least, this third option, restructuring the parameters of the market, will provide the requisite uniformity in many different fertility-industry practices and will also ensure the ability to track donors and the resulting offspring. In addition to continuing existing requirements on the safety of the gametes themselves and on reporting about cycles involving donor eggs and embryos, the federal government should establish standards for fertility clinics and bank certification, rather than relying on individual states or industry groups. The requisite reporting should include the use of donor sperm and the identity of sperm providers, with this information provided to a national registry. Without some type of a uniform registry at the federal level for keeping track of donors, donors will continue to be able to misrepresent not just the number of times that they have donated but the quality of their gametic materials and, indeed, their qualifications; without better and mandatory regulation not just of the safety practices of intermediary agencies but also of their business practices, financial abuses will continue. Egg donation is typically one of the last steps in a couple's infertility treatment (although it is one of the first steps for gay men), so recipients often have little incentive to check the accuracy of the claims of the providers. And without at least minimal disclosure requirements to ensure informed consent on behalf of egg donors, donors may be manipulated into repeatedly agreeing to potentially risky procedures, either because of the money or because of altruism.

Women sell not just labor but parts of their bodies when they provide eggs to others (or when they gestate babies for others). Our employment laws provide some protection against worker exploitation through minimum-wage laws, antidiscrimination provisions, and overtime guarantees. Requiring basic procedural rules for structuring the gamete market serves the interests of all involved by providing guarantees of safety and freedom from exploitation. Although informed-consent laws may have minimal impact, they provide notice to those who read the underlying agreements. The parameters of informed consent are further discussed in chapter 11.

Returning to the case of *Johnson v. Calvert,* consider that the court rejected the donor's claim to a physician-patient privilege because there was no evidence, it asserted, that the donor ever consulted the Cryobank for medical diagnosis and treatment. Instead, the donor sought merely to make money from the sale of his sperm and was thus not subject to the protections offered by the privilege. Sale of the good did not subject him to the same privacy rights. Although we might think differently about privacy in connection with a sale of "goods" than in connection with a sale of "personhood,"[73] treating sperm and eggs as the sale of goods might help allay concerns about the identity of the providers. This is an example of how the concept of commodification may be useful because it allows us to separate out the "good" from the privacy interests of the provider. Viewing gametes as commodities should diminish privacy concerns. Ascribing financial value and using commodification discourse does not necessarily destroy all other values that gametes may contain.[74]

The proposal for a regulated market will please neither the Nothing But nor the Hostile Worlds advocates, although it draws from both positions. It recognizes the complexities of donating eggs, of acting as surrogates, of providing sperm so that someone else can have a child, and of providing medical services in connection with these transactions.

9

What Is Wrong with Technology?

ALTHOUGH—INDEED, BECAUSE—reproductive technology produces babies, it also produces cultural controversies. In addition to confusing issues surrounding the identity and meaning of parenthood, and beyond the implications of our failure to regulate them, the new reproductive technologies tap into profound and deeply held moral values. Ironically, although legal regulation of the reproductive technologies treats parenthood, identity, and genetics separately, cultural opponents of the reproductive technologies conflate creating babies with a series of social problems.

First, making babies outside the human body allows children to have only one known legal parent, so the technologies can facilitate single parenthood and child rearing outside the heterosexual family. Indeed, some commentators see the technologies as threatening the institution of marriage itself. Second, the technologies, because they appear to allow humans to "play God" by bypassing naturally occurring biological processes and permitting parents to select traits, are contrary to the moral beliefs of many people. Third, in addition to the issues of exploitation of gamete providers and surrogates, reproductive technologies are class based, typically involving the transfer of gametes from economically (although not necessarily socially) lower classes to wealthier people, and they generally benefit white people. And, finally, because the technologies may result in embryos, they have gotten mixed up with issues of cloning and stem-cell research.

This chapter explores the cultural and moral concerns that come along with advances in reproductive technologies. The discussion identifies four main issues triggered by reproductive technology: (1) the ability of technology to allow for only one legal parent, (2) the concern that beneficiaries of reproductive technology are playing God by altering natural reproduction, (3) the unavailability of reproductive technology to certain socioeconomic classes, and (4) the conflation of reproductive technologies with more controversial issues like cloning and stem-cell research.

The chapter recognizes various religious, historical, and philosophical objections with different aspects of reproductive technology, including preimplantation genetic diagnosis, the moral status of embryos, and embryos as property. The chapter investigates how domestic and foreign courts and legislatures have approached reproductive technology issues, as well as the power of private contracts in donor and surrogacy agreements.

Should Every Child Have Two Parents of the Opposite Sex?

Biologically, of course, a woman's egg and a man's sperm must meet to create a child. From this simple biological fact spring a variety of arguments concerning marriage and children's rights that are based in the fundamental concept that children should live in married, heterosexual families. Consequently, advocates believe that children should have two parents and suggest either that single parents not be allowed to choose to construct families or that when a single parent has a child through gamete donation, a second parent of the opposite sex must be identified. These advocates believe that reproductive technologies threaten marriage as a heterosexual institution by facilitating reproduction by single parents and by gays and lesbians and that reproductive technologies also threaten children's rights to grow up in marital households and know their biological origins.

Decoupling Male-Female Marriage

Groups such as Focus on the Family explain that although gays and lesbians might be able to produce children through sperm donation, "The problem with a pair of homosexuals raising children isn't that they couldn't love them; it's that Moms and Dads are different, and children need one of each. Having 'two Moms' or 'two Dads' just isn't the same. This is common sense"[1] The pregnancy of Mary Cheney in 2007, the lesbian daughter of Vice President Richard Cheney, brought widespread condemnation from such groups. The Concerned Women for America criticized Cheney's behavior as "unconscionable" and "injur[ious to] her child."[2] In their legal challenges to gay marriage, advocates have repeatedly argued in court cases that allowing same-sex marriage would profoundly undermine one of the fundamental purposes of marriage, which is to procreate.[3] Reproductive technologies, which allow for procreation outside the traditional male-female family, challenge the legally privileged status of marriage.

In a report on changing notions of parenthood, the Institute for American Values decries the threat to children who are not raised in a married family with a mother and a father through developments such as using surrogacy or donor sperm or eggs. The institute calls for a five-year moratorium on any legal changes that would "broadly undermine the normative importance of mothers and fathers in the lives of children."[4] As an example of an appropriate initiative, the institute notes that in Italy, only married couples (or those in stable heterosexual relationships) can use assisted reproductive technology.[5]

Demooring Children

The claim that reproductive technologies are a threat to traditional marriage is combined with the claim that the erosion of traditional marriage would be disastrous for children and would endanger the norm of the nuclear family. Making the links as clear as possible, two writers warn in the *National Review*,

> Artificial reproductive technologies [by] allowing homosexual partners to create their own children either with donor eggs or donor sperm, or with surrogates, or even perhaps by means of cloning, would further erode the ideal of children being conceived and raised by their natural parents.[6]

As these writers note, facilitating the creation of a child by two partners of the same sex does, indeed, challenge the traditional family form; of course, adopted children are neither conceived nor raised by their "natural" parents either.

David Blankenhorn is one of the most respected and thoughtful advocates of this position involving concern for the resulting children. He argues that family rights are being reconceptualized so that people can form families of choice in whatever manner they would like to do so. He identifies assisted reproductive technology as the most significant source for this reconceptualization, but he also blames the increasing legal equality of nonmarital and marital relationships and the acceptance of gay marriage. These changes result in "the phenomenon of erasing the biological basis of parenthood from law and replacing it with the idea of the state-defined 'legal' parent . . . [which is] contrary to the best interest of children" as it precludes them from knowing, and being brought up by, their "two natural parents."[7] The reproductive technologies, he alleges, allow adults' rights to create their own families of choice at the expense of children's developmental needs. Accordingly, activists should develop children's rights to be raised with a marital unit, to have their biological heritage preserved, and to have the opportunity to know their biological progenitors rather than being raised as "genetic orphans."

The overall argument, then, both within and outside the legal academy, suggests that contemporary family law should encourage two parents, one of each sex, for every child.[8] If society does allow single women to form families through artificial insemination by donor, professor Marsha Garrison argues in the *Harvard Law Review*, then the applicable paternity rules should be the same as for conception by sexual means, and the "donor" should be deemed the legal father.[9] Garrison's argument is that existing precedent establishes the two-parent family as the model, and there is no reason to depart from this model when it comes to single-parent families formed through ART. She explains, "outside the AID [artificial insemination by donor] context, our legal system grants no parent, male or female, the right to be a sole parent. . . . There is simply no logical basis for a one-parent policy applicable only to single AID users."[10] Similarly, Maggie Gallagher, the president of the Institute for Marriage and Public Policy, blogged that the law allows single mothers to "strip" their children of the right to have a father through contracts that women sign with sperm banks that maintain the secrecy of the sperm provider.[11]

The "But"

The condemnation of single-parent and gay and lesbian families is based on a view of such families as "deviant" and "bad" for children. If, instead, the focus is on the commitment of these parents to their children, then these families can be viewed as moral and deserving of support. Changing the lens from external structure to internal caregiving provides a new perspective.

Studies on single—parent families show that, even controlling for income, children may experience higher levels of behavioral problems and lower standards of living than in two-parent married families. Yet other variables, such as parental warmth[12] and the relationship between the child and the male parent (whether he is a stepparent or an adoptive or biological parent) are also important. The lack of social support for single parenting certainly provides a partial explanation for some of these differences.

In their early-twenty-first-century comprehensive review of children raised in lesbian and heterosexual households, sociologists Judith Stacey and Timothy Biblarz explained that there are few significant differences between the children raised in the different types of households in terms of anxiety, depression, self-esteem, and other measures of social and psychological adjustment.[13] Other research has compared children raised in biological and adoptive families, finding that adoptive parents are similarly likely to demonstrate a high degree of attachment and commitment to children. As sociologist Laura Hamilton and her colleagues concluded in 2007, "our study suggests that the presence of nonbiological parents (or absence of biological parents) alone may not cause lower parental investment."[14]

Children do not necessarily need two parents, or two parents of the opposite sex, to thrive, and the imposition of a second parent not only infringes on the single parent's rights as a parent but, as a practical matter, may not benefit the child. Although the two-parent model generally is beneficial for children, forcing all families into that model does not benefit children. Indeed, when parents are forced to marry each other, or when a single parent marries someone else, children do not necessarily thrive.

Recognizing that single parents form families, and providing them with the legal support to do so, reflects changing historical circumstances in which increasing numbers of women and men are creating these families with increasing amounts of social acceptance. In the 1990s, one of every three births took place outside marriage, one of every two marriages ended in divorce, and over half of American children born during the decade are expected to spend some part of their childhood in a single-parent family. Simply saying that single-parent families should be coerced into looking like two-parent families, or that single people should not have access to reproductive technology simply on the basis of their marital status, does not take into account the changing historical circumstances surrounding families, nor does it account for the differing reasons underlying the formation of one- or two-parent families.

The Ethics Committee of the American Society for Reproductive Medicine suggests that all member programs provide equal access to reproductive services for single, gay, and lesbian patients, regardless of the program's moral objections to such treatment. After reviewing objections to this equal treatment, including concerns that children of gay and lesbian parents would be socially isolated, the ASRM concluded, "we do not believe that unmarried persons or gays and lesbians harm their children by reproducing outside of heterosexual marital relations."[15]

Is Technology Antimoral?

Are we becoming suprahuman? In Virginia, antichoice protesters set up pickets in front of a fertility clinic, claiming that "IVF kills babies."[16] The Catholic Church condemns any use of the new reproductive technologies, whether it be artificial insemination by husband or donor, egg donation, or IVF. According to the Official Catechism of the Catholic Church,

> 2376. Techniques that entail the dissociation of husband and wife, by the intrusion of a person other than the couple (donation of sperm or ovum, surrogate uterus), are gravely immoral. These techniques (heterologous artificial insemination and fertilization) infringe the child's right to be born of a father and mother known to him and bound to each other by marriage. They betray the spouses' "right to become a father and a mother only through each other."
>
> 2377. Techniques involving only the married couple (homologous artificial insemination and fertilization) are perhaps less reprehensible, yet remain morally unacceptable. They dissociate the sexual act from the procreative act.[17]

Kelly Romenesko, a French teacher, claimed that she was fired by the Appleton, Wisconsin, Catholic school district when she asked for leave so that she could undergo in vitro fertilization.[18] According to the district, she was told that IVF was contrary to the moral teachings of the Catholic Church and thus violated her employment contract, which required her to "uphold the teachings of the Roman Catholic Church" and "act in accordance with Catholic doctrine and Catholic moral and social teachings."[19] By contrast, the Focus on the Family organization, which seeks to "spread the Gospel" by helping to preserve traditional families, draws a careful distinction between using egg and sperm providers from within the immediate family and using more distant providers. It believes that the latter would involve "'play[ing] God'—to create human life outside the bonds of marriage . . . most conservative Christians would agree that this practice is morally indefensible from a biblical perspective."[20]

Another critique comes from the Left. Do the ARTs privilege biological relationships over other types of families? Deborah Wald, a lawyer who helps people form nontraditional families, writes in her blog,

> We have over 100,000 children in foster care in California alone, and national estimates are that there are well over 100,000 children in foster care nationally that have been cleared for adoption and are just waiting for good homes. Add to that another 400,000 embryos in storage. And yet there is an industry starting to convince people NOT to adopt children who desperately need homes (after all, they may be damaged goods) and NOT to accept donated embryos (after all, they have already been "discarded" by someone else) but instead to CREATE NEW EMBRYOS from new eggs and new sperm, chosen on the basis of the academic credentials and good looks of the donors, among other things.[21]

The final, related critique concerns fears of genetic engineering. Aside from bans on cloning, there are no limits on manipulating eggs and sperm to produce what some have termed "transhumans." The process of preimplantation genetic diagnosis (PGD) allows for the testing of embryos formed through IVF before they are placed in the woman's uterus. PGD can screen for essentially any condition currently subject to genetic testing, ranging from cystic fibrosis to sex to hereditary deafness.[22] On its website, the Genetics and IVF Institute describes PGD as an "exciting technology with incredible potential to increase your chance of a healthy pregnancy" and then, in an ethically neutral fashion, lists the various types of screening available, including "Gender Selection."[23] Approximately three-quarters of all IVF clinics offer PGD; those that have declined to do so most commonly explain their decision as based on a lack of resources, although some clinics also cite ethical and moral concerns.[24] PGD allows patients to discard embryos with undesirable characteristics. German law bans the creation of an embryo unless it will be used for a pregnancy, effectively prohibiting the use of PGD, while other countries regulate the purposes of PGD, precluding, for example, PGD for sex selection without a valid medical purpose.[25]

PGD raises a series of ethical issues, ranging from those concerned about the potential destruction of embryos for any reason to those concerned about the impact on people with disabilities.[26] As writer (and IVF mother) Beth Kohl explains, "PGD is a thrilling scientific accomplishment. . . . But it gave me the creeps. I pictured American minivans teeming with Nazi archetypes, Indian kindergarten classes without a single girl."[27]

Yet PGD itself does not allow for the creation of designer embryos; the analysis is limited to an examination of the already-existing gamete. What critics fear even more is the creation of "superembryos," or embryos that have been specially enhanced. Harvard philosopher Michael Sandel suggests that we are experiencing "a kind of moral vertigo. To grapple with the ethics of enhancement, we need to confront questions largely lost from view in the modern world—questions about the moral status of nature, and about the property stance of human beings toward the given world."[28] To help us out of the vertigo, Sandel identifies a fundamental problem with genetic enhancement, which is a "drive to mastery" that may result in the destruction of our "appreciation of the gifted character of human powers and achievements,"[29] with disastrous effects on many characteristics that make us human, like humility and responsibility.

Perhaps the line should be drawn, as New York Times columnist Nicholas Kristof suggests, at "any effort that goes beyond the curative to enhance the germ line DNA of our offspring . . . fiddling with the heritable DNA of humans to make them smarter, faster or more pious—or more deaf."[30]

Cloning and Stem-Cell Research

In November 2006, Missouri voters considered Amendment 2, which provided that any form of research on stem cells permitted under federal law would also be permitted under Missouri law. Its opponents crafted several arguments, including that the amendment would allow for the creation of life, only then to kill it. But the argument closest to the issues in this book provided a link between egg donation and stem-cell research. In the Vitae Caring Foundation's campaign against the amendment, it aired a television commercial that began with an image of what appears to be a college dormitory, with a woman's tearful voice saying, "Sure, I signed the consent form, but I didn't really read it. I needed money to pay my college bills so I sold my eggs to the fertility clinic. The procedure was really painful and my mom was upset. Now I find out that it might cause kidney failure, ovarian tumors and sterility. Some women even die from it." As she speaks, the camera focuses on the college student's body, coiled in an almost fetal position. At the end, a calm voiceover proclaims, "Embryonic stem cell research will require millions of eggs, and women will pay a terrible price."[31]

Unlike the less controversial adult stem cells, which only generate specific types of tissues (skin cells only generate more skin), embryonic stem cells are believed to be capable of becoming any part of the body. When scientists take out cells from a blastocyst, they destroy the blastocyst but create cells that appear to be capable of reproducing themselves indefinitely and could create, it is hoped, virtually any tissue in the body. Although scientists are finding replacements for embryonic stem cells, the Missouri advertisement echoes the concerns of other organizations that, by allowing for the "harvesting" of eggs, artificial reproduction reflects the move "toward a society that views some human lives as fit for laboratory experimentation for the benefit of others."[32] The Institute for American Values warns that a woman's physician, her "most trusted advisor in her often years-long effort" to overcome infertility, might ask if she would donate any extra eggs for research.[33] These twin evils—experimenting on potential children and taking advantage of women—pervade the rhetorical arguments against stem-cell research.

The status of embryos—are they potential children or simply blastocysts with no personhood?—has engaged moral philosophers throughout the academic world. Princeton philosopher Robert George claims that each embryo is a potential human being who must be protected and given the same rights as any other human being. Consider this headline from the nonprofit LifeSiteNews.com service: "UK Court Denies IVF Appeal: Woman's Frozen Embryonic Children Must Die."[34]

Harvard philosopher Michael Sandel does not support genetic engineering but nonetheless believes that embryos are an appropriate subject for scientific research. He argues that embryos are *not* human beings, and their potential is comparable to the potential of an acorn to become an oak tree.[35] Although an embryo may become a child, arguing that the two are morally equivalent provides an example of a particular type of philosophically flawed argument that was known to the ancient Greeks.[36]

Echoing Sandel's argument, advocates of stem-cell research point out that embryonic stem cells are not children and that no woman will be forced to donate her unused eggs for research. Although stem cells from adults can also be used for research, the most promising research is based on embryonic stem cells, cells taken from an approximately five-days-old, 150-celled organism called a blastocyst, and cells taken from the umbilical cord.[37] There are approximately four hundred thousand unused embryos that are being stored nationwide. Although fertility specialists may prefer to refer to the embryos as "clumps of cells," they are, for many people, including many of those who have created the clumps, much more than that. On the other hand, not every blastocyst will become a baby; even if the blastocyst were developing inside a woman, there is only about a 30–40 percent chance that it would result in a successful pregnancy.[38]

Asking a woman to donate leftover eggs or embryos for research provides her with additional choices once she has completed her fertility treatments. Many women are uncomfortable with destroying unused eggs, and many couples do not want to destroy their embryos; allowing them to choose to donate this material to others facing infertility or to those undertaking groundbreaking research simply adds to the list of available options.

Too Many Embryos?

A final controversy concerns the disposition of excess embryos, an issue that, in some ways, can be neatly divided into conservative and liberal, right and left positions, at least when it comes to potentially destroying embryos. The issue is, however, more complex and requires an examination of the different interests involved in the right to procreate. As we think about how to handle gametic material, of the intertwined nature of market and familial relationships, of choice and commodification and control, an examination of the dilemma of extra embryos provides insights into the practical and theoretical difficulties. Excess embryos are an inevitable byproduct of a successful IVF attempt, particularly as physicians transfer fewer embryos per cycle. One possibility might be to fertilize only the number of eggs that the recipient wants implanted; given the uncertainties in predicting which fertilized eggs will become likely candidates for implantation, however, this possibility is unrealistic. Instead, there are three options for excess embryos: destroy them, freeze them, or donate them either for research or to another couple.

When the embryos have been created by a single person, dispositional issues are quite straightforward: in all states except Louisiana, only that individual has authority over them. When they are jointly created by a heterosexual or gay couple, however, each individual may have a different preference. At the time of creation, they may agree and sign a dispositional directive. Subsequently, however, what happens if one changes his or her mind? Or what if there is no written agreement? Only a few states require that the creators specify, in advance, how to dispose of excess embryos. And only a few cases have gone to court after couples who have created preembryos have split up or one has died. These cases challenge our conceptions of embryos as individuals, as property, or as something in between. If the embryos are simply excess body parts, then they are private property; if they are children, then they have quite separate and distinct and nonproperty interests. As a middle ground, they may instead be considered quasi-property, property for some purposes but not all.[39] Almost two decades ago, Texas law professor John Robertson explained, "While differing views of early embryo moral status exist, there is wide consensus that embryos deserve 'special respect' because they have completed the first steps after fertilization toward becoming a newborn child."[40]

Even though they may be deserving of special respect, embryos still constitute property, just like eggs and sperm. Casual statements such as "Embryos do deserve special moral status"[41] are virtually meaningless without an explanation of what this means and why this might be so. Granting embryos special moral status may begin the slide down what many of us fear will be the slippery slope that results in Louisiana's legal treatment of embryos as "juridical persons." Moreover, embryos are simply the few-days-old union of egg and sperm, which, when considered separately, are not believed worthy of the same special status by most of the same people. Embryos become people only after they have been gestated for a little less than nine months; just ask the many disappointed IVF patients who have not gotten pregnant after the transfer of multiple embryos.

That being said as a jurisprudential matter, I must confess that my husband and I kept our extra embryos on ice for more than a decade. When it came time for us to dispose of them, I did feel an emotional connection to them and found it difficult simply to flush them down the drain.

Nonetheless, given the multiple meanings of property in our country, ranging from entitlements to welfare benefits to ownership of land, concluding that embryos are property decides little but the starting point from which analysis should proceed. The notion of property as involving ownership of a concrete object, say a house, is deeply engrained in our legal history. We can contrast property rights with other types of rights, such as privacy. Whereas property protects the right to control objects, privacy protects the rights inherent in an individual's identity. As law professor Radhika Rao articulates the difference, "A person does not 'own' his or her body under the right of privacy. Instead, privacy envisions the body as an integral part of the person. . . . the law of property differentiates between the owner and that which is owned."[42]

More modern analysis of property builds on this distinction, expanding our conception of what property actually means. Property involves relationships among people with respect to things, and though property is traditionally thought of as a bundle of rights—the rights to exclude, possess, use, and transfer—this conventional description is incomplete. Moreover, the meaning and scope of property protection may vary depending on the context; property rules respond to social needs and can change over time in response to changes in those needs. Some types of property, such as historic sites and beaches, are protected; some intentions concerning even one's own property are illegal; some types of property are sacred. When it comes to embryos, we may choose to provide some special protections, but that does not negate their status as property. In a classic article from 1972, Guido Calabresi and Douglas Melamed suggest that society must first define who is entitled to have something and then decide how strongly to protect that entitlement. One set of rules would prevent anyone else but the owner from ever having the entitlement, unless the owner decided to sell it; another set of rules would protect against any interference with that entitlement other than through court action; and a third set of rules would prevent sale or other action taking away that entitlement (e.g., the right to be free from slavery).[43] Thus, saying that something is property, that one is entitled to create embryos and keep them, is a separate issue from how strongly that entitlement will be legally protected.

When it comes to legal protections and safeguards concerning embryos, few states have adopted legislation addressing the implications of embryo disposition and storage, although the number is growing. A 1998 American Bar Association (ABA) report found that only two states— Florida and Louisiana—had enacted legislation addressing zygote-disposition agreements,[44] although today several other states including California, Connecticut, Massachusetts, and New Jersey require that IVF clinics provide patients with information to help them make informed choices concerning embryo disposition.

The first two states to regulate this area took very different approaches, and the later set of states have dealt with this issue in the context of stem-cell research. In Florida, the legislation dates from 1993 and is part of the law that governs domestic relations and, more specifically, the determination of paternity. Florida law requires that couples undergoing in vitro fertilization enter into a written agreement that provides for the disposition of zygotes (as well as eggs and sperm) in the event of death, divorce, or other "unforeseen circumstances." If there is no written agreement, then the gamete providers are given joint dispositional authority;[45] if one provider dies, then the other person has control over the zygote.[46] Texas provides somewhat more limited direction in its laws concerning the parent-child relationship. Although it does not address dispositional issues, the statute, enacted in 2001, allows a divorced spouse to withdraw consent to the use of gametic material prior to implantation, unless the spouse had consented, prior to the divorce, to the use of the materials postdivorce.[47]

Whereas Florida and Texas include embryo disposition within their family law statutes, Louisiana takes a different approach and absolutely precludes the destruction of zygotes. A 1986 Louisiana law declares that an in vitro fertilized ovum is a juridical person to whom the in vitro fertilization patients "owe . . . a high duty of care and prudent administration."[48] If the patients renounce their "parental rights," then the juridical person is available for "adoptive implantation."[49] The zygote can be disposed of only through implantation.[50] After the renunciation, but prior to implantation, the physician is deemed the zygote's temporary guardian until adoptive implantation can occur.[51] If there is a dispute between the progenitors, then the same standard that applies in child-custody cases—the best-interest test—applies to the embryo.[52] In Louisiana, then, an agreement may not direct zygote disposition other than implantation. Other options, such as donation for research or destruction, are prohibited. Under this approach, frozen zygotes cannot be destroyed because doing so would be destroying life.[53] The constitutionality of this law is questionable in light of current abortion jurisprudence.[54] In Australia, zygotes must be freed for surrogate implantation and cannot be destroyed.[55]

A few other states require informed consent before the use of sperm, eggs, or zygotes but do not specify the terms of the informed consent or otherwise require that the parties address the disposition of this gametic material.[56] California has a detailed law that requires the clinic to provide information on possible embryo dispositional alternatives, and the state even requires the clinic to provide a form to patients setting out possible outcomes—but does not require the patient to sign the form before proceeding with the ART. Although Massachusetts does in fact require that patients execute an informed-consent form, that form does not necessarily require the patient to make a choice regarding embryo disposition, and the informed-consent provision is preceded by a section concerning stem-cell research and followed by one about the availability of umbilical tissue for research.[57] These provisions are typically included as part of a state's legislative scheme concerning stem-cell research (true in California, Connecticut, and New Jersey), rather than as part of a state's policy toward ethical medical practices or personhood. Indeed, approximately one-quarter of all U.S. states prohibit embryos from beings sold for research.[58]

Judicial Dispositions

In the absence of legislative guidance, courts have developed a variety of approaches to deal with the issues outlined in the preceding sections, and, somewhat surprisingly, they have not necessarily given deference to the parties' contracts. In the divorce context, courts primarily consider whether to force someone to become a parent, and intent at the time of the agreement appears to be less important. In the death context, the same issues arise concerning whether to force someone to become a parent. In both family law and estates law, if there are differing intents, then courts generally seem to find in favor of the person who does not want to procreate, regardless of the existence of prior agreements or statements of intent.[59]

What is at stake in these cases is not just control over embryos but control over the decision to become a parent. Initially, the first group of cases decided in the late twentieth century supported the enforcement of express agreements relating to zygote disposition. In the 1992 case of *Davis v. Davis*,[60] one of the first such cases, although there was no contract, the court indicated its preference for an enforceable contract over a seeming failure to anticipate the contingency of divorce.[61] Six years later, in the New York case of *Kass v. Kass*,[62] the contract was not for procreation but for donation of the prezygotes to research.[63] In *Davis*, the court developed a quasi-property analysis.[64] There was no pre-IVF agreement on what to do with excess zygotes.[65] The court pointed out that the zygotes' value was in their potential to become children, so the "essential dispute here [was not over property but] ... whether the parties [would] become parents."[66] To resolve that dispute, the court articulated a three-part test that began with deference to the "preferences of the progenitors"; if their prior preferences were unclear or if they could not agree, then any prior agreement should control; finally, in case of a dispute without the existence of a prior agreement, then the court should evaluate each party's relative interests in using the embryos, with the party seeking to avoid procreation generally prevailing, unless the other party has no "reasonable possibility" of otherwise becoming a parent. The court accorded great deference to the terms of a prior agreement as well as to the wishes of the party seeking to avoid parenthood.[67] In *Kass*, the contract provided,

> In the event of divorce, we understand that legal ownership of any stored pre-zygotes must be determined in a property settlement and will be released as directed by order of a court of competent jurisdiction. Should we for any reason no longer wish to attempt to initiate a pregnancy, we understand that we may determine the disposition of our frozen pre-zygotes remaining in storage. . . .
>
> The possibility of our death or any other unforeseen circumstances that may result in neither of us being able to determine the disposition of any stored frozen pre-zygotes requires that we now indicate our wishes. THIS STATEMENT OF DISPOSITION MAY BE CHANGED ONLY BY OUR SIGNING ANOTHER STATEMENT OF DISPOSITION WHICH IS FILED WITH THE IVF PROGRAM. . . .
>
> In the event that we no longer wish to initiate a pregnancy or are unable to make a decision regarding the disposition of our stored, frozen pre-zygotes, we now indicate our desire for the disposition of our pre-zygotes.[68]

Although the agreement specifically contemplated the destruction of the embryos, the wife subsequently expressed her opposition to doing so. The court nonetheless upheld the contract.[69]

In later cases, however, courts refused to enforce prior express and even unambiguous contracts that would compel one donor to become a parent against his or her will, relying on public policy considerations rather than the written words of an agreement.[70] The underlying theme in these cases is judicial respect for the right not to procreate, regardless of the potential existence of a contract to the contrary.

In *A.Z. v. B.Z.*, a Massachusetts case decided in 2000, the signed agreement stated that if the parties "[s]hould become separated, [they] both agree[d] to have the embryo[s] . . . return[ed] to [the] wife for implant."[71] When the couple divorced, the husband objected to being coerced into parenthood.[72] The trial court refused to enforce the agreement, referring to the unforeseen changes in circumstances between the signing of the agreement and the divorce four years later.[73] On appeal, the Massachusetts

Supreme Court also refused to enforce this agreement, holding that it was a violation of public policy to force someone to become a parent.[74] This policy consideration trumped even the express terms of the agreement.[75] The court split legal hairs, observing that although the couple had signed a form specifying what to do with the frozen embryos if they "become separated," they had not defined the term "'become separated.' Because this dispute arose in the context of a divorce, we cannot conclude that the consent form was intended to govern in these circumstances. Separation and divorce have distinct legal meanings." The court concluded, "we would not enforce an agreement that would compel one donor to become a parent against his or her will. As a matter of public policy, we conclude that forced procreation is not an area amenable to judicial enforcement."[76]

Similarly, in the 2001 case of *J.B. v. M.B.*, a New Jersey state court refused to force a woman to become a parent.[77] When the husband and wife consented to undergo in vitro fertilization, they agreed that they would relinquish all control of their gametic material to the IVF program upon divorce (unless court order provided otherwise) or upon death of both of the parties (unless a will provided otherwise).[78] Unlike most of the other cases, it was the husband who wanted to enforce the agreement, seeking to preserve the zygotes for his future use or for donation to an infertile couple.[79] The wife opposed any use of the zygotes.[80] The court refused even to let the issue of whether the wife had earlier agreed to donate unused zygotes to go to trial because, even if the embryos were destroyed, the husband's right to procreate remained unaffected, whereas implanting the zygote would infringe on the wife's ability not to procreate.[81] The court agreed with the rationale of *A.Z.* and concluded "that a contract to procreate is contrary to New Jersey public policy and is unenforceable."[82]

The trend of unenforceable contracts, and of refusing to foist parenthood on an individual, continued in *Litowitz v. Litowitz*,[83] decided by a Washington state court in 2000. The couple created a zygote using the husband's sperm and an egg provided by another woman.[84] The wife sought enforcement of an implied contract allegedly constructed by the couple's "plan" to parent other children and evidenced by their prior decision to preserve the zygotes created by a surrogate egg donor.[85] The contract provided that upon death of both parents, the zygotes would be disposed of, but it said nothing about divorce.[86] The contract stated that a court could make a decision upon the parties' petition.[87] The court ruled in favor of the husband, who did not want to procreate or become primary parent but who instead wanted to donate preembryos to someone else.[88] The court followed *Davis,* holding that it would not "read into the contracts an implied promise that [the husband] would continue with the parties' family planning after the dissolution."[89] "Absent any evidence that [the husband] 'intended to pursue reproduction outside the . . . marital relationship' with [the wife]," the court was "unwilling to create such an obligation."[90] The court does say in dicta that "at least one court, because of public policy concerns, has said it would not enforce even an unambiguous agreement 'that would compel one donor to become a parent against his or her will.'"[91]

Litowitz clearly implicates the parties' desires to have children.[92] The husband did not want to be a parent and instead sought to donate the zygotes for adoption; the wife wanted the zygotes so that she could arrange a surrogate pregnancy.[93] In Iowa, regardless of what an agreement signed at the time of IVF actually provides, the individuals can subsequently change their minds; then, unless both parties agree to use or destroy their embryos, the embryos remain in frozen limbo.[94] This has the effect of preventing either person from becoming—or not becoming—a parent.

In yet another divorce suit, Augusta and Randy Roman tried IVF and, as part of the informed-consent process, signed a document in March 2002 directing that any excess embryos be discarded if the parties divorced. The night before implantation of three successfully fertilized embryos, Randy withdrew his consent to the procedure, and in December Randy filed for divorce. Although the parties agreed on how to divide all other marital property, they could not agree on how to dispose of the frozen embryos. Randy asked the court to follow the parties' written agreement, while Augusta asked the court to allow her to become a parent. The trial court found that the embryos were marital property and that it was "just and right and a fair and equitable" result to award Augusta the embryos. An appeals court, however, upheld the validity of the document that the parties had signed in which they agreed to dispose of the embryos if they were divorced.[95]

British law ultimately reaches the same result as U.S. law, requiring both parties to give consent before implantation can occur and allowing either party to withdraw consent until the time of implantation. Natallie Evans found this out the hard way. She is a British woman who created embryos with her partner, Howard Johnston, before undergoing treatment for ovarian cancer. He withdrew his consent for her to use the embryos, and even though she had no other chance at creating biologically related children, she was not allowed to keep them.[96]

Notwithstanding decisions spanning a fifteen-year period in different states, the legal approaches to embryo disposition share four characteristics. First, courts recognize the tensions in their decisions between contract enforcement and respect for the right not to procreate. As the New Jersey court explained in *J.B. v. M.B.*, "Our conclusion is not inconsistent with Davis . . . or Kass . . . because neither decision enforced a contract to procreate, despite expansive dicta regarding the enforceability of agreements between progenitors."[97] Ultimately, courts have overridden clearly stated intents, in support of a public policy that privileges one party's right not to procreate over the other party's right to procreate.[98] Moreover, although courts may claim that embryos are not property, the claim is somewhat disingenuous. Property concerns relationships among people with respect to a thing, with ownership guaranteeing certain rights. When the progenitors agree, they decide what to do with the embryos and can destroy, cryopreserve, or donate the embryos for research or to another couple. It is only when the creators disagree that courts struggle with what to do. In that situation, courts must decide between conflicting rights to the same "thing"; granted, the "thing" has the capacity to become a person, and that capacity provides the basis for courts' decisions to resolve the conflict in favor of the person who does not want to use or donate the embryo. In each of the cases, the courts have decided against allowing the embryos to be implanted, grounding this result either in the terms of the contract itself or in terms of public policy.

Second, all the cases recognize that the initial decisions concerning disposition of embryos rests with their creators and that, other than in Louisiana, embryos do not (as of yet) have a separate legal existence that requires either implanting or destroying them. The cases that rely on public policy examine the capacity of the embryos not just to create a child but also, more importantly for the parties involved in each case, to create a parent. The question of whether embryos are either property or quasi-property because of their potential for human life has legally been irrelevant; it is only pursuant to the Louisiana approach of treating embryos as full "juridical persons" that the issue of the embryo's status becomes relevant.

In the landmark case of *Roe v. Wade*, the Supreme Court made four potentially contradictory statements concerning the constitutional status of prenatal life: it first held that "the word 'person' as used in the Fourteenth Amendment, does not include the unborn."[99] It then held, as a critical component to its trimester framework, that the State has an "important and legitimate interest in protecting the potentiality of human life."[100] It explained that "a legitimate state interest in this area need not stand or fall on acceptance of the belief that life begins at conception or at some other point prior to live birth. In assessing the State's interest, recognition may be given to the less rigid claim that as long as at least potential life is involved, the State may assert interests beyond the protection of the pregnant woman alone."[101] And although it catalogued a number of cases in which states had accorded rights to unborn children, it refused to decide whether life begins at conception, holding instead that "the unborn have never been recognized in the law as persons in the whole sense."[102] After *Roe*, many states enacted laws that they felt were necessary to upholding respect for human dignity by restricting or banning research on fetuses—often defined to include embryos.[103]

Clarifying the nature of the state interest in protecting potential life, the Supreme Court in the 1992 *Casey* decision observed that the state has an interest, "from the outset of the pregnancy," in protecting both the life of the pregnant woman and "the life of a fetus that may become a child."[104] Nonetheless, in an opinion authored by Justice Sandra Day O'Connor, the Court recognized that the decision of whether to undergo an abortion was the woman's, to be made without mandating any involvement on behalf of her husband (or any other potential father).

The Supreme Court reiterated, in the 2007 decision of *Gonzales v. Carhart*, its support for the state's interest, "from the inception of the pregnancy," to provide "protect[ion of] the life of the fetus that may become a child."[105] Expanding on this concept, the Court referred generically and broadly to the state interest in the "unborn" yet also upheld the state's right to "show its profound respect for the life within the woman,"[106] which an embryo formed in vitro is not.

Commentators have raised questions about the implications of these Supreme Court decisions for embryos, although the Court has never directly addressed the status of embryos. Legal scholar Jack Balkin spells out the consequences if a state grants equal status to a woman and an embryo: "The state would have to prohibit almost any manipulation or use of fertilized ova that causes their mutilation or destruction, including discarding embryos not used for in vitro fertilization."[107] The Court's observation that the state's interest begins at "the outset of pregnancy"[108] could be interpreted to include fetal life, even though an embryo is not, medically, a fetus. The explicit emphasis on the government's interest in protecting fetal life suggests that states can experiment with the legal status of embryos.

And the longstanding federal ban on stem-cell research, which means no experimentation on embryos for entities receiving federal funds,[109] suggests the political nature of the moral status of embryos.

Finally, the disposition of extracorporeal embryos (those that are frozen and exist outside a body) implicates very different legal rights and interests when contrasted with the disposition of embryos within a woman's body (those involved in abortion). For abortion, the Supreme Court has placed the decision squarely in the hands of the woman, but for frozen embryos, courts have listened very carefully to the voices of both potential parents. Abortion is a woman's decision because it focuses on her body; disposition of embryos requires responding to the decisions of both progenitors.

Dividing Embryos, Debating Technology, and Unifying Approaches

Debates over the moral status of embryos and over the alienability of other gametic materials have divided U.S. approaches to the reproductive technologies. Given the depth and fervency of these beliefs, there are questions on how to promote dialogue in order to develop a more coherent approach to regulating the technologies. One possible means of resolving some of these conflicts is through using a cultural cognition model. This model studies how different belief clusters are correlated with varying attitudes to culturally significant issues, such as gun-control laws, and then analyzes how to affect these attitudes to enact consensus legislation. The approach might help provide a framework for resolving existing conflicts on reproductive technology issues, such as commodification and additional regulation.

Such an analysis compellingly suggests several important lessons for issues involving strongly held views on reproductive technology: (1) more information, such as about the utility of stem-cell research, will not necessarily change underlying beliefs; (2) as various political theorists have shown, beliefs about reproductive technology are part of a larger worldview that includes related perspectives on other (nonrelated) issues; (3) on such culturally contested issues, both sides can feel respected even if their positions are not dominant; and (4) the law can reinforce and help to implement any cultural compromises that have been reached, but it does not, by itself, create those compromises.[110]

In a series of studies, the Yale Cultural Cognition Project has focused on how people interpret empirical evidence that is contrary to their strongly held positions.[111] One project, for example, examines how the gun debate is affected by people's cultural beliefs.[112] The conventional view is that exposure to additional empirical information can affect understanding and perception of such contentious issues. Instead, the authors conclude that empirical evidence is interpreted in conformity with individuals' cultural worldviews rather than analyzed separately as mere "objective" information. Evidence is challenged through a series of psychological mechanisms, such as "biased assimilation," which is "the tendency of individuals to condition their acceptance of new information as reliable based on its conformity to their prior beliefs."[113] Consequently, when many people are confronted with new scientific information on issues that are "culturally disputed, . . . men and women in white lab coats speak with less authority than (mostly) men and women in black frocks."[114]

The authors of the article establish models through which individuals interpret the world, using labels such as hierarchical/egalitarian and individualist/communitarian.[115] They articulate a Breakthrough Politics model to encourage deeply divided groups to talk to one another. Instead of promoting change through providing empirical information, they suggest that dialogue is most likely to occur with three steps: expressive overdetermination (policies that are rich enough that both sides have a stake in them); identity vouching (figures associated with both sides affirm a particular policy); and discourse sequencing (achieving compromise only after developing the richer policies and ensuring their articulation by key identity figures).[116] (For example, the recognition of the importance of "creation care" by the head of the Evangelical Association of American shows identity vouching on the issue of global warming.) A French abortion law that allows a woman to obtain an abortion upon a certification of personal "distress" provides an example of the three steps: it is, the authors assert, "a policy that allows both religious opponents to abortion and feminists each to believe that the law is respecting their beliefs."[117] In a somewhat similar vein, linguist George Lakoff observes that contradicting another person's facts is unconvincing because "[f]rames trump facts. His frames will stay and the facts will bounce off. Always reframe,"[118] that is, set out your ideas in your language within the context of your values. And Lakoff advocates using value-laden talk, with values that are universally shared.

These studies suggest that compromise is possible even on highly contested issues, such as the moral status of embryos or the sale of gametic material. I am not, however, entirely sanguine that this approach would work for all the reproductive technology issues. The nature of the views on these issue stems from religiously based beliefs that are, from an evolutionary perspective, designed to divide rather than to create conciliation. Nonetheless, particularly given our federalist system in which states can experiment with alternative programs, some compromises are possible. And as discussed in the final part of this book, even when consensus is not possible, the pace of change, the ongoing uncertainty in family formation, requires some resolution.

PART IV

Baby Steps Forward

10

Baby Steps

Going to Market

> Given that a largely unregulated market for fertility services already exists in the United States, any new regulation must offer benefits as well as restrictions if it is to encourage individuals to stay within the system in the face of increased inconvenience or expense.[1]

GIVEN STATE VARIATION in legal approaches and the lack of cohesiveness in thinking through the issues of identity, parenthood, and marketing, we need to develop coherent sets of laws that recognize the interrelated aspects of these issues. The final part of the book argues for new approaches. Each chapter addresses one of the three main concerns of this book: the technology market, parenthood determinations, and identity formation.

How do we regulate the reproductive technology market? Other chapters have explored supply and demand, cost and price. This chapter examines if, when, and how to regulate market suppliers directly, focusing on the fertility clinics and those who utilize the clinics: potential parents and donors. However, market oversight is only one aspect of fertility regulation. Any laws applicable to the market must recognize the relationships being created when gametes are transferred between people. Although the market requires distinct rules, these rules must be part of the larger context that places making children into a cultural context.

There is already some regulation from federal, state, and industry groups. The important legal issues regarding the fertility market concern what additional safeguards are appropriate. Professor Judith Daar, a leader in issues of reproductive technology and the law, suggests two different kinds of regulation that might be appropriate:

First, regulation can focus exclusively on the providers who render the ART services. Regulation in this area might include licensure of ART personnel, certification of ART facilities, reporting requirements for all aspects of initiated procedures, including patient demographics and pregnancy success rates, and standardization of clinical techniques. The goal behind regulation aimed at providers would be to assure quality and uniformity in the practice of reproductive medicine. . . .

Second, regulation can be geared at the relationship between providers and consumers. These laws would focus primarily on the interaction between doctors and patients. For example, state laws could be drafted to require word-specific, written informed consent for any ART procedure. Or laws could be designed to sanction misconduct in the practice of reproductive medicine, such as egg or embryo theft.[2]

A third type of market regulation, perhaps implicit in the first two, affects those whose bodies are involved with ART services: the donors and the recipients. These laws might, for example, prevent exploitation of gamete providers, protect recipients against discrimination in service provision based on familial status, race, or income, and preclude, to the extent possible, multiple births by limiting the number of embryos transferred.

All three types of regulation are interrelated and appropriate for the commoditization of gametic material. Notwithstanding the comparatively few abuses or scandals that have been reported or litigated, problems of market oversight remain. There is no mandate that IVF laboratories meet accreditation standards, nor is there any sanction when clinics fail to report, or fail to report accurately, their success rates. Although individual states recognize various tort or contract suits for medical malpractice, require some minimal levels of consent, and mandate some certification, not only is there enormous variation among states, but there are also no minimum requirements that are imposed on all states.

Given the comparative lack of federal regulation of many other areas of medical practice and treatment, it is reasonable to question whether ARTs should be treated differently. The answer, of course, depends on what aspects of ARTs are being regulated. The physician-patient relationship is, ideally, close and confidential. Imposing various requirements of informed consent, however, does not undercut the relationship but should, instead, support it. We cannot—and should not—regulate what is said, in privacy, by a physician to his or her patient, but we can regulate the products that are available for discussion and the parameters in which they are used.

Ensuring that gametes are handled appropriately, that genetic tests are accurate, and that medical procedures are safe does not interfere with what patients discuss with their doctors. Similarly, protecting gamete donors from exploitation or ensuring access to treatment options without discrimination appear to be appropriate concerns for regulation.

This chapter argues for a coherent set of laws in dealing with the technology market: if, when, and how to regulate market suppliers directly, focusing on the fertility clinics and those who utilize the clinics (potential parents and donors). There is currently some regulation in place, but additional safeguards that cover all aspects of the market are necessary. For instance, communication between patient and provider should still be kept confidential; however, informed-consent regulation provides even stronger protection of this relationship. The chapter addresses other questions regarding regulation, including which aspects of ART should be regulated by whom: the federal government, the states, or the industry itself.

There is a series of important principles to think about in regulating the gamete trade, according to Debora Spar, a Harvard Business School professor: providing accurate information, evaluating equity issues concerning who has access to the technologies, drawing lines between what it is legal to sell and what it is illegal to sell, considering cost issues, and determining the parameters of parental choice, such as creating transhuman children or only implanting embryos of one sex.[3] These principles provide the basis for thinking about a series of issues concerning the market structure, but, as the preceding chapters have shown, there are additional issues concerning the regulation of market participants and the legal framework in which people become parents (or relinquish any rights to doing so) with which they are intertwined.

Implementing these principles requires difficult policy choices in a series of areas. One of the first issues, beyond what should be regulated, is who should regulate. Increased regulation of the fertility industry could come from any of the three sources currently regulating: the federal government, state governments, or the industry itself. Each one of these options has benefits and drawbacks, and the ideal solution may consist of a combination of all three, depending on the issue. Controlling the market, including collecting information that could be useful for identifying donors and limiting the number of donations, might best be left to the federal government, while states could continue to decide parentage issues, albeit with more uniformity (as discussed in the next chapter), and the industry could regulate actual clinic practices.

The primary benefit of federal-government regulation (most likely through the FDA) is standardization—consumers could count on at least a minimal level of regulation at each sperm bank, even if they order specimens from another state. Federal regulation could unilaterally preempt states' efforts so that, for example, clinics could satisfy one standard set of safety measures regardless of where they are located. Another benefit of federal regulation is the enforcement power of the federal government. Although federal government funds are not unlimited, more money for enforcement could be provided by the federal government than by either state governments or industry groups. The FDA also has the power to be quite flexible with the regular publication of guidance documents. Because many fertility clinics follow the guidance documents, they could be used as a testing ground for new potential regulations. If a particular guidance was found suitably effective in reducing disease transmission or other problems, it could then be turned into an enforceable regulation. This "proving ground" for regulations would lessen the risk of unpredicted financial or medical consequences.

Some people suggest that the federal government should not be involved in this type of regulation because family law issues have traditionally been left to the states.[4] Although it is important to recognize the role of the states in establishing family laws, federal regulation in this area will not necessarily usurp states' prerogatives. The FDA's regulation of sperm banks and minimum medical standards for donors would not impinge on states' right to determine and manage the familial relationships created by artificial insemination or states' ability to consider and ensure the best interests of donor-conceived children.

State regulation, though helpful in many individual cases, is too inconsistent at the moment to offer the kind of assurance that artificial insemination clients need. Families ordering sperm from out of state (a common occurrence, especially if significant genetic concerns narrow the possible donor pool) must take on the responsibility of learning the regulations for the specimen's originating state and deciding for themselves if those regulations are adequate. Although self-education is a necessary aspect of all medical treatment, learning the regulations in multiple states places an enormous burden on gamete recipients. Moreover, clinics would benefit from one uniform standard, rather than needing to comply with the laws of different states.

Finally, the professional organizations that are currently advancing the state of regulation by proffering guidelines lack "established mechanisms to police compliance with these guidelines."[5] Membership in these groups and compliance with their guidelines are both strictly voluntary. Conscientious consumers might know about the organizations' existence and standards and choose only to work with an accredited bank or recruiter; competition might then encourage other banks to seek accreditation. One cannot assume, however, that all consumers are conscientious, thereby allowing unscrupulous banks to cut corners and cut prices to attract patients who are already under financial strain from other fertility treatments. Nonetheless, the accrediting organizations have improved the state of gamete provision, and they should continue to perform their standard-setting function and serve as a voice in the ongoing debate over this technology.

As one more example of regulatory failings, consider the information available on fertility-clinic websites. The fertility industry's two most prominent groups have adopted advertising guidelines that are mandatory if a clinic wants to remain a member of the Society for Assisted Reproductive Technology. These guidelines require, for example, that the clinics not mislead consumers into assuming that their chances of pregnancy are higher than they actually are and that the clinics comply with the Federal Trade Commission's policies on advertising.[6] The Federal Trade Commission, which is the federal agency responsible for consumer protection and the prevention of anticompetitive practices, has brought complaints against fertility clinics for misrepresenting their success rates.[7] But a study of Internet advertising published in 2007 found that "the majority of fertility clinic websites do not follow the 2004 SART/ASRM mandatory guidelines for advertising," perhaps because, the authors explain, the clinics did not know about the guidelines.[8] Ensuring that these guidelines are enforced—and disseminated to the clinics—would provide much stronger protection for patients. Doing so might require congressional action to amend the 1992 Fertility Clinic Success Rate Act to strengthen its implementation and clinic monitoring.

The federal government would also be able to establish uniform standards for access and price controls. Regardless of whether the U.S. Constitution requires equal access to infertility services based on marital status, sexual orientation, or income, policy choices regarding access could be made at the national level rather than by each individual state.

Depending on who is excluded, however, there may be drawbacks to one federal standard in this area. In Britain, the Human Fertilisation and

Embryology Authority does not regulate access to infertility treatment based on the patient's sexual orientation or marital status; however, such policies are addressed by individual providers and vary between clinics.[9] Martha Ertman expresses a concern that if it were not the market but "public law [that] was the sole determinant of who could become a parent . . . , then many gay people would likely be excluded," as has happened in other countries.[10] This is a significant potential disadvantage; nonetheless, a policy that excludes based on discriminatory criteria is speculative and may be illegal.

In addition to access issues, requiring comprehensive insurance coverage of infertility may simply result in better medicine. Full insurance appears to be associated with fewer embryos transferred and with fewer multiple births;[11] in turn, these effects translate into reduced costs for the premature babies associated with multiple births. Requiring all employers to offer insurance for infertility treatment and diagnosis could be done at the national level, so that we would not have the patchwork of existing state regulation in this area.

What Should Be Regulated?

Federal regulation is best suited to ensuring procedural protections within the market by, for example, setting standards for genetic testing of donors, reporting requirements concerning successes and failures of the technologies as well as donor identification, informed consent, and basic medical safety practices such as numbers of embryos to be transferred and related issues.

The question of how infectious disease should be regulated in the United States was partially answered by the FDA regulations implemented in 2005. Although the goal of keeping infectious diseases, including HIV, out of the gamete industry is laudatory, there is considerable debate on the methods for achieving that goal. A federal standard would reduce conflict but might enshrine problematic practices. For example, the FDA recommended avoiding "high-risk" donors in its guidance document. This guideline included a recommendation that gay men be banned from donating sperm, a ban that many sperm banks have adopted since the issuance of the guidance document. Ironically, however, under this guideline, a heterosexual man who had sex with a heterosexual woman who was infected with HIV would be able to donate one year later, whereas a gay may in a long-term monogamous relationship would be precluded from donating.[12] Despite the questionable ban on gay men's donating sperm, the FDA is in a position to take on a role more like that of the British Human Fertilisation and Embryology Authority. Vesting one government organization with the authority to oversee, license, and monitor the clinics performing gamete transfers would create a uniformity that is currently lacking.

Compensation, counseling, and education are areas that could be improved quickly. The AATB rules on compensation could be implemented nationally by the FDA to forbid compensation for anything other than lost earnings or costs directly attributable to sperm donation,[13] or the FDA could limit the amount of payment for each kind of gamete. Potential donors should not be expected to cover the costs of their own donation, but we might decide that it is important that donation remain primarily an act of goodwill, not commerce. Counseling and education should also be mandated by the FDA to potential donors and recipients. Patients and their families should be educated about the potential dangers of passing both genetic and communicable diseases through donation, and they should be aware of the precise meaning of the donor's chosen anonymity status. The ASRM recommends that egg-donation programs implement counseling and disclosure guidelines to ensure that donors understand the consequences of their actions.[14] These precautions will help both donors and patients make informed decisions about a process that may seem quite simple before birth but can become ever more complicated as the resulting child grows up.

Existing FDA regulations leave open the difficult question of genetic testing.[15] The high costs associated with such testing may serve as a deterrent to prospective parents, and the fact that every human carries some recessive genes that could cause a genetic disorder may result in a dangerous reduction of the donor pool. The practical balance currently in place at many entities—testing every donor for cystic fibrosis and testing particular donors based on medical and family histories and ethnic background—may be the best approach to achieving a midpoint between cost and safety. As testing becomes cheaper and more precise through developments in technology, testing requirements could be increased to provide greater safety without increasing cost.

The FDA could move quickly to include two important items in the next guidance document: (1) mandatory testing for cystic fibrosis mutations in every donor and (2) instructions for evaluating medical and family histories to achieve the maximum level of predictability for genetic disorders. The guidance document should also include an instructional set of "red flags" for more common genetic disorders—if A is identified anywhere in the medical history, then a test for B must be performed before releasing the specimen for use. These two measures would increase the confidence and safety of patients, particularly those who use one of the numerous unaccredited sperm banks in the United States. The FDA should also include genetic-testing guidelines for the most common genetic disorders found in at-risk groups including Ashkenazi Jews, Cajuns, French Canadians, and African Americans. Although the debate over fertility-industry regulation in the United States is far from over, especially in the field of genetics, important steps have been made in the past few years toward uniformity and safety, and the measures suggested here would be another positive development for all patients and donor-conceived offspring.

Clinics should also be required to limit the number of embryos that can be transferred into one woman, as is done in some European countries. The number of women pregnant with multiples has increased dramatically because of IVF. From 1980 to 2003, the percentage of women pregnant with twins increased by 75 percent. The American Society for Reproductive Medicine has developed guidelines on the number of embryos that should be transferred, recommending that only one or two embryos should be transferred for women under the age of thirty-five and for those between the ages of thirty-five and thirty-seven with a "more favorable" prognosis.[16] In the United Kingdom, the Human Fertilisation and Embryology Authority has proposed that women be limited to one embryo per IVF attempt.[17] Although a limit may be frustrating for infertile couples who have spent thousands of dollars trying to conceive, it nonetheless would, as a public health measure, decrease the number of multiple births and, as a private matter, decrease the emotional (and financial) effect on families of suddenly coping with triplets.

Moreover, multiples do not just cause difficult pregnancies for the mother; studies have shown that children born from reproductive technologies have potential severe health impairments. The risk appears to be not from the technology itself but from the risk of being a multiple. Consider the following two headlines from the summer of 2007: "IVF Risks Mostly Due to Multiple Births" and "More Health Risks Found in IVF Babies."[18] The underlying study to which these headlines refer did find that even nonmultiple IVF children have a slightly higher risk of abnormalities than non-IVF children, but it found that these risks are primarily due to the reasons that people use IVF in the first place: their age and genetic factors. Other experts opine that the biggest problem in reducing multiple births in IVF patients is the result of a lack of insurance coverage and overaggressive patients.[19]

Donors

The number of times that one person can provide eggs or sperm to another person is an important issue on multiple levels. As Melissa, who is Donor 811 at the Fairfax Genetics and IVF Institute, explains, she is willing to "donate as many times as the clinic will allow her to": "I was surprised by how easy it was."[20] How many times is enough?

Beyond the philosophical issues of exploitation, there is a series of physical limitations. Egg donation has both short- and long-term risks. The most common short-term complication for oocyte donors is ovarian hyperstimulation syndrome (OHSS). Indeed, the donation procedure itself is actually *controlled* oocyte hyperstimulation, designed to produce the maximum number of mature eggs, and a mild form of OHSS is considered almost inevitable.[21] Severe OHSS is rare but can be fatal, with symptoms that include kidney and liver dysfunction and respiratory distress. Some studies have shown that severe OHSS may be less common in donors than in women undergoing IVF, partially because donors typically stop receiving drugs after the eggs have been retrieved, while IVF patients continue with additional procedures and hormones in their attempts to conceive.[22] On the other hand, the medical risk increases based on the number of donations.[23] To minimize OHSS, researchers are studying new drug protocols and possible genetic markers.[24]

A second risk, beyond simply taking hormones, concerns the oocyte retrieval process itself, which is a surgical procedure that requires repeated punctures of the vaginal wall and ovarian follicles. As with any other surgery, complications are possible, including vaginal bleeding and infection. Although the procedure is generally done on an outpatient basis, physicians usually use some form of sedation. Thus, the risks inherent in anesthesia, such as stroke and respiratory failure, are also present.[25]

Finally, the long-term risks of oocyte donation include various gynecological cancers, such as breast, ovarian, and uterine. Several medical studies have shown that women who repeatedly undergo treatment with fertility drugs have an increased risk for these cancers, as do repeat oocyte donors. However, the evidence is based largely on infertile women undergoing IVF, and several causes of infertility are acknowledged to cause cancer as well.[26] Disentangling the data is difficult, but initial analysis suggests that healthy donors do not necessarily share the same increased risk for breast and ovarian cancer, although the extent to which fertility treatments do affect those cancers for healthy donors is uncertain. On the other hand, the data on the risk of uterine cancer for healthy donors is sparse but of more concern.[27] Moreover, researchers do not know whether repeated donations can affect the donor's future fertility, and they are still uncertain about the psychological consequences.

The short- and long-term health risks involved in oocyte donation are numerous and potentially serious, and most policymakers believe that these risks require further research. Nonetheless, the ASRM concluded that although "there are no clearly documented long-term risks" for egg donors, "because of the possible health risks . . . it would seem prudent to consider limiting the number of stimulated cycles for a given oocyte donor to approximately six."[28]

There are few existing laws concerning multiple gamete donation, and those that exist focus on the well-being of the resultant offspring. Some states suggest limits in the number of children that may be conceived using any single gamete donor to prevent incestuous relationships developing between two donor offspring of different families, who would be biological half siblings.[29] But there are no statutes limiting who may donate, how frequently, or how many times in any time period. Many fertility clinics do limit donation cycles per donor to six and some to as few as three,[30] but these limits are entirely self-imposed, and a donor with proven fecundity is valuable to these clinics. Moreover, a donor can register with multiple clinics. There are well-publicized stories of women who have donated at double the recommended limit.[31]

For sperm donors, the primary issue is not exploitation or health or future fertility but how many related children should result. Any form of donation, either egg or sperm, involves the potential for "inadvertent consanguinity," when a donor has provided gametes to different families and the resulting children do not know of their shared genetic heritage.[32] Many sperm banks impose a limit on the number of children who can be born from one person's donated sperm. The ASRM recommends taking into account the geographical area and population base for a particular donor, but it suggests a limit of twenty-five births per donor.[33] This limitation makes sense, and it should be incorporated into the FDA's rules for sperm donors. In an age of easy travel, donor secrecy, and limited understanding of genetics, reducing the number of children that can be born from each donor reduces the possibility of inadvertent consanguinity.

A final issue concerns how to implement the informed-consent and counseling requirements discussed earlier. For both kinds of gamete donors and for embryo donors, the informed-consent process should include issues relating to the ultimate disclosure of their identities, as well as medical risks. The informed-consent process should begin early to ensure that all involved parties understand the implications of the treatment. Egg donors are often not provided with sufficient information concerning potential risks.[34] This may be a deliberate choice in order to maximize the potential donor pool, given the demand for eggs. The informed-consent process for both recipients and donors could include a counseling component as well.

Various professional organizations, including both the Family Law Section of the American Bar Association and the ASRM have already developed guidelines for the informed-consent process.[35] At the least, full disclosure should include a discussion of the known and potential health risks from donation and of the donor's choice of how to dispose of any unfertilized eggs. Clinics should implement various measures to provide information early, allow patients to ask questions, and assure patients that the informed-consent process is confidential and that decisions concerning the ultimate disposition of their gametic material will not be disclosed to anyone involved in their treatment.[36]

If other recommendations discussed in chapter 12 concerning confidentiality are adopted, then the informed-consent process must include an acknowledgment that the donor understands that his or her identity will be released once a child reaches the minimum age. To ensure that adequate medical information about donors is available to the clinics, recipients, and children, donors could also be required to provide information concerning the future development of any serious health conditions. The documents should also include a recognition that, unless there is a contrary agreement, providing egg, sperm, or embryos to another person irrevocably and legally transfers any claim to parental rights from the donor to the recipient. Sperm banks and embryo- and egg-donation clinics and recruiters could be mandated to provide at least one hour of counseling for patients.

Ultimately, although the uniformity achieved through federal regulation is entirely appropriate for market issues, it is also critical that the federal government avoid extensive oversight of the types of families that can be created with assessments of parental commitment, age, health, and other factors. Such a family-by-family judgment is better left to the states and individual banks if it is to be considered at all. The state has long eschewed the responsibility of determining who should give birth to children, focusing instead on the postbirth welfare of children.[37] What the federal government can do, however, is to structure a market that is fair to participants.

11

Five-Parent Families?

A Parenting Proposition

THE CURRENT LAWS on the identity of parents for children born through the new reproductive technologies are complex, confusing, and inconsistent, varying from state to state and often depending on marital status. A nonmarital woman may be the only legal parent of a child born through artificial insemination—or may not, depending on the state and whether any contractual agreement will be enforced. A woman who gestates another couple's embryo may be the mother—or may not, depending on the state. A man who provides sperm may be the father—or may not, depending on the state where the donation occurs and whether he is married to the mother. The laboratory of states that is the hallmark of our system of federalism provides the opportunity for states to experiment with different approaches to the parenting issues until national consensus exists. But the confusion as to whom we recognize as a parent or nonparent serves neither parents nor children. Changing the identity of parents when a child is two years old, or even five months old, does not provide the continuity and stability of care that children need and is a disservice to all the adults who so desperately want a child. Encouraging adults to forum shop, to move from one state to another, in order to become a parent makes an already potentially complex medical procedure into a complex legal procedure.

When several adults all claim to be the parent, the indeterminacy of the concepts both of "parent" and of the child's best interests gives judges the discretion to choose any factors they deem relevant to the custody award. When the biological mother is married and the biological father—or the other potential biological mother—is not, the biological mother wins.[1] When it comes to the new reproductive technologies, and there are arguably several potential mothers, the mother who belongs with the biological father wins. Similarly, in the surrogacy context, the biological father wins against a gestational mother. Thus, the biological mother who is not married to the biological father invariably loses against a traditional-appearing nuclear family; she wins, of course, when she is married to the biological father and is part of a nuclear family herself. The inconsistencies cross state lines but also cross technologies, so that the laws applicable to a sperm provider may be different from those that apply to an egg provider or embryo donors.

Instead of the continued indeterminacy of definitions of parenthood, which perpetuate the differential treatment of mothers and fathers, and of married and unmarried parents, of those who use known or unknown gamete providers, several potential solutions are explored in the pages that follow. Each solution sets out a different test for determining who can exercise parental rights. The first involves using biology as the basis for parenthood. A second would accord primary parent status solely to the mother, elevating the "mother-child dyad" over other family forms. A third uses intent as the basis for recognizing parenthood. The final proposal combines elements of several other approaches, suggesting that parenthood be determined based on a combination of biology or adoption and nurturance. Each of these solutions has problems in conception and application, however. What each solution does show is the significance of classifying parents for reproductive technology purposes, and the implications of such redefinitions for the child's interests.

Assimilation

Under contemporary law, the integration of alternative families into existing family law has taken the form of treating the two types of families similarly. Yet donor-created families are, in some ways, significantly different from conventional biological families and are more comparable to adoptive families.

First, the process of creating a family through donated gametes is very different from the process of creating a biological family. A third party is necessarily inherent in the creation process, and, almost always, some members of the medical profession are involved.

On the other side, many scholars and activities argue that contemporary family law fosters two parents for every child, regardless of the parents' marital status, so "fairness demands that status be determined by similar legal standards."[2] Thus, for single women who choose artificial insemination by donor, this approach suggests that the applicable paternity rules should be the same as for conception by sexual means, and the "donor" should be deemed the legal father.[3] Such an approach definitely provides certainty: all children will have two parents.

Yet there are problems with this approach. Attempting to fit new family forms into existing family structures, without adjusting those structures, straitjackets the new families and fails to recognize the rights of either parents or children. When contemporary courts refuse to acknowledge the rights of a lesbian co-parent, they are using blood rather than functioning relationships as the defining characteristic. When they grant rights to a sperm donor over the objections of the mother, blood and tradition again become the definition of family form.

This two-parent preference, regardless of context, relies on the heterosexual marital family as the only norm for deriving regulatory standards. Instead, laws that apply to new family forms must examine the actual function, and functioning, of these families to ensure the fairest regulation.

Further, the two-parent-for-every-child approach requires that courts determine an underlying consensus about widely acknowledged and shared background principles. In the law, stare decisis seems to supply such background principles.[4] History thus helps provide a reasoned basis for examining why principles are as they are and whether this trajectory should be followed. As sociobiologists observe, it is not necessarily the "best" genes that continue but rather only those that enhance survival; thus, individuals have the ability to move "beyond" their genetic heritage. Similarly, it may not be the "best" principles that have developed but rather only those most likely to survive appellate review at any given time. We have some choice as to how to apply those principles. Consequently, rather than analogizing unlike cases to one another, it becomes important to examine the underlying purpose of families, rather than their specific form. When it comes to these purposes, it is somewhat easier to develop consensus principles that should inform, and serve as a background for, legal decision-making. Moreover, in using past principles and cases as a guide, it is critically important to examine their development to ensure that they make sense in a changed environment.[5]

When the legal system struggled with interpreting early adoption statutes, past cases involving biologically based families could provide only limited guidance. Adoption was a newly developing status, even though it created an otherwise recognizable relationship and, in many cases, ratified an existing relationship. Similarly, today, when the law struggles with issues relating to single-parent families or the visitation rights of gay and lesbian parents to non-biologically-related children, reliance on past decisions must be carefully limited based on their sets of sufficiently dissimilar facts. If the law defines families as two parents (one man and one woman) with their child(ren), then legal actors will try to change the new families to fit into this image. If families are defined as intimate arrangements for the protection of adult intimacy and/or the nurturing of children, then there is an obvious need for protecting and promoting such arrangements.

Examining what is like and unlike between donor and biological families confronts a central paradox. Seeking to treat donor families like biological families is, in some ways, quite radical, because it is an acknowledgment that familial relationships can be formed in different ways. Yet this approach has, historically, been seen as conservative, because it seeks assimilation rather than a recognition of difference. Moreover, the radical aspect of this action is undercut by the narrowness of the assimilative process; only certain types of donor families could ultimately be recognized as legitimate. The "assimilation without recognition of difference" model does provide short-term benefits for a specific group. It is, however, ultimately flawed for three reasons: (1) the failure to recognize differences precludes responding to alternative needs; (2) groups with differences are foreclosed from those benefits; and (3) the model itself remains reified and unable to change.

Biology

One deceptively simple rule would reinforce the rights of the genetic parents, requiring that custody be awarded based solely on biology. Genetics would determine the identity of the parents. This solution is effective in the conventional custody situation, when a married couple seeks a divorce and the husband and wife are, typically, the biological parents. It is also effective for determining paternity, since there can be only one biological sperm donor, and, under this approach, he would be the father, regardless of the mother's marital status. This rule is, however, problematic when it comes to determining maternity; moreover, it ignores other values that our culture finds significant.

As discussed earlier, most state laws use a mixture of biological and emotional connections to determine paternity; although there is no distinction between the rights of married and unmarried mothers, there are significant distinctions between the rights of married and unmarried fathers. Marriage makes the difference as to whether men will be defined as a parent. Using biology alone to establish a bright-line rule would require dissolving the distinctions between married and unmarried fathers and simply recognizing paternal rights that are vested in the man who contributed the sperm.

An approach based solely on biology is, of course, easy to administer. It simply requires DNA tests. And it serves to protect the rights of all biological parents, regardless of the circumstances in which they conceived. If a nonmarital woman becomes pregnant with donor sperm, and she does not know the identity of the sperm provider, a biologically based approach might require the sperm provider to be labeled the father, even if he has no intention of ever asserting paternal rights. Moreover, strict biology would mandate that the egg and sperm providers would always be declared the legal parents, precluding use of gametes by other people who seek to establish parenthood.

Biology is clearly a complex solution to the surrogacy cases, when the determination of the biological mother may be in question. In common law, she who gave birth was considered to be the mother, but she who gave birth was also both the gestational and the genetic mother.[6] When a gestational mother and a genetic mother each seek to be declared the mother, however, biology provides no simple answer. Even though courts have found that the gestational mother is, essentially, an incubator with no other relationship to the baby that she "hatches," this is contrary to other medical evidence regarding the impact of gestational actions on the fetus. Consequently, one of the other methods explored in this book must decide the issue.

There are, in addition, more theoretical problems with the biological approach. As a society, we may want to choose—and, in fact, we already have chosen—other values, such as nurturance, over biology. Some of these values defend the parental rights of married men, who may not be biological fathers but who have functioned as social fathers. Or the intent of the parents may be an important factor to consider in deciding who should be declared the parents, such as by protecting the rights of a lesbian co-mother who has not biologically contributed to the child.

Biology can be a rigid basis for deciding on parental status; it confers rights based simply on DNA evidence rather than an examination of intent or nurturing behavior.

Mother-Child Dyad

Several scholars have suggested that the core familial unit to be recognized is the relationship between mother and child. Martha Fineman argues that a mother-child dyad should be the primary familial affiliation.[7] She explains that other adults may be included: "fathers, or nonprimary caretakers who have sexual affiliation to the primary caretaker, are certainly free under my model to develop and maintain significant connections with their sexual partner and her children *if she agrees to such affiliation.*"[8] Under this model, the (biological) mother thus has control over the child's development of familial relationships with anyone else. The mother-child dyad form gains additional support from the work of Yale Child Study Center authors Joseph Goldstein, Anna Freud, and Albert Solnit, who advocate that custody, and other forms of control, be awarded to the one person who is the sole psychological parent.[9]

This perspective definitively resolves disputes by recognizing the decision-making authority of only one parent. There will be no more parental conflicts, because only the mother will have legally cognizable rights. Thus, unwed fathers would be unable to veto the biological mother's consent to adoption, and mothers would not be required to notify the sperm donors of their pregnancy. Presumably, in the surrogacy context, only the mother would have any parental rights, although deciding between the gestational and the genetic mother would be difficult.

One problem with this perspective is that it perpetuates stereotypes about women and the use of rigid gender boundaries. Although women do, in fact, provide a disproportionate share of caretaking, this is not true of all women.[10] The mother-child dyad perpetuates an ideology in which only women are encouraged to be caretakers.

A second problem with this perspective (although perhaps a benefit to its proponents) is the lack of rights for fathers and, even if determination of the primary caretaker is gender-neutral, for others with whom children have developed strong emotional attachments. Fineman believes that gender-neutrality in family law has only disadvantaged women, but there are many persuasive arguments in favor of according rights to fathers and other parental figures. First of all, regardless of the merits of single-parent families, it is hard for one individual to raise a child. Thus, practically speaking, the mother may not be the sole decision-maker. Second, to the extent that any individual(s) have formed significant relationships with the children, these relationships will have no legal significance. Thus, neither married nor unmarried fathers nor lesbian co-mothers could exercise any rights.

Intent

Another method for designating those entitled to all the rights associated with parental status is to consider intent. This approach privileges intention over a concrete biological or genetic tie.[11] Accordingly, when the proposed parents deliberately and explicitly expend efforts to create a child, their intentions should be respected. This approach has most frequently been applied to the surrogacy context, in which the commissioning parents—those who, preconception, take actions to bring about the child's existence—are deemed the intended parents. By signing a contract in which they agree to pay someone else for her "services" in helping to create a child, they deserve to be named the parents. But the approach may also be useful in the adoption context, in which the people who want and are caring for the child, who have taken the child after he or she is relinquished, could be deemed the intending parents. This approach appears to assume that the birth mother did not intend to get pregnant and/or to keep the baby, while the adoptive parents have undergone an intrusive home study and otherwise indicated their extremely strong intent to raise a child. Similarly, the unwed father who is unaware of the pregnancy or the child, or who is uninvolved with the child, could be termed an unintentional parent who has not chosen the rights and responsibilities of parenthood. The law could elevate conscious and deliberate choice as the indicia of parenthood; in the words of legal scholar Marjorie Schultz, this would mean that "bargained-for intentions determin[e] legal parenthood."[12] One problem with this approach, however, is that intent can, and in the contested cases does, change. The gestational mother may not have initially intended to keep her child, but as the pregnancy progresses, she may change her mind. Intent regarding parental status frequently changes; we do not force women who, prebirth, intend to put their children up for adoption to actually do so after birth.[13] Or the "intending parents" may have wanted only a genetically normal, healthy child, while the child born to the surrogate is not. An unwed father may not have intended to create a child but may change his mind as the pregnancy progresses or after he meets the child. At what point in time do we respect intent?

A second problem concerns the meaning of intent and choice. All choice is socially constructed, and there is a debate over when to respect choice and when to act paternalistically. Should we respect the surrogate mother's initial choice? Or should we, as some critics suggest, instead look at the culture that "forced" her into such a choice and respect her later decision to keep the child? Another problem is that the intent model assumes legal acceptance of surrogacy, an assumption that is true in some states but not in others.[14] Finally, it seems harsh toward the biological parents to cut off their rights without allowing them second thoughts. Although biology is not an appropriate test by itself, the intent approach makes it totally irrelevant.

Decisions of State, Stating Decisions

There are various approaches to the complex issues of how to define the parents of any child produced through ART, depending on whether we choose to prioritize marriage, intent, biology, genetic connection, or gestation and on whether we recognize only marital families or the diversity of family forms that may use ARTs. The Uniform Parentage Act, which is one solution, still does not address many of the parenting issues regarding gay and lesbian parents, and in its first five years of existence, it has become law in only seven states. Because the UPA must be enacted by each state legislature, the process is time-consuming and ensures variation depending on state policies and politics. Moreover, the UPA is focused on intent, particularly in its validation of gestational contracts, and it does not recognize the possibility of recognizing parental rights in more than two people, the potential of awarding visitation but not full custody rights to, for example, a surrogate who changes her mind.

Family law continues to struggle with the treatment of families without conventional biological connections. To some extent, this struggle occurs whenever technology intersects with the law, although there are some reproductive technologies that require no legal change. For example, increasingly reliable home fertility or pregnancy tests are legally neutral, and aside from the need to regulate their safety and reliability, they do not have other legal implications for parental identity. A simple yes or no letting a woman know that she is pregnant, or a simple fertility test that diagnoses problems with egg or sperm, has no relevance to legal issues of parenthood. Home DNA tests, however, may not be as neutral when it comes to legal parenthood. Imagine a child who tests herself and one parent only to discover no biological relationship. And the use of surrogacy and donor gametes does require change.

Laws are changed in two different ways: (1) Congress or state legislatures enact uniform laws of widespread application, or (2) common law courts, as they decide each case before them, may interpret existing law in such a way as to dramatically change future applications of those same laws. For example, historically, in deciding whether artificial insemination within a marriage constitutes adultery, courts applied existing adultery and parentage law to cover situations that could not have been anticipated when these laws were first enacted, thereby binding other courts to reach the same conclusions. The same criticisms that are more generally applicable to the interaction between technological innovation and the law apply to the ways that the law has changed (or not) in response to the new reproductive technologies: existing law simply does not cover the new situation, it is responding too slowly, or current laws that may appear to address the technologies cannot be applied coherently (for example, the adultery laws are somewhat nonsensical as applied to donor eggs and sperm).

Judges can, and have, changed the laws regarding the use of ARTs. Lesbian co-parents have more rights because of a trilogy of California Supreme Court decisions from 2005 that conferred the legal status of parent on the lesbian partner of a legal mother. But courts only decide the cases in front of them; it is up to legislatures to make broader changes. Accordingly, as in other areas of technology, legislatures and courts might address reproductive technology in any number of ways. First, they might develop completely new laws, treating the technology as requiring the development of new approaches, such as Louisiana's ban on disposing of embryos. Second, they might simply clarify or expand existing law by analogizing new situations to current law, for example, specifying that donor eggs are treated in the same way as donor sperm. Third, they might repeal existing laws, such as the legal inability to contract out of parenthood. And finally, courts and legislatures might simply abstain and wait for more clarity on the technology itself.[15]

Each of these methods describes various contemporary approaches to definitions of legal parents in families formed through the new technologies. As a general matter, there has been an effort to use the second approach, of analogizing new situations to those that have arisen under existing law. Indeed, contemporary attempts to regulate "artificial" families, like adoption laws in the late nineteenth century, struggle with the utility of the existing template of the marital family. When alternative families look like the nuclear family—when there is only one mother and one father for a particular child, even if that father is not the biological father[16]—then these families are more likely to gain the same rights and privileges as the traditional family form. When alternative families look different—two parents of the same sex or one parent of either sex—then adapting family law is more difficult. The normative need to enshrine a single family form (as discussed in chapter 4) is aligned with cultural concerns over the decline of the family and what is best for children. Nonetheless, a focus on how children are actually living and what they actually need may result in changing the template.

Differences inherent in the new family structure, such as a child having two parents of the same sex and possibly a third parent of the opposite sex, need to be acknowledged as realities with legal consequences. Rather than a narrow application of analogical reasoning that relies on an empirically outdated model of the ideal family, family law can use a broader approach that recognizes the dilemmas presented by actual families. Forcing all families to conform to a single model harms all members of the unit. Using the two-parent, heterosexual biological family as the template against which to measure, and to conform, other families is not the wisest approach. As discussed earlier, sperm donors have repeatedly received extensive visitation rights over the objections of the biological mother and her partner,[17] based on analogizing the parent-child relationship to existing familial forms. In other cases, lesbian or gay partners who have planned families together but who then separate after the child's birth without legalizing the second parent's relationship may also face imposition of the traditional parenting model when the second parent's rights are not recognized.

When contemporary courts refuse to acknowledge the rights of a lesbian co-parent, they are again using blood rather than functioning relationship as the defining characteristic. When they grant rights to a sperm donor over the objections of the mother, blood and tradition again become the definition of family form. Using blood-based, two-parent, marital families as the prototype to which all other families are analogized utterly fails to recognize the complexity of family forms. Accordingly, courts and legislatures should recognize the rights of lesbian and gay co-parents who have contributed to the creation of a child and participated in child rearing. Single parents should be allowed to raise children without the necessity of second-parent involvement through mandating responsibility for the sperm provider.

The government has different options concerning parenthood regulation. First, it can mandate rules of general application that individuals cannot challenge. Thus, even if a couple tried to set the terms of their own agreement—for example, guaranteeing an egg/sperm donor certain rights or nonrights—they could not do it. The state would simply mandate the role of a sperm donor, with no possible changes. Or a state might provide that all children must have one mother and one father, with no exceptions.

Second, the state can set default rules, with accepted means of contracting around these rules. For example, in the absence of an agreement otherwise, a state might provide that a sperm provider would be the legal father, although a written agreement could circumvent this; or the law might provide (as it does in many states) that a sperm provider who does not intend to serve as a parent is not the father and, going even further, allow known providers to contract out of any paternal rights that they might otherwise have.

My proposal uses the second approach, letting people work out their own parenting arrangements, balancing biology and intent and the potential genetic contributions of more than one person. The basic principle is that intent controls. In the absence of a written agreement otherwise (oral agreements are extremely difficult to prove because they invariably involve one person's word against another, and this is parentage, after all), egg and sperm providers—whether known or unknown—have no parental rights at all based on their biological contributions. Moreover, when the parties enter into an agreement providing that an intending parent or parents will be the legal parents, then the agreement controls everyone's status. In general, then, intent is the deciding factor, and signing an agreement indicates status. The solution to the current uncertainty of parentage laws requires that states recognize written agreements between donors and recipients.

Once the intending parents sign, they should never be able to renege. The purpose of requiring a written agreement and full disclosure of relevant information is to ensure informed consent to the intending parents' roles as parents. If one did seek to renounce parental rights, then he or she would have to proceed in the same way as any other parent: relinquish the child for adoption. Nor should the egg and sperm providers be able to claim parenthood based simply on biological connection after they have signed a written agreement providing otherwise. Of course, if a provider can prove functional parentage (as in the *E.G.* case in California, discussed in chapter 1), then he or she should be allowed to proceed on this separate claim. The only other exception to the categorical enforcement of parenthood rights by agreement would be for gestational and genetic surrogates, who, as in the adoption context, should have at least one week following the birth of a child in which to decide to keep the child.

The more complicated situations involve establishing a default rule that applies when there is no agreement between the parties. For an unknown donor, this is straightforward: the donor has no parental rights (even if he or she could be identified). With a known donor, however, there are two potentially difficult situations when conflicts may arise. First, the donor may want rights, and the recipient may claim that the donor should receive none. Second, the recipient may want the donor to take on various responsibilities, and the donor may not want to do so. To prevent these conflicts, a state should enact legislation requiring that recipients and known donors enter into written agreements concerning their future responsibilities. These written agreements should control the outcome. In the absence of an agreement, courts must balance different policy considerations, determining whose interests should receive priority: the recipient or the donor or the resulting child. These situations are, however, fact specific and should not be resolved through a default rule that privileges one set of interests.

In addition, to ensure certainty for parents and children, for donors and recipients, the intending parents should be able to seek a prebirth judicial declaration of parental rights—or, in an even more efficient process, a prebirth birth certificate from the state's health department—that sets out the names of the parents. Prebirth parentage declarations have numerous benefits, ensuring that the intending parents are the legal parents of the child and will be involved in the birth experience. Moreover, this process guarantees that their names will go on the birth certificate that is filled out after the child is born. This also means that the hospital can discharge the baby to the care of the intending parents. These declarations are similar to prenuptial agreements in that they are advance determinations of rights and relationships that precede the triggering event (the birth of a child or a marriage).

In states without such laws, a second parent of the same sex should be able to adopt a child created through donor eggs or sperm. In states that allow same-sex marriage or provide that civil unions and domestic partners should be treated like married couples for parenting purposes, these statutes could be amended to provide greater certainty for parental authority. These states should provide some method for judicial recognition of parenting relationships, which should help ensure that other states will, under the Full Faith and Credit Clause, accept such relationships. Legal recognition of both parties as parents avoids the contentious issue of the interstate recognition of gay marriages, civil unions, or domestic partnerships.

One statutory reform might mandate the automatic issuance of birth certificates with both same-sex parents' names. A second reform could require the automatic issuance of a certificate of adoption or an automatic declaration of parentage when a child is born into a same-sex relationship.

With private contracts and legislative action, the special legal problems facing gay and lesbian parents can be mitigated, and their legal status and rights as parents can be affirmed. And that is certainly in the best interests of their children.

State law also must recognize that individuals who sign certain contracts (perhaps on model state forms) can relinquish parental rights. Without these contracts being validated by the law, the general rule is that parenthood cannot be created or denied through an agreement. Instead, parenthood is created by statute or denied by courts based on a determination of what is in the child's best interests, and this often means making sure that men do not contract out of their child-support obligations. Consequently, a contract between a donor and the intending parents will not be binding by itself unless this proposal becomes law. Known donors should be able to rely on such a relinquishment, as should the recipients of their gametes.

Subsequent events, such as living with a child and creating a functional parent-child relationship, provide an alternative method for establishing parenthood. Thus, in the E.G. case discussed chapter 1, the egg donor had signed away any rights based on her genetic contribution but had then lived with the children and her partner for several years, and the children thought of her as their mother. The appropriate outcome was not to void the contract, as the court did, but to recognize that the egg donor had become the mother through her actions subsequent to the egg provision.

Finally, state laws in this area must pass a nondiscrimination principle. More than forty states have enacted legislation banning gay marriage; there is certainly a risk that state legislatures might enact burdensome and discriminatory rules when it comes to access to the new reproductive technologies. Indeed, there are models internationally of such restrictive legislation, as discussed in chapter 9, including Italy's ban on anyone who is not married or in a stable heterosexual relationship from using IVF. The current lack of uniformity among states has allowed gays, lesbians, and single women in some states to use the new technologies, to engage in surrogacy agreements, and to form alternative families. In a federalist system, with more than fifty jurisdictions, states have been able to experiment with their approaches to these issues, allowing for a diversity of family forms to develop.

The risk from uniform parentage laws is that all states will go the way of Italy. Given the response to gay marriage, this is certainly a possibility. But states are already free to develop their own rules. If, however, the uniform parentage statute provides for equal access, regardless of sexual orientation, gender identity, or marital status, then it would provide a model for state responses that accepts alternative families. A model equal-access statute at least suggests the appropriate direction for state law in accepting gay, lesbian, and single-parent families.

The law can require men and women to decide on parentage in advance of their use of reproductive technologies to ensure certainty for all involved. Becoming involved with reproductive technology is not a casual undertaking, and the informed-consent and disclosure processes for both recipients and donors must handle not just medical risks but also legal outcomes. Just as patients precommit themselves to the technology, they can precommit to their roles once a child is born. Accordingly, sperm, egg, and embryo banks and fertility clinics should, as part of the informed-consent process, use state-provided forms that disclose and clarify parentage choices. These forms could be retained by the facility or kept in a central state registry. Although this proposal adds another regulatory layer to the ART process (we do not ask couples having a baby to sign numerous documents), people who choose to use this technology have already ventured outside the privacy of their bedrooms to create a child.

Without clarity concerning parenthood, donors may be concerned about their obligations to any resulting children, and recipient parents may be concerned about the security of their legal rights. Consequently, to ensure predictability and smooth transactions, to protect parents, gamete providers, and offspring, states must enact laws shielding donors from parenting obligations and transferring those legal obligations to recipients, in the absence of written agreements otherwise.

12

Finding Out

TO CONFRONT THE delicate issue of whether to disclose the identity of gamete providers, this chapter reframes the issue from a rights-based view to one weighing the relative interests and practical concerns of all the parties—providers (donors and industry), legal parents, and offspring. The discussion emphasizes arguments in favor of identity disclosure, addressing the most common objections to disclosure. The chapter closes with recommendations on how to implement what I term "limited disclosure." The discussion also identifies different strategies used by other countries, analyzing whether those methods would be desirable or even permissible within the United States' legal system.

Discussions of gamete identity disclosure are often framed as children's right to know versus their parents' and the donors' right not to disclose. In journalist Liza Mundy's book on reproductive technology, for example, she asks, "Do children—who after all are the point of all this, the point of everything everybody goes through—have the right to know the truth and the whole truth of their origins? Do children have a right to know the identity of their donor? . . . What happens if the rights of the child conflict with the rights of the parents? Whose reproductive freedom is it? And who is going to make these decisions?"[1] Dr. Robert Nachtigall, in his sensitive 1993 examination of these issues, suggested that the child's best interests, framed as a need to know, may conflict with the parental preference for secrecy.[2] Columnist Ellen Goodman wrote a column advocating disclosure that was titled "Kids' Right to Know Trumps Sperm Donors' Right to Anonymity."[3]

But framing the issue solely in terms of rights is wrong: it confuses the issues of confidentiality and privacy, establishing schemes of competition, rather than focusing on the interests of all involved. This framing also seems to contemplate either open or closed identity, rather than conceptualizing a limited disclosure once the child reaches a certain age. First, of course, when we talk about children, it is important to recognize that we are talking about people who will become adults, capable of exercising their own rights. Indeed, some have begun to refer to themselves as donor adoptees. Second, once we begin to discuss the importance of balancing rights, we enter an area of compromise. Do we privilege donors' rights? Offsprings' rights? Recipients' rights? Asking these questions requires an analysis of each set of competing interests. Our traditional method for providing protections has been through the development of specific legal rights. Yet rights discourse is complicated, particularly when it is applied to children. Children's rights and interests exist for them as individuals—and the older they become, the stronger are their rights—and more contextually, for them as family members. Until they are capable of articulating their own needs, they are dependent on their caretakers and on the state to protect them. When parents and children's interests diverge, however, respecting children's interests does not mean overlooking adults' interests. Nor should recognizing adults' interests mean trivializing children's interests. Although it is critical to respect children's rights and relationships, to make decisions that are in their best interest, and to listen to their needs, parents' rights can also be respected.

This is why, most fundamentally, we need to reframe the issue so that we are not talking about competing rights. Recipients are, almost invariably, intensely interested and conscious of the characteristics of the gamete provider. Should it come as any surprise that their children may be similarly interested? Moreover, as a culture, as parents, we emphasize that we want what is best for our children. The option to learn the identity of their genetic parents is in the children's best interests (as discussed in chapter 6). Ultimately, we must redefine gamete provision as something other than a single transaction, as a sale that involves a longer-term responsibility.[4] The provider is not simply sustaining an already-existing life, as is true of organ and blood donors, but provides the possibility of creating life, a life with a substantially similar genetic heritage.

Beyond the jurisprudential debates of privacy and individual rights, there are more practical reasons to tell a child about his or her origins. Because the parents may have shared the information with other people in their lives, there is a risk of accidental disclosure to the child. Second, as the child grows older, medical information about one-half of his or her genetic pool becomes more important, even as technology provides more data about our genetic background.[5] Third, knowledge of origins protects against unknowing incestuous relationships; without information about one's genetic origins, offspring conceived from gametes of the same donor may marry each other. This was dramatically illustrated in early 2008 in the United Kingdom, when twins, who had been adopted by different families, married each other. Their marriage was ultimately annulled, but this occurrence in the adoption context supports the case for "limited disclosure" (one U.S. sperm donor estimated that he could potentially have almost five thousand children).[6] "Limited disclosure," rather than "open identity" or even "mandatory disclosure," is the appropriate terminology to use for this information.

Why Not Disclose? Objections

Regardless of the practical difficulties of mandating disclosure, there is a series of more complicated objections to ending anonymity. The primary arguments against information disclosure center on pragmatic concerns about the supply of gametes and the difficulty of implementing a disclosure system, as well as more philosophical concerns about the distinction between legal and genetic relationships and the rights of privacy of everyone involved: the parents, the gamete providers, and the children.

Biology and Destiny

Focusing on biological information raises the danger of genetic essentialism, or genetic determinism, a concept that suggests that a person is merely the sum of his or her genes and that behavior can be predicted based on genetic information. As Dorothy Nelkin and Susan Lindee explain, "DNA in popular culture functions, in many respects, as a secular equivalent of the Christian soul. . . . Fundamental to identity, DNA seems to explain individual differences, moral order, and human fate . . . relevant to the problems of personal authenticity."[7] The gene has been seen as the "unifying concept" of the field of biology, with a virtually "iconic status" that makes it capable of explaining us to ourselves.[8] Mandating identity disclosure may suggest that genetic origins are superior to socially and legally created parenting relationships[9] and thereby contribute to the danger of overemphasizing one's biological composition. In the context of adoptees who are seeking information about their biological parents, critics have charged that the adoptees are overly concerned with biology and are seeking to elevate biological relationships over adoptive relationships.

Some argue that advocates of open records are so concerned about the biological connection between parent and child that they are antiadoption. One of the more thoughtful proponents of this position, Ellen Herman, suggested that the movement toward open records and reunions may "reinforce the entirely conventional view that birth parents are real, adopters artificial, and identity incomplete and inferior without benefit of blood."[10] And professor Wayne Carp, in his insightful discussion of the history of closed adoption records, suggests that the adoption-rights movement maintains as one of its primary convictions that biological ties are superior to adoptive ties.[11]

These criticisms show, I think, a potential insecurity that the search for a biological past, by definition, prioritizes biological relationships over legal and functional relationships. On this perspective, any recognition that blood ties could have significance seems threatening to the whole concept of non-biologically-related families. On the other hand, as Donor Sibling Registry founder Wendy Kramer has observed in her blog, parents "rise above their own discomfort to do what they know is best for their kids."[12]

Although I advocate the disclosure of the gamete provider's identity, I do not justify it because of the genetic information that it will provide[13] but because it is in children's best interests and for the fertility market. Knowing the identity of a biological progenitor may help the child in his or her identity development, but it is certainly not the only factor in that development; genetic information, though potentially helpful, does not reveal everything about a person's identity. What this information can do, however, is aid children who feel a connection to a biological past.

The mere knowledge of one's genetic information is not, by itself, determinative of one's identity, or even of one's physical reality. Genes play some role in diseases, but environment plays a significant role as well, even with respect to the expression of genetic diseases.[14] Knowing that a parent has developed cancer, heart disease, or depression does not definitively indicate that the child will do so as well. Genes do not provide knowledge about a person's culture, family, friends, or moral beliefs.[15] Obtaining genetic information does not allow an adoptee or a child of gamete provision to predict, or even to explain, all of his or her personal characteristics and traits. For example, studies of adoptees whose biological parents were alcoholics do indicate that they have a much higher than normal probability that they will also become an alcoholic.[16] Nonetheless, most such children will not become alcoholics: 82 percent did not. Moreover, studies of female adoptees of alcoholic birth parents do not indicate the same increased probability.[17] Genes are complex and can only be understood in a larger biological and social context.[18] Nonetheless, a genetic history does contain useful information about potential medical conditions, and it may provide some grounding for those children who want to know more, helping them shape future behavior.

Wanting to know about one's genetic history does not, then, mean that every aspect of one's life will suddenly be explained. Instead, having the same genetic heritage creates the opportunity for a connection between parent and adult offspring that the state must not foreclose. As professor James Nelson points out, "Why . . . regard a biological connection to the future as a vital part of the identity of adults, but not see biological connectedness to the past as an equally vital part of the identity of children?"[19] Given the importance to many parents of having a genetic connection to their child, it should be unremarkable that children are themselves interested in learning about those to whom they have a genetic connection. In the case of gamete provision, when couples establish a genetic attachment between one of them and a child, it should not be surprising that children would want to know about other aspects of their genetic heritage. Establishing this continuity with both the future and the past is understandably important to many offspring.

The forms that gamete providers must fill out are extremely detailed with respect to their family health histories, and much of this information is disclosed to potential recipients. Sperm providers frequently undergo extensive screening as well as a complete physical examination.[20] Recipients can choose egg or sperm providers based on a specified number of traits. For example, it is possible to choose race, ethnic ancestry, height, weight, physical build, hand coordination, vision, approximate IQ score, and college grade-point average for egg providers.[21] Cryogenic Laboratories offers the following: "Simply send us a photo of the individual you would hope for your offspring to resemble. Our staff will then rank the resemblance of the donors you've selected."[22] The bank may even collect an audiotape of the providers.

The full disclosure of anonymous information at the time of gamete provision—information that goes well beyond simple genes—along with corresponding secrecy of the identity of the person, seems itself to be an example of genetic essentialism on the part of the intending parents. They do not want to know the actual person; they simply want to know his or her genes and a great deal of other information as well. A primary rationale for requiring disclosure of nonidentifying genetic information is to allow prospective gamete recipients to guard against any dangers that might be posed through "faulty" genes. As a secondary rationale, sperm banks report that many of their clients are looking for a good genetic match: "Sperm banks have found that most of their clients seek donors who share their ethnic background and personal interests."[23]

As exemplified by Ellen DeGeneres's frustration with the process of seeking a sperm donor who looks like her (mentioned in chapter 1),[24] lesbian couples seem to be as interested as heterosexual couples in attempting to match the sperm provider's characteristics with those of the non-biologically-related partner.[25] By contrast, the purpose of disclosing the identity of biological relatives is to aid the adoptees and the various parents in their personal and emotional development, not solely to provide genetic information (although this may be an important by-product).[26] Indeed, a birth mother recently petitioned a court so that she could inform the adoptive family of various predispositions toward medical conditions.[27]

Ultimately, the reasons that adoptees or gamete children seek information go far beyond genetically related rationales. The information provides additional background to their full identities: genetic, emotional, and even cultural. Regardless of how happy children are, and have been, in their families, they still may want and need additional information about their origins. Adoptees who have searched and found their birth mothers generally report a more positive self-perception together with a more holistic sense of identity.[28] Studies of donor children will undoubtedly show similar results.

Privacy Interests

A second critical argument against information disclosure centers on the privacy rights of everyone involved: the social/legal parents, the gamete providers, and the child. The argument against providing identifying information relies, in large part, on the history of nondisclosure and on the use of nondisclosure to protect the interests of all involved in the process. The traditional articulation of the fundamental right to privacy, however, does not comprehend the various interests at stake in the gamete-provision cases.

Existing privacy law has developed from many sources and takes many forms, ranging from electronic surveillance to abortion. For our purposes, it is useful to focus on sexual decision-making. Privacy within family law has two primary, and interrelated, meanings. First, privacy can mean privatization, the use of internal rather than external norms and, thus, the legal ability of those within the relationship to control their own rights and responsibilities, such as through prenuptial contracts, cohabitation agreements, or separation agreements. There has been a general movement since the last third of the twentieth century to allow for increased private contracting before, during, and at the end of marriage, as well as between cohabiting couples. States have adopted different standards for judging these contracts, sometimes applying general standards of contract law and, at other times, stressing the nature of the fiduciary relationship between marital partners. Although these contracts have been upheld when they relate to obligations between intimate partners, courts are far stricter when these agreements affect the rights of children through child support or child custody, generally holding that the state must decide these issues under a best-interest-of-the-child test.

Second, as discussed earlier, privacy can denote a protected sphere, the right to engage in any activities that one chooses within that sphere. Beginning in *Skinner v. Oklahoma,* the 1942 Supreme Court case striking down mandatory sterilization laws, and continuing into the contraception and abortion cases, courts have recognized a right to decide whether or not to beget a child. It was only in 1965, in *Griswold v. Connecticut,* that the Supreme Court directly addressed the concept of sexual decision-making other than in the context of eugenics. *Griswold* protected marital sexual decision-making, locating it in the penumbras of various constitutional rights rather than grounding it explicitly in a constitutional guarantee. (But, as professor Jed Rubenfeld points out, the Court has consistently found "fundamental rights [that] exist unspecified in the Constitution.")[29] Although the Constitution does not explicitly recognize any forms of familial privacy, to claim that the Constitution does not at least suggest such rights would represent a constrained and strained view of the Bill of Rights. Seven years after deciding *Griswold,* the Court confronted the question it had not explored in that case of whether the right to privacy extends to individuals, including the unmarried. In answering yes, the Court extended the right of sexual decision-making to the individual. In stirring, and potentially quite expansive, words, Justice Brennan declared, "If the right of privacy means anything, it is the right of the individual, married or single, to be free from unwarranted governmental intrusion into matters so fundamentally affecting a person as the decision whether to bear or beget a child."[30] In 2003, in one of its broadest pronouncements on privacy, *Lawrence v. Texas,* the Court allowed the right of privacy to protect same-sex sexual intimacy, an opinion that may help gay and lesbian parents seeking to use ART. The abortion cases have similarly been decided pursuant to privacy jurisprudence. Because of a woman's privacy right in her own body, she is not required to inform, much less seek permission from, the potential father that she is seeking an abortion.

Privacy is not a monolithic construct and is not always good: it has allowed domestic violence and other forms of exploitation to occur within the family. The story of the 1971 Supreme Court case *Wyman v. James* illustrates other aspects of privacy within the family. Barbara James, a public-welfare recipient, refused to allow her caseworker to visit her home. She told her caseworker that she would provide any information that was relevant to her continued receipt of welfare but that the caseworker could not make a home visit. At the time, New York State law required home visits to public-welfare recipients once every three months to verify information concerning eligibility for welfare, provide professional counseling, and prevent welfare fraud. Moreover, New York law specified that a child would be eligible for aid only "if his home situation is one in which his physical, mental and moral well-being will be safeguarded and his religious faith preserved and protected."[31] Although a three-judge federal district court struck down the home-visit requirement, the Supreme Court reversed the decision. The majority opinion in *Wyman* focused on distinguishing between a true constitutionally protected search and the "visitation" at issue, which was neither forced nor compelled nor sanctionable with criminal penalties. The majority found that even if in some sense the home visit was a search, it was not unreasonable. The majority upheld the termination of James's welfare benefits upon her refusal to comply with the home-visit requirement.

Justices Marshall and Brennan wrote a strong dissent, explaining,

> It is argued that the home visit is justified to protect dependent children from "abuse" and "exploitation." These are heinous crimes, but they are not confined to indigent households. Would the majority sanction, in the absence of probable cause, compulsory visits to all American homes for the purpose of discovering child abuse? Or is this Court prepared to hold as a matter of constitutional law that a mother, merely because she is poor, is substantially more likely to injure or exploit her children?[32]

As these questions show, family privacy varies with the class of the family. Wealthier families have received more protection for their familial decision-making, and lower-income families have not received the same privacy entitlements. Examining the class-based variations in privacy protection helps illustrate that privacy is not an absolute concept but is dependent on other aspects of the individual's life. Indeed, the case's discussion of privacy provide conflicting notions of whose rights and interests merit protection at any one time, thereby challenging the presumed confidentiality of donors.

When we discuss privacy in this context, there is actually a group of possible harms from disclosure of information beyond the boundaries within which one expects the secret to be kept, including breach of confidentiality and intrusion into decision-making.[33] At the same time, however, there may be harms from nondisclosure, such as children who feel betrayed by not knowing their origins. It is, consequently, important to recognize that privacy, though constitutionally protected, is not absolute and requires balancing various interests.

The history of secrecy in gamete provision appears to be based on the need to protect gamete donors from obligations toward the children produced and the need to protect family members from the shame of infertility. Once there is legislation clarifying the relational and parental obligations for both marital and nonmarital children (as discussed in chapter 10), then donors will be clearly protected from additional legal obligations. The stigma of infertility and the fear of rejection will not, however, be dissolved by legal action. The historical shame associated with infertility is facing several challenges. In light of the increasing use of donor gametes by single parents and gay and lesbian parents, many of the consumers of ART are not confronting infertility. Moreover, as children and parents engage in increasingly open discussions of sex and sexuality, fertility and infertility, this may dissolve the legacy of stigma. As the social justifications for privacy become more questionable, the legal issues become more salient. The discussions of personhood and privacy in adoption cases, which provide the closest analogies, address conflicting notions of whose rights and interests merit protection at any one time.[34] The whole notion of privacy—the right to be let alone—has developed as protection for individuals from state interference; because donor anonymity is a privately created status involving a relationship between families, the traditional formulation of the doctrine is problematic. For gamete and egg donors, the privacy interests should be analyzed with a recognition that the state has been—or should be—involved in defining their status as parents or as nonparents as well as in the secrecy of their identities.

The term "privacy" includes a series of different "rights," some of which have been recognized by the federal Constitution and some of which have developed in other contexts. Jeffrey Rosen argues that in the reproductive-rights area, the Supreme Court has labeled as privacy what is better conceived of as an individual's right to make reproductive decisions, in contrast to a "more focused vision of privacy that has to do with our ability to control the conditions under which we make different aspects of ourselves accessible to others."[35] Disclosure of the identity of sperm and egg providers implicates both aspects of privacy, the interests of the ultimate parent(s) in making intimate reproductive choices and the interests of the gamete providers in controlling the circumstances under which they become—or do not become—known. In addition, disclosure implicates a third kind of privacy, the interests of the child in the choice of whether to learn more about him- or herself.[36]

Some feminists have analogized the adoption/gamete-provision decision to that made by women choosing to undergo an abortion, claiming that the same right to privacy protects both.[37] The argument is that there is a fundamental right to make decisions regarding reproductive choices without intervention.

This argument works very well in the abortion context, when a woman is deciding what to do with her own body. It works much less well when, after a woman or a man has decided what to do with her or his body, there is now a child with separate and independent needs and interests who is deciding what to do with his or her body. Children have independently recognized rights that exist apart from, and sometimes in conflict with, those of their (different sets of) parents.[38] Moreover, whatever constitutionally protected interests donor-conceiving parents—or the donor him- or herself—may have in controlling a child's access to information while the child is a minor weaken considerably once a child reaches majority.

The privacy interests of all involved in gamete provision can appear to preclude disclosure. Few cases other than *Johnson* involving identity disclosure have reached the courts. Even in *Johnson*, the disclosure of the genetic parent's identity was incidental to the tort claims being brought against the clinic that had provided the defective sperm. The court did, however, examine the 1973 Uniform Parentage Act (UPA)—which allows for donor insemination records to be inspected based on a court's finding of "good cause"—to decide whether the donor could be required to appear at a deposition, even though the Johnsons and the sperm bank had entered into a contract that protected the donor's anonymity. The court noted that there were no reported decisions concerning the UPA's "good cause" standard. Nonetheless, the court found that "insemination records, including a sperm donor's identity and related information contained in those records, may be disclosed under certain circumstances."[39] Although the court was not called on to decide the circumstances under which a court would disclose these records to a child based on the UPA, the court did not foreclose this option. It suggested that, if the contract "conflicts with California's compelling interest in the health and welfare of children," then the court might order disclosure.[40]

The only reported case dealing with a child's attempt to find out the identity of his biological father probably does not involve donor sperm. Minor J. was born in 1989 to Ms. and Mr. J. His parents were divorced in 1995. Although both Minor J. and Mr. J. had assumed that Mr. J. was the biological father, DNA tests challenged this assumption. Minor J. sued his mother in 2006, seeking to require her to reveal the identity of his biological father. A trial court refused to allow the case to proceed because Minor J. was considered the legal child of Mr. J.; Mr. J. was married to Ms. J. when Minor J. was conceived and born. Minor J. appealed, arguing that he had a right to information about his biological father, but an appellate court rejected his claims.[41]

And in another sperm-identity case, albeit with a twist, Michael Hayes sued an Oregon fertility clinic to determine if his sperm was mistakenly used to inseminate a stranger rather than, as he had intended, his fiancée. M.H., as he is known in the court papers, wanted to establish a relationship with the child who *might* have been born. The woman who received the sperm—who had not revealed whether she gave birth to a child— wanted to be left alone, without revealing her identity (in the court papers, she is known only as "Jane Doe").[42] She alleges that she was forced to take a morning-after pill and even offered a free abortion. The judge has prevented M.H. from finding out whether he is a father, again using the marital presumption to shield the woman and her husband from further scrutiny.[43]

The analogies between the donor's claim to privacy and those claims asserted in the adoption context are quite strong. In both cases, there is a claim of a promise of confidentiality, and there is a claim that disclosing information violates privacy interests. In both cases, state statutes have typically specified that disclosure is available upon a showing of "good cause," and ultimately, courts have decided that good cause can sometimes trump these privacy interests. This does not mean that disclosure will be easy; one sperm donor described, in the very public forum of the *New York Times*, the ambivalence of his potential meeting of a donor child: "Thinking about such an encounter has always provoked anxiety and excitement in me. I've been . . . worried about potential possible financial liability. . . . But I've also felt excited."[44]

In light of the multiple meanings of privacy, and potential conflicts between different privacy interests, our deference to privacy interests must, in the words of privacy scholar Daniel Solove, "depend upon the circumstances of each situation. . . . We must focus on the relationships in which information is transferred and the uses to which information is put."[45] When it comes to donor-conceived adults' interest in information about their origins, information can be transferred only to them, not to the public, and they generally seek the information to help them understand themselves better.

Retroactivity

The disclosure of donor information is most controversial with respect to gamete donation that took place under a sealed-records regime. Opponents argue that unsealing these records unfairly breaches promises of confidentiality made to gamete providers and the recipient parents.

Although initially appealing, such breach-of-promise arguments are ultimately unpersuasive. First, the confidentiality is protected by private agreements, not by state laws; the state can change rules governing contracts when required by public policy, such as a child's best interest. Moreover, courts have uniformly rejected such vested-rights arguments in other areas of family law relating both to personal rights and to property rights. For example, courts have held that the application of no-fault divorce laws to marriages entered into under a prior fault-based regime did not violate the vested rights of "innocent" spouses who wished to preserve a marriage. Courts have firmly rejected the assertion that family members have a legally protected interest in having their rights and obligations remain static. These cases indicate that popularly elected legislatures retain the authority to alter the contours of state-created family law structures and that neither promises nor expectations about the continuing consequences of those structures rises to the level of a vested constitutional right. As a middle ground, disclosure for gamete provision prior to a certain date might occur through a mutual registry, established either by the government or privately, such as the existing Donor Sibling Registry.

Supply and Demand

Requiring that gamete providers agree to the possibility of information disclosure may be risky in terms of supply. One of the primary—and strongest—arguments against disclosure of the identity of gamete providers is that it will have a negative effect on the supply of sperm and eggs. If gamete providers know that they can be found, the argument goes, then they may be less likely to give gametic material out of fear that an unknown child will come knocking on their door twenty years later, whereas current practices appear to protect their ongoing anonymity.

Studies have repeatedly shown that about half of both egg and sperm donors would not participate if anonymity were removed—but that the other half would continue to provide gametes.[46] Indeed, a 2007 study of egg donors found that almost 90 percent would donate without any guarantee of anonymity.[47] Early studies from countries that have moved toward mandatory donor identification similarly showed that donors were less willing to provide gametes if they knew their identity would be disclosed.[48] Even the future possibility that a law will require such disclosure may have a dampening effect.[49] Indeed, after Sweden enacted legislation in 1985 that mandated the identification of gamete providers when the child reached the age of eighteen, there was some concern that the legislation had caused a severe decline in the number of sperm donors.[50] Subsequently, however, there appears to be an increase in the number of sperm providers, and fears that donor-identity release requirements would inhibit semen provision have been allayed.[51] Similarly, after New Zealand mandated the release of identifying information, there was an initial decline; rates stabilized, however, after the first year.[52]

In the United Kingdom, there was similar concern over decreasing numbers of donors once national law precluded anonymous donation in April 2005, but the actual situation is more complicated. The well-known Bourn Hall fertility clinic even advertises on its website that its "successful sperm bank" helps overcome the "national shortage" and that embryo, egg, and sperm are available when patients need them.[53] And the number of men providing sperm in the United Kingdom actually increased by 6 percent in the first year after anonymity ended.[54] Thus, although requiring the release of information may have some initial impact on the number of donors, predictions of drastic long-term effects appear overblown.

Moreover, such legislation may result in the development of new methods to recruit other donors,[55] and the publicity associated with new laws may encourage different types of donors to come forward. By changing advertising techniques to emphasize helping others rather than the amount of payment, banks may be able to recruit donors who care less about money and more about facilitating the creation of families.

In the comparable context of adoption in the United States, open records have not compromised the integrity of the adoption process. Indeed, as professor Joan Hollinger observes, more than 80 percent of the biological mothers who have relinquished children for adoption in Michigan since 1980 have consented to the disclosure of their identity when their children become adults.[56] In the adoption context, then, giving a child access to information about a biological parent may not compromise the decisions of the biological parents.

Similarly, in the context of gamete donation, the requirement that children receive access to donor information will not necessarily result in a dramatic decrease in donors.[57] However, in contrast to the situation in the United Kingdom, where more sperm donors registered in the year following the disclosure requirement than in the previous year, in Canada, when payment for sperm donors was cut off, the sperm supply decreased dramatically.[58] What seems likely is that mandating open-identity programs will attract different men to donation: men who are older than the current pool of donors, who already have children, who believe that donating sperm is an altruistic act, and who assume that open-identity programs are appropriate.[59] There are fewer data on the impact of mandated disclosure for egg and embryo providers, although the adoption data do seem pertinent.

The critical policy questions are whether the risk of a temporary shortage in gametic material is balanced by allowing access to information for gamete-donor children. Although the sale of gametes may be a commercial transaction for the seller, it has much broader implications for the children ultimately created; it is their interests and, in many cases, the interests of their parents and the donors that are respected through a disclosure regime.

How to Disclose: A Recommendation

As a policy matter, all adults involved with ART—gamete providers, recipients, and gamete offspring—should have access to identifying records once the child reaches the age of eighteen. Other countries that have adopted limited disclosure have enacted national laws that apply to anyone involved in the reproductive technology business. As discussed later in this chapter, in the United States, these laws could be enacted state-by-state or by the federal government. Each state would be required to enact a uniform law mandating that fertility clinics, sperm and egg banks, and physicians' offices maintain records for each child born through donor gametes. If states are unwilling to adopt uniform legislation, then Congress can enact a federal law, with regulations promulgated by the FDA as part of its oversight authority.

Calls for allowing gamete children access to identifying information are not new. In a 1986 groundbreaking article, legal scholar John Robertson suggested that "[t]he welfare of offspring is a sufficient basis for limiting reproductive contracts. The state may enact—and arguably should enact—policies that protect offspring's need to know their genetic and gestational roots."[60] And in 1980, medical ethicist George Annas called for physicians to maintain records on each donor so that donors could be matched with any resulting children.[61] Anonymity, he believed, might be in the best interest of the donor but not of the child.

Where this issue is addressed in current U.S. law, the language typically comes from the 1973 Uniform Parentage Act, discussed earlier in conjunction with *Johnson*.[62] The 2002 UPA does not address this issue at all. Consequently, in the states that enacted the 1973 UPA, at least, gamete providers could not have been promised absolute confidentiality, since insemination records can be opened upon a judicial finding of good cause. Although *Johnson* is the only case concerning the use of this standard for donor gametes, courts have interpreted "good cause" quite narrowly in the comparable context of adoptees seeking access to their birth records.[63] A few courts have allowed birth-record disclosure based on an adoptee's severe psychological need to learn about the identity of his or her biological parents.[64] Using this statutory opening to access gamete-donation records, however, is inherently cumbersome; it requires a lawsuit together with an underlying claim that satisfies the good-cause standard. Moreover, most of the existing good-cause statutes apply only to sperm provision, not egg donation.

Some observers have suggested a middle ground in which donors and recipients could each choose anonymity or identity. In effect, this "dual track" structure, a system that is in place in Iceland, would require few changes in the law in the United States, where recipients already have such an option available through an increasing number of gamete banks. Rather than placing a societal value judgment on identified or anonymous donation, and taking sides on such a contentious issue, continuing the current situation is value-neutral. Moreover, a major benefit is that it preserves choice, allowing parents and donors to decide how much disclosure they want, and thereby having little impact on the supply of donated gametes; a major drawback, however, is that some children may not know their biological origins or even know that they do not share gametes with one of their parents.[65]

Parents want what is best for their children, and numerous studies and organizations have called for disclosure. Preserving choice for parents and donors should not trump the ability of children to know their parents, a fundamental right seemingly guaranteed by international human-rights treaties, including Article 7 of the 1989 United Nations Convention on the Rights of the Child. Indeed, in Britain, Joanna Rose claimed that the European Convention on Human Rights, which guarantees a right to family life, entitled her to disclosures concerning her biological father. A High Court Judge, who did not decide on whether the Convention or British law had been violated, nonetheless held that a child conceived through donor insemination has the same right as anyone else to obtain information about his or her identity.[66] When Britain changed its laws to allow children born after 2005 to learn the identity of their donors, the chair of the British fertility regulatory agency hailed the new law as a significant component of "responsible parenting."[67] Because not all donor children are covered through this law, the British Department of Health provided funding for a voluntary registry, UK DonorLink, to allow donors and children to indicate their mutual desire to be contacted. Moreover, the register of the British Human Fertilisation and Embryology Authority provides nonidentifying information about donors to children conceived between 1991 (when it started collecting information) and 2005 (the point at which children are entitled to identifying details). Although the United States has not ratified the Children's Rights Convention and is not bound by the European Convention, we do often look to other countries to determine children's rights.

To ensure that children know that their biological and legal parents are different people, the birth certificates of children conceived with donor gametes could be stamped with "by donation" next to the mother and/or father's name.[68] Although this places pressure on parents to inform their children of their biological origins, it also ensures that, regardless of whether parents inform their children, the children will know. Such a system is already being considered in Britain. In late 2007, a group of members of the British Parliament recommended such a step, suggesting that birth certificates indicate the donor status of a child with a special stamp or by including the words "from donor."[69] The proposal was highly controversial. The chief executive of the Bourn Hall Clinic—the fertility clinic founded by Patrick Steptoe and Robert Edwards, who helped create Louise Brown, the first IVF baby born in the world—wrote that requiring birth certificates, which are public documents, to include information about a child's conception via donor gametes was an unfair intrusion into the privacy of the parents and might discourage donors from coming forward.[70] Moreover, given the public nature of birth certificates, which may be used in applying, for example, for a passport, such a system would permit many additional people to learn about the child's origins. On the other hand, the proposal recognizes the right of children to know how they have been conceived regardless of whether their parents provide them with this information.

An alternative is the "shadow," or secondary, birth certificate, which would be available to any donor-conceived child at the age of eighteen. This "shadow" certificate would include the name of the donor and would be available when the donor-conceived adult requested a copy of his or her birth certificate. Because this certificate would be automatically issued to the donor-conceived child, parents would still not necessarily have to tell a child of his or her origins. The shadow certificate would not be available to the public, so the recipient could then choose whether to use the original or the shadow certificate. Although donors could not be promised anonymity under such a system, they could file statements with the registry indicating whether they would—or would not—like to be contacted. Donors could change these statements at any time. When a child contacted the registry, the registry would release the identifying information together with the most recent statement of donor intent. Such contact/no-contact preference statements are already part of the law in several states concerning adoptees' birth records.[71] Correspondingly, a contract between a donor and a fertility clinic, bank, or even a recipient that precluded the release of identifying information would be unenforceable.

Changing current law will be difficult. A variety of interests—clinics, some recipients, some children, and many past, present, and future donors—are opposed. The culture of gamete use has come to value secrecy or, at least, the choice of identity release. In the analogous context of open records for adoption, advocates have proceeded state-by-state, using law-suits, lobbying, and referenda in an ongoing effort to change the existing closed-records situation.

Adults created through gamete provision have a strong interest in having access to information about their biological origins. Regardless of whether anyone involved actually seeks this information, there are a variety of arguments for making it available. First, for the now-grown child, this information may be critical to a sense of identity. Moreover, the private nature of the process has never accorded with the realities of the experiences of all provider families. Finally, although permitting access may disrupt the expectations of donors and recipients who have relied on continued secrecy, this secrecy has been guaranteed and maintained through private contracts and court enforcement, with little public involvement.

Focusing on the concept of identity, and particularly on its fluidity, suggests that the appropriate solution is one that allows for change over time. At the time a child is born, it is the parents' and providers' identity issues that are most critical. The Supreme Court has recognized the importance of deferring to parents' wishes. In the 2000 case of *Troxel v. Granville*, in which the Court considered the constitutionality of Oregon's visitation statute as applied to the paternal biological grandparents of children, the Court's plurality opinion focused on the rights of parents to raise their children without interference. The Court held that the visitation statute at issue conflicted with the parents' rights to care, custody, and control of their children. *Troxel* appropriately recognizes the constitutional significance of an ongoing parent-child relationship and the consequent assumptions that children are best cared for by their parents, who are presumed to make decisions that are in their children's best interests. Respecting the donor's desire for confidentiality is also consistent with the broad deference accorded to individual privacy rights.

As the child matures, however, the child's identity should begin to predominate. By the time the child reaches the age of majority, the child's need to construct his or her own identity may include the need to know his or her gamete providers. At this point, the child's status as an adult diminishes any claim that anyone might assert to make decisions on behalf of the child. This analysis suggests that there should be a strong presumption of open records at the election of the now-adult child created by donor gametes.

Children's right to know includes two interrelated parts: the right to know that one has been conceived through donor gametes and the right to know the donor.[72] Requiring that parents tell their children of their donor-conceived status is highly problematic; not only is it difficult to enforce, but it is highly intrusive of intrafamilial relationships. Implementing a system like that in the United Kingdom, where clinics must report all assisted reproductive cycles to a central authority, allows children to check whether they result from donor gametes. Donors should also be required to update their information when the child turns eighteen.

A 2006 Model Assisted Reproductive Technology Act, proposed by the Family Law Section of the American Bar Association, would require the state to maintain records concerning the identity of gamete donors and recipients but would permit donors to choose to remain anonymous.[73] Another suggestion for model legislation would require the release of medical and genetic information but not identifying information.[74] These proposals recognize the importance of providing information in some contexts but do not go far enough by requiring full disclosure. Congress should enact legislation (1) requiring that fertility clinics, sperm banks, and physicians' offices maintain records for each child born through donor gametes and (2) guaranteeing that gamete offspring have the right to access those records.

The alternatives of fertility-industry or state-by-state implementation of these mandates are both inadequate. The fertility industry and its associated professional associations certainly have a strong stake in ensuring the effectiveness of such a registry and must play a role in monitoring and maintaining this registry. Nonetheless, they are not the only stakeholders who must be involved. Governmental mandates can ensure widespread participation and can sanction entities that do not report. There is also the concern, as expressed by Wendy Kramer of the Donor Sibling Registry, that if such a registry is industry operated, then it "is only a fearful reaction to the possibility of the FDA imposing its own regulations and will only serve to protect this industry's own best interests."[75]

State implementation[76] is similarly problematic. First, even if uniform legislation is developed, states might modify the legislation prior to enactment, so the registration and disclosure requirements could vary dramatically. Second, children might not know the state in which their parents obtained gametic material or underwent fertility treatment and so might need to engage in searches of multiple state registries. Third, even if states attempted to coordinate their registry systems, it would require yet another oversight body to ensure the necessary cooperation. Finally, it is more efficient to establish one system for information collection and retention, rather than mandate that all fifty states set up their own systems.

This federal legislation could also include the additional mandates for regulation of the fertility industry discussed in earlier chapters, including limits on the number of offspring from one donor. These limits become more feasible with the existence of a nationally based registry.

Failing to disclose donor information values contract over connection. We imagine that explicit contracts, between gamete providers and gamete banks and between banks and recipients, that guarantee secrecy are more important than the children's need for information and the donors' and recipients' need for closure and connection. We live in a culture that respects kinship based on blood ties.[77] It is perfectly possible and completely desirable to challenge concepts of families based solely on blood by emphasizing intention and nurture, but it is also important to acknowledge that genetic ties may be important for a variety of reasons. Without essentializing the notion of genetic connection, children may still want to know where they came from.

Ultimately, a failure to disclose the identity of gamete providers reinforces the notion of the "exclusive"[78] and traditional family. It suggests that recognizing a child's need for disclosure threatens parental rights, instead of acknowledging the validity of the child's interests and the increasing pertinence of genetic information. And it denies the possibilities for connection that biology can create. The secrecy surrounding adoption and early sperm donation developed during a period of pronatalism, a celebration of the nuclear family and of heterosexual motherhood and a corresponding condemnation of single mothers;[79] gamete use challenges the traditional family by allowing the creation of alternative families. As we rethink what it means to belong to a family, we should rethink outdated approaches based on the stigma of infertility. Allowing for the release of a donor's identity recognizes that biology is not everything but that a child's identity develops through multiple sources. Releasing this information, however, does not change the identity of the child's parents. Disclosure allows only the affected donor-conceived adult to obtain the access he or she deserves.

Conclusion

AFTER TWELVE CHAPTERS about the law of reproductive technology, there remain myriad unanswered questions about daily occurrences in the field. How old is too old? Should sixty-three-year-old women be able to have babies? Should doctors be able to take eggs from kindergarten children undergoing cancer treatment, mature the eggs, and freeze them for when the child wants to become a mother? Should a mother be able to donate eggs for her seven-year-old infertile daughter? Should a fertility clinic's insurance cover reproductive mishaps?

This book has focused on pushing the legal system to respond to these difficult issues. The easy cases—the ones in which known donors and recipients harmoniously work out their own relationships and definitions of themselves as parents, in which recipients and gamete providers agree on a price through a clinic that protects the safety of the gametic material and respects the providers, in which the parties agree on how to dispose of excess embryos—serve as illustrations of the types of transactions and arrangements that the law should facilitate. The hard cases—the ones that form the core of this book—illustrate the need for legal default rules to help people structure their transactions and to provide a safety mechanism for when these transactions fail.

My goal has been to suggest that we think about these issues of parenthood, children's identity, and marketization in an integrated and rigorous manner and not ask all the same questions each time we come across a new issue in the field. The technology is forcing the legal system to decide on the fundamental meaning of family—and of reproduction. We must consider the consequences of the current structure and develop new policy options for all involved in the market, the recipients, donors, industry, and children. This requires a cohesive and coherent approach that addresses the trio of issues together—market, parentage, disclosure—and then allocates regulatory responsibility among the federal and state governments and industry groups.

The technology pressures the law to respond. The difficulty today, as has always been the case in our approach to family law, is determining how existing legal standards and institutions must adapt and expand and change to acknowledge the transformation in how families are created. Decisions on how to regulate the technologies will have a powerful impact on all participants in the fertility market, and they will also profoundly affect the ability to become a parent.

Moving forward requires legal action at the state and federal levels and must preserve a role for industry self-policing as well. The federal government should continue its oversight of the testing of gametic material through national legislation and should implement uniform standards for clinic and gamete-bank certification. Moreover, the federal government should require, similar to what is currently done in the United Kingdom, that fertility clinics provide fuller reports on the use of donor sperm, eggs, and embryo, including the identity of the donors. This information would be maintained by a central registry that would allow donor-conceived children access to identifying information about their donors when the children turn eighteen. Although each state has its own fertility market, federal action is necessary to protect donors and to ensure uniformity by mandating disclosure and setting limits on the number of times an individual can provide eggs or sperm to another person. The fertility industry should continue to recommend adoption and compliance with its guidelines concerning the number of embryos to be transferred. The federal government might choose to allow clinic and bank oversight through industry self-regulatory organizations rather than perform all such certifications through federal inspection.

The states should continue to regulate access and parentage issues, subject (of course) to constitutional guarantees of equality. The danger of federal legislation that would restrict access by nonmarital individuals to the new reproductive technologies is persuasive; allowing states to regulate access should help to ensure diversity in access. Even if one state refused to permit gay, lesbian, or single individuals to use donor eggs, sperm, or embryos, that individual is likely to be able to travel to take advantage of another state's less restrictive access laws. Although I believe that such restrictions violate U.S. constitutional protections for reproductive autonomy, until there is a Supreme Court opinion or congressional legislation guaranteeing this access, states can enact their own laws. As for parentage, there are similar issues concerning the potential for discrimination. Moreover, the long history of family law in the United States also supports the appropriateness of states' enacting their own laws. Model legislation should provide that donors have no rights in the absence of a written agreement, and states can then choose to adopt this legislation or modify it.

Notes

Notes to the Introduction

1. Centers for Disease Control and Prevention, "Assisted Reproductive Technology Success Rates: National Summary and Fertility Reports" (2007), available at http://www.cdc.gov/ART/ART2005, 13.

2. Jürgen Habermas, *The Future of Human Nature* (Malden, MA: Polity, 2003), 24.

3. Ibid., 25. Although I disagree with Habermas's argument that this then should result in "ensur[ing] the contingency or naturalness of procreation" (ibid., 25–26), I agree on the significance of "modernity having become reflective" (ibid., 26). For me, this book is reflecting on what modernity has wrought.

4. See, e.g., Janet Dolgin, *Defining the Family: Law, Technology, and Reproduction in an Uneasy Age* (New York: New York University Press, 1999), 246.

5. National Campaign to Prevent Teen and Unplanned Pregnancy, "Unplanned Pregnancy: Key Data" (2007), http://www.thenationalcampaign.org/resources/pdf/FactSheet-KeyData.pdf.

6. The ASRM has approximately nine thousand members, seven thousand of whom are physicians, and publishes a leading obstetrics/gynecology scholarly journal, *Fertility and Sterility*. See American Society for Reproductive Medicine, "History and Purpose," http://www.asrm.org/history.html.

7. Liza Mundy, *Everything Conceivable: How Assisted Reproduction Is Changing Men, Women, and the World* (New York: Knopf, 2007), 43 (quoting Kim Gandy, then president of NOW); see Claudia Kalb, "Should You Have Your Baby Now?" *Newsweek*, Aug. 13, 2001, p. 40.

8. Nancy Gibbs, "Making Time for a Baby: For Years, Women Have Been Told They Could Wait until 40 or Later to Have Babies; but a New Book Argues That's Way Too Late," *Time*, Apr. 15, 2002, p. 48.

9. Ibid.

10. Lisa Marcus, "Fertility Goddess," *Women's Review of Books* 20 (Feb. 1, 2003): 15.

11. See "About Us," Our Bodies Ourselves website, http://www.ourbodies ourselves.org/about/default.asp.

12. For an articulation of these conflicting positions, see Karey Harwood, *The Infertility Treadmill: Feminist Ethics, Personal Choice, and the Use of Reproductive Technologies* (Chapel Hill: University of North Carolina Press, 2007).

13. Nicole Bartner Graff, "Note: Intercountry Adoption and the Convention on the Rights of the Child: Can the Free Market in Children Be Controlled?" *Syracuse J. Int'l L. & Com.* 27 (Summer 2000): 405, 430.

14. This paragraph is drawn from Naomi Cahn, "Family Issue(s)," *U. Chi. L. Rev.* 61 (1994): 325, 341–345, which reviews Elizabeth Bartholet, *Family Bonds: Adoption and the Politics of Parenting* (Boston: Houghton Mifflin, 1993).

15. For documentation of the following discussion, see Cahn, "Family Issue(s)," 342–43.

16. Harwood, *Infertility Treadmill*, 102, 160.

17. See Martha M. Ertman, "What's Wrong with a Parenthood Market? A New and Improved Theory of Commodification," *N.C. L. Rev.* 82 (2003): 1, 41–42.

Notes to Chapter 1

1. Information about the Johnson family is based on "The Bad Seed," *Dateline NBC* (NBC television broadcast, Mar. 1, 1998); *All Things Considered* (NPR radio broadcast, Aug. 24, 2000).

2. This information is drawn from the California Cryobank website: http://www.cryobank.com/sbanking.cfm?page=2&sub=126.

3. *Johnson v. Superior Court*, 80 Cal. App. 4th 1050, 1057 (2d Dist. 2000), *modified*, 101 Cal. App. 4th 869 (2d Dist. 2002).

4. Julie Marquis, "Gift of Life, Questions of Liability: LA Couple Are Suing a Sperm Bank over Their Daughter's Illness, Claiming the Donor Should Have Been Rejected; They Seek to Know His Identity, but the Bank Is Balking in the Name of Confidentiality," *L.A. Times,* Aug. 9, 1997, p. A1.

5. Cal. Fam. Code § 7613(a) (2007).

6. Quoted in *Johnson*, 80 Cal. App. 4th at 1056.

7. Denise Grady, "Sperm Donor Seen as Source of Disease in 5 Children," *N.Y. Times,* May 19, 2006, p. A16.

8. Denise Grady, "As the Use of Donor Sperm Increases, Secrecy Can Be a Health Hazard," *N.Y. Times,* June 6, 2006, p. F5.

9. *K.M. v. E.G.*, 118 Cal. App. 4th 477, 482 (1st Dist. 2004), *rev'd* 117 P.3d 673 (2005).

10. Most of the facts in this paragraph are drawn from Peggy Orenstein, "The Other Mother," *N.Y. Times Magazine,* July 25, 2004, p. 24.

11. Amanda Paulson, "Modern Life Stretching Family Law," *Christian Science Monitor,* Aug. 10, 2004, sec. USA, p. 1.

12. Maura Dolan, "After Gay Parents Split Up: Custody Can Fall into a Legal Gray Area When Nontraditional Families Dissolve; Courts Haven't Kept Up with Social and Technological Changes," *L.A. Times,* July 22, 2004, p. A1.

13. Cal. Fam. Code § 7613(b) (2007). This provision is adapted from the Uniform Parentage Act (1973).

14. *K.M.,* 117 P.3d at 682.

15. As John Robertson explains, although adoption and foster parenting can provide parenting experiences, only [artificial reproductive techniques] enable one or both partners to have some biologic tie to their children. John A. Robertson, "Assisted Reproductive Technology and the Family," *Hastings L.J.* 47 (Apr. 1996): 911, 912.

16. E.g., Sperm Bank of California, "Comprehensive Donor Screening," http://www.thespermbankofca.org/pages/page.php?pageid=24.

17. Egg Donor Fertility Bank, "Egg Donor Program," http://www.eggdonor-fertilitybank.com/?dl=1.

18. See Cryogenic Laboratories, Inc., a Genetic and IVF Institute Cryobank, "Choosing a Donor," http://www.cryolab.com/Default.aspx?section=selection&page=choosingADonor.

19. Gay Becker, Anneliese Butler, and Robert D. Nachtigall, "Resemblance Talk: A Challenge for Parents Whose Children Were Conceived with Donor Gametes in the US," *Soc. Sci. & Med.* 61 (2005): 1300, 1303.

20. *If These Walls Could Talk 2,* (HBO television broadcast, Mar. 5, 2000).

21. "Egg Donor Ethics," *Religion and Ethics Newsweekly* (PBS television broadcast, Sept. 1, 2006), available at http://www.pbs.org/wnet/religionandethics/week1001/cover.html.

22. See, e.g., David Adamson, "Regulation of Assisted Reproductive Technology in the United States," *Fam. L.Q.* 39 (2005): 727, 728–29. Adamson observes,

> There is a widely held perception that ART is unregulated in the United States. This is entirely inaccurate, since we have more regulation than most countries. There are a number of possibilities why this perception has developed: absence of a socialized health care system with its attendant controls; absence of a single national regulatory body; limited insurance coverage for infertility services; illegal, immoral, irresponsible, and unethical behavior by a few practitioners; minimal federal involvement in reproductive research; rapid scientific advances; different values and ethics perspectives on reproductive medicine; a media presentation of reproductive issues that focuses on harms and sensationalism; and absence of regulation regarding some sensitive issues involving the practice of medicine and personal choices. Regulation in the United States has been, however, very fragmented.

23. See National Conference of State Legislatures, "State Laws on Frozen Embryos" (updated July 2007), http://www.ncsl.org/programs/health/Embryo-Disposition.htm (listing state laws and legislation regarding the use and storage of frozen embryos).

24. Lori Andrews and Nanette Elster, "Regulating Reproductive Technologies," *J. Leg. Med.* 21 (2000): 49.

25. See Nancy Polikoff, "Breaking the Link between Biology and Parental Rights in Planned Lesbian Families: When Semen Donors Are Not Fathers," *Geo. J. Gend. & L.* 2 (2000): 57, 63 n. 28.; Ami S. Jaeger, "Statutory Overview of Collaborative Reproduction," in *Adoption Law and Practice,* ed. Joan Heifetz Hollinger (New York: Matthew Bender, 2008), § 14.05. Most of these statutes address situations involving the obligations of married parents and unknown donors.

26. Helen M. Alvare, "The Case for Regulating Collaborative Reproduction: A Children's Rights Perspective," *Harv. J. on Legis.* 40 (2003): 15 (citing voluntary ASRM guidelines advising that "[d]onors and recipients and their partners should execute documents that define or limit their rights and duties with regard to any offspring.")

27. Ibid., 27 (noting that Florida statute requires donors to relinquish all rights and obligations with respect to resulting children and citing that North Dakota, Oklahoma, Texas, and Virginia make the intended mother the legal mother while relieving the egg donor of all rights and obligations). Laura M. Katers, "Arguing the 'Obvious' in Wisconsin: Why State Regulation of Assisted Reproductive Technology Has Not Come to Pass, and How It Should," 2000 *Wis. L. Rev.* (2000): 448 (stating that the legal relationship of the egg donor to the child is uncertain in most states).

28. Quoted in Jill Callison, "Web Site Offers Chance to Meet and Gain Insight," *Argus Leader,* Sept. 10, 2006, p. 1A.

29. E.g., *Paretta v. Med. Offices for Human Reproduction,* 195 Misc. 2d 568 (N.Y. Misc. 2003); *Andrews v. Keltz,* 2007 N.Y. Slip Op. 27139 (N.Y. Misc. 2007).

30. See Judy Peres, "Setting Limits on High-Tech Baby-Making: The Law Has Not Kept Up with Reproductive Science; Partly Because the Issues Are Difficult to Discuss," *Chicago Tribune,* July 26, 1998, p. C1.

31. E.g., Margaret Radin and Radhika Rao, "Property, Privacy, and the Human Body," *B.U. L. Rev.* 80 (2000): 443.

32. Mary Lyndon Shanley, *Making Babies, Making Families: What Matters Most in an Age of Reproductive Technologies, Surrogacy, Adoption, and Same-Sex and Unwed Parent* (Boston: Beacon, 2002), 149.

33. See George Lakoff, *Moral Politics: How Liberals and Conservatives Think* (Chicago: University of Chicago Press, 2002), 5–7.

34. See, e.g., *Jhordan C. v. Mary K.,* 224 Cal. Rptr. 530 (Ct. App. 1986); *Thomas S. v. Robin Y.,* 618 N.Y.S.2d 356 (1994); see Polikoff, "Breaking the

Link," 57; see Shanley, *Making Babies, Making Families*, ch. 5 (discussing general framework for thinking about the rights of known sperm providers). In one case, for example, a sperm donor sought additional visitation rights beyond those to which he had previously agreed in writing. *In re Matter of William "TT" v. Siobhon "HH,"* NYLJ, Oct. 2, 2000 (Albany Fam. Ct.) (The court awarded the donor additional rights on the basis that the children "were fortunate to have two biological parents [the mother and the father] who love and care for them.") Courts have a tendency to try to find two parents of the opposite sex for children. See Naomi Cahn, "Reframing Child Custody Decisionmaking," *Ohio St. L.J.* 58 (1997): 1.

35. See Polikoff, "Breaking the Link," 57.

36. Martha A. McCarthy and Joanna L. Radbord, "Family Law for Same Sex Couples: Chart(er)ing the Course," *Can. J. Fam. L.* 15 (1998): 101, 130–31 n. 83.

37. Nancy D. Polikoff, "Lesbian and Gay Parenting: The Last Thirty Years," *Mont. L. Rev.* 66 (2005): 51, 54.

38. See David Crary, "Many Adoptees Seeking Open Birth Records," *Charleston Gazette*, Nov. 13, 2000, p. P4C.

39. Nina Burleigh, "Are You My Father? Donor-Inseminated Children," *Redbook* 192 (Mar. 1999): 108.

40. Roy Eccleston, "Dear Dad (Whoever You Are . . .)," *Australian*, Apr. 19, 1998, 12.

41. Mary Linton, "Donor Offspring Believe They Have a Right to Know Their Biological Identity," *Toronto Life*, Sept. 13, 2000.

42. Rainbow Flag Health Services, "Known Donor Insemination," http://www.gayspermbank.com/index1.html.

43. The bank explains that it developed the first "Identity Release Program" and that almost 75 percent of its families have used donors who are in this program. The Sperm Bank of California, "Home," http://thespermbankofca.org/pages/page.php?pageid=1&cat=1.

44. Fertility Plus, "Donor Sperm, Donor Egg, Surrogacy & Embryo Adoption Resources," http://www.fertilityplus.org/faq/donor.html.

45. Pacific Reproductive Services, "The Sperm Bank with the Most 'Willing to Be Known' Donors," http://www.pacrepro.com/index.htm (all five donors in the December 2000 catalogue indicated a willingness to be known).

46. California Cryobank Sperm Bank, "Open Donor Program," available at http://www.cryobank.com/opendonorFAQ.cfm (the bank's "Openness Policy" emphasizes the importance of mutual consent before the release of any information).

47. Jonathan Eig, "An American Family," *Offspring* (Dec./Jan. 2001): 92.

48. Amy Harmon, "Are You My Sperm Donor? Few Clinics Will Say," *N.Y. Times*, Jan. 20, 2006, p. A1.

49. *Guardianship of I.H.*, 834 A.2d 922 (Me. 2003).

50. See Margaret Jane Radin, *Contested Commodities* (Cambridge, MA: Harvard University Press, 1996), 15; Margaret Jane Radin, "Market Inalienability," *Harv. L. Rev.* 100 (1987): 1849.

51. ASRM Ethics Committee, "Financial Compensation of Oocyte Donors," *Fertility & Sterility* 88 (2007): 305, 307.

52. President's Council on Bioethics, "Reproduction and Responsibility: The Regulation of New Biotechnologies" (2004), 171, available at http://www.bioethics.gov/reports/reproductionandresponsibility/_pcbe_final_reproduction_and_responsibility.pdf.

53. E.g., Lori B. Andrews and Lisa Douglass, "Alternative Reproduction," *S. Cal. L. Rev.* 65 (1991): 623, 679–80; Andrews and Elster, "Regulating Reproductive Technologies," 40.

54. See Polikoff, "Breaking the Link," 57.

55. See *Troxel v. Granville*, 530 U.S. 57 (2000); Naomi Cahn, "Models of Family Privacy," *Geo. Wash. L. Rev.* 67 (1999): 1225; cf. Barbara Bennett Woodhouse, "Who Owns the Child? *Meyer* and *Pierce* and the Child as Property," *Wm. & Mary L. Rev.* 33 (1992): 995.

56. Barbara Bennett Woodhouse, "Are You My Mother? Conceptualizing Children Identity Rights In Transracial Adoptions," *Duke J. Gend. L. & Pol'y* 2 (1995): 107, 127–28; see Shanley, *Making Babies, Making Families*, 1–33 (discussing the need to see a child in context).

Notes to Chapter 2

1. This chapter is adapted from chapter 6 of Helena Michie and Naomi Cahn, *Confinements: Fertility and Infertility in Contemporary Culture* (New Brunswick, NJ: Rutgers University Press, 1997), with permission of Helena Michie.

2. Roni Caryn Rabin, "With New Test, Men Can Have At-Home Fertility Screening," *N.Y. Times,* June 4, 2007, p. A12.

3. Genosis, "Genosis PLC Preliminary Results Announcement," press release (May 2007), available at http://cms.genosis.rroom.net/uploads/documents/FINAL%20PRELIMS%20v271.pdf.

4. See Cheryl Miller, "Blogging Infertility," *The New Atlantis*, 19 (2008): 79.

5. Peggy Orenstein, *Waiting for Daisy* (New York: Bloomsbury, 2007), 58.

6. Much of this description is based on a series of patient information booklets available through ASRM, http://www.asrm.org/Literature/patient.html.

7. Advanced Fertility Institute, "Causes of Infertility," http://www.fertilitydocs.com/causesof.html.

8. Carmen De-Navas Walt, Bernadette D. Proctor, and Robert J. Mills, "Income, Poverty and Health Insurance Coverage in the United States: 2003," U.S. Census Bureau, Current Population Reports: Consumer Income (Aug. 2004), 15 (table 5), available at http://www.census.gov/prod/2004pubs/p60-226.pdf.

9. Julie Vargo and Maureen Regan, *A Few Good Eggs: Two Chicks Dish on Overcoming the Insanity of Infertility* (New York: HarperCollins, 2005), 224.

10. Daniel A. Potter and Jennifer S. Hanin, *What to Do When You Can't Get Pregnant: The Complete Guide to All the Technologies for Couples Facing Fertility Problems* (New York: Marlowe, 2005), 35, 123.

11. Ellen Sarasohn Glazer and Evelina Weidman Sterling, *Having Your Baby through Egg Donation* (Indianapolis: Perspectives, 2005), 211, 214.

12. Melinda Beck, Debra Rosenberg, Pat Wingert, and Mary Hager, "The Infertility Trap," *Newsweek*, Apr. 4, 1994, p. 30.

13. See "Welfare = Clomid = WTF?" The Angry Pharmacist weblog, the angrypharmacist.com/archives/2007/01/welfare_clomid.html#comments.

14. Cara Birrittieri, *What Every Woman Should Know about Fertility and Her Biological Clock* (Franklin Lakes, NJ: New Page Books, 2004), 206.

15. Ibid., 19.

16. Quoted in Mark Dagostino, "My Struggle to Have a Baby," *People*, Aug. 13, 2007, p. 79.

17. Carrie Friese, Gay Becker, and Robert D. Nachtigall, "Rethinking the Biological Clock: Eleventh-Hour Moms, Miracle Moms and the Meanings of Age-Related Infertility," *Soc. Sci. & Med.* 63 (2006): 1550.

18. Ibid.

Notes to Chapter 3

1. Steven Kotler, "The God of Sperm: In an Industry Veiled in Secrecy, a Powerful L.A. Sperm Peddler Shapes the Nation's Rules on Disease, Genetics—and Accidental Incest," *L.A. Weekly*, Sept. 26, 2007, available at http://www.laweekly.com/news/news/the-god-of-sperm/17290/.

2. Eric Surrey, "What Is SART?" Society for Assisted Reproductive Technology website, http://www.sart.org/WhatIsSART.html.

3. Douglas T. Carrell, Deborah Cartmill, Kirtly Jones, Harry Hatasaka, and Matthew Peterson, "Prospective, Randomized, Blinded Evaluation of Donor Semen Quality Provided by Seven Commercial Sperm Banks," *Fertility & Sterility* 78 (July 2002): 16, 20.

4. M. Cho and F. Licciardi, "Egg Donors Significantly Under-Report Their Weights," *Fertility & Sterility* 86, supp. 1 (Sept. 2006): S138.

5. Larry Palmer, "Book Reviews," *Jurimetrics J.* 38 (Winter 1998): 223, 234–35.

6. Barry Stephen Verkauf, "Artificial Insemination: Progress, Polemics, and Confusion: An Appraisal of Current Medico-Legal Status," *Hous. L. Rev.* 3 (Winter 1966): 277, 282.

7. Gaia Bernstein, "The Socio-Legal Acceptance of New Technologies: A Close Look at Artificial Insemination," *Wash. L. Rev.* 77 (2002): 1035, 1039–41.

8. Ibid., 1046–48.

9. Wilfred J. Finegold, *Artificial Insemination* (Springfield, IL: Charles C. Thomas, 1964), 5.

10. Ibid., 6; Center for Reproductive Medicine, "History 1500–1900," http://www.repromed.org.uk/history/history_1500.htm.

11. Andrew Chang, "Anonymous Sperm Donation in an Era of Technology, Bioethics, and Business," *Yale J. Pub. Health* 3 (Spring 2006): 3, available at http://www.yaleph.com/archive/vol3no3/article3.html.

12. Bernstein, "The Socio-Legal Acceptance of New Technologies," 1061.

13. "Substitute Fathers," *Newsweek* (Sept. 1943): 87, 88.

14. Bernstein, "The Socio-Legal Acceptance of New Technologies," 1067.

15. Ibid., 1071.

16. David Plotz, *The Genius Factor: The Curious History of the Nobel Prize Sperm Bank* (New York: Random House, 2005), 167–68.

17. Bernstein, "The Socio-Legal Acceptance of New Technologies," 1075–76.

18. Alfred Koerner, "Medicolegal Considerations in Artificial Insemination," *La. L. Rev.* 8 (1948): 484, 491.

19. Ibid., 490.

20. California Cryobank Sperm Bank, "Sperm Banking History," http://www.cryobank.com/sbanking.cfm?page=2&sub=126 (accessed Oct. 2, 2007).

21. Ibid.

22. U.S. Congress, Office of Technology Assessment (OTA), "Artificial Insemination: Practice in the United States: Summary of a 1987 Survey—Background Paper," OTA-13P-BA-48 (Washington, DC: U.S. Government Printing Office, Aug. 1988), available at http://www.princeton.edu/~ota/disk2/1988/8804/8804.PDF.

23. Ibid., 4.

24. Karen M. Ginsberg, "Note: FDA Approved? A Critique of the Artificial Insemination Industry in the United States," *U. Mich. J. L. Reform* 30 (Summer 1997): 823, 826 (although the number of sperm banks used is not specified, "[b]y 1993, more than 80,000 women were undergoing AI each year, resulting in the conception of more than 30,000 babies").

25. OTA, "Artificial Insemination," 11.

26. Ibid., 53–54.

27. Ibid., 54–55.

28. Ibid., 55.

29. See David Plotz, "Collected 'Seed,'" *Slate* (2001–2005), http://www.slate.com/id/2119808/.

30. See Liza Mundy, *Everything Conceivable: How Assisted Reproduction Is Changing Men, Women, and the World* (New York: Knopf, 2007), 112.

31. Finegold, *Artificial Insemination*, 25. Alan Guttmacher wrote the introduction.

32. Ibid., 40.

33. Ibid., 33–35.

34. Centers for Disease Control, "2005 ART Report: 2005 ART Cycle Profile," fig. 29, available at http://www.cdc.gov/ART/ART2005.

35. "Golden Eggs: Drowning in Credit-Card Debt and Student Loans, Young Women Are Selling Their Eggs for Big Payoffs; But Can They Really Make the Right Medical and Moral Decisions When They're Tempted with $15,000?" *Boston Globe Magazine*, June 25, 2006, p. 18; CDC, "2005 ART Report: 2005 ART Cycle Profile."

36. ASRM Ethics Committee, "Financial Compensation of Oocyte Donors," *Fertility & Sterility* 88 (2007): 305.

37. James W. Akin, Katrina A. Bell, Diana Thomas, and Jeffrey Boldt, "Initial Experience with a Donor Egg Bank," *Fertility & Sterility* 88 (Aug. 2007): 497, 500.

38. Extend Fertility, "Set Your Own Biological Clock," http://www.extendfertility.com/why/.

39. Aina Hunter, "Later Baby," *Village Voice*, Dec. 13, 2005, p. 14.

40. Rene Almeling, "Selling Genes, Selling Gender: Egg Agencies, Sperm Banks, and the Medical Market in Genetic Material," *Amer. Soc. Rev.* 72 (June 2007): 319.

41. Sharon M. Covington and William E. Gibbons, "What Is Happening to the Price of Eggs?" *Fertility & Sterility* 87 (2007): 1001.

42. ASRM, "Psychological Assessment of Gamete Donors and Recipients," *Fertility & Sterility* 77, supp. 5 (June 2002): 11.

43. This description draws on my own analysis of egg and sperm banks as well as that of Almeling, "Selling Genes, Selling Gender," 319.

44. Natalie Adsuar, Julianne E. Zweifel, Elizabeth A. Pritts, et al., "Assessment of Wishes Regarding Disposition of Oocytes and Embryo Management among Ovum Donors in an Anonymous Egg Donation Program," *Fertility & Sterility* 84 (Nov. 2005): 1513.

45. Almeling, "Selling Genes, Selling Gender," 334.

46. Finegold, *Artificial Insemination*, 67.

47. Bernstein, "The Socio-Legal Acceptance of New Technologies," 1069 (citing Verkauf, "Artificial Insemination," 298; Bernstein focuses on the parenthood legal issues and the uncertainty regarding the family.)

48. U.S. Congress, Office of Technology Assessment (OTA), "Infertility: Medical and Social Choices," OTA-BA-358 (Washington, DC: U.S. Government Printing Office, May 1988), 15–31. OTA also issued an extensive summary of the research underlying the report, which included an analysis of questionnaires from more than fifteen hundred physicians and from fifteen commercial sperm banks. OTA, "Artificial Insemination."

49. See Gail H. Javitt and Kathy Hudson, "Public Health at Risk: Failure in Oversight of Genetic Testing Laboratory," Genetics and Public Policy Center

report, available at http://www.dnapolicy.org/images/reportpdfs/PublicHealth AtRiskFinalWithCover.pdf.

50. *American Association of Bioanalysts v. Shalala,* 2000 U.S. Dist. LEXIS 2603 (D.C. 2000).

51. President's Council on Bioethics, "Reproduction and Responsibility: The Regulation of New Biotechnologies" (2004), ch. 2, available at http://www.bio-ethics.gov/reports/reproductionandresponsibility.

52. Judith Daar, "ART and the Search for Perfectionism: On Selecting Gender, Genes, and Gametes," *J. Gend, Race & Just.* 9 (2005): 241, 254–55.

53. 42 U.S.C. § 263a-2(i) (2007) (restricting both the federal government and the states from establishing, as part of the certification program, "any regulation, standard, or requirement which has the effect of exercising supervision or control over the practice of medicine in assisted reproduction technology programs"); see also Margaret Foster Riley and Richard A. Merrill, "Regulating Reproductive Genetics: A Review of American Bioethics Commissions and Comparison to the British Human Fertilization and Embryology Authority," *Colum. Sci. & Tech. L. Rev.* 6 (2005): 1, 4.

54. Lori Andrews and Nanette Elster, "Regulating Reproductive Technologies," *J. Leg. Med.* 21 (2000): 35; *Fed. Reg.* 64 (July 21, 1999): 39374.

55. Centers for Disease Control, "Implementation of the Fertility Clinic Success Rate and Certification Act of 1992: A Model Program for the Certification of Embryo Laboratories," *Fed. Reg.* 64 (July 21, 1999): 39374.

56. President's Council on Bioethics, "Reproduction and Responsibility," 150.

57. 42 U.S.C. § 263a-1 (2007).

58. Centers for Disease Control, "2003 Assisted Reproductive Technology (ART) Report: Commonly Asked Questions," http://www.cdc.gov/ART/ART2003/faq.htm#4.

59. Nanette R. Elster, "ART for the Masses? Racial and Ethnic Inequality in Assisted Reproductive Technologies," *DePaul J. Health Care L.* 9 (2006): 719, 723.

60. *Fed. Reg.* 70, no. 20 (Feb. 1, 2005): 5187–88, available at http://a257.g.akamaitech.net/7/257/2422/01jan20051800/edocket.access.gpo.gov/2005/pdf/05-1787.pdf.

61. Information about Westat is available on its website, http://www.westat.com/about/index.cfm.

62. Centers for Disease Control, "Assisted Reproductive Technology Success Rates: National Summary and Fertility Clinic Reports" (2006), 5, available at http://ftp.cdc.gov/pub/Publications/art/2004ART508.pdf.

63. Ibid., 499.

64. Ibid.

65. There is one other possibility for ensuring that clinics' claims match their practices. The Federal Trade Commission, which has the authority to monitor marketing claims, has sporadically investigated fertility clinic advertisements.

66. Surrey, "What Is SART?"

67. Valerie L. Baker, Marina O. Gvakharia, Heather M. Rone, James R. Manalad, and G. David Adamson, "Economic Cost for Implementation of the Food and Drug Administration 21 Code of Federal Regulations Part 1271 (FDA 21 CFR Part 1271) in an Egg Donor Program," *Fertility & Sterility* 86, no. 3 (Sept. 2006): S178–79.

68. Betsy Streisand, "Who's Your Daddy? Sperm Donors Rely on Anonymity: New Donor Offspring (and Their Moms) Are Breaking Down the Walls of Privacy," *U.S. News & World Report*, Feb. 13, 2006, p. 53.

69. Helen M. Alvare, "The Case for Regulating Collaborative Reproduction: A Children's Rights Perspective," *Harv. J. on Legis.* 40 (2003): 1, 28.

70. 21 C.F.R. § 1271.75 (2007).

71. Ibid., §§ 1271.85(a) and (c).

72. Ibid., § 1271.80(c).

73. Ibid., § 1271.85(d).

74. Ibid., § 1271.60 (a).

75. N. Garrido, J.L. Zuzuarregui, M. Meseguer, et al., "Sperm and Oocyte Donor Selection and Management: Experience of a 10-Year Follow-Up of More than 2100 Candidates," *Human Reprod.* 17 (Dec. 2002): 3142, available at http://humrep.oxfordjournals.org/cgi/content/full/17/12/3142.

76. 21 C.F.R. § 1271.90(a)(2).

77. Ibid., § 1271.75(e).

78. Ibid., § 1271.170.

79. Ibid., § 1271.160.

80. Ibid., § 1271.47.

81. Ibid., § 1271.47(c).

82. Food and Drug Administration, "Guidance for Industry: Eligibility Determination for Donors of Human Cells, Tissues, and Cellular and Tissue-Based Products (HCT/Ps)" (2007), available at http://www.fda.gov/cber/gdlns/tissdonor.pdf.

83. Leland Traiman, "Creating Life? Examining the Legal, Ethical, and Medical Issues of Assisted Reproductive Technologies: Guidelines but No Guidance: GaySpermBank.com vs. FDA," *J. Gend., Race & Just.* 9 (Spring 2006): 613, 619–620. This section is drawn from a paper prepared by Rachel Hull.

84. 21 C.F.R. § 1271.75(d).

85. FDA, "Guidance for Industry," 15–16.

86. "Gays to Be Banned as Sperm Donors," Associated Press, May 5, 2005, available at http://www.365gay.com/newscon05/05/05050sperm.htm (quoting Leland Traiman).

87. Quoted in Marc Kaufman, "Gay Groups Assail Sperm Bank Rule," *Washington Post*, May 7, 2005, p. A2.

88. See Eugene Volokh, "Sperm Banks and Gays," The Volokh Conspiracy weblog, May 16, 2005, http://volokh.com/posts/1116248831.shtml.

89. Michael Fumento, "Sperm Donation a Matter of Health, Not Rights," Michael Fumento website, May 19, 2005, http://www.fumento.com/disease/sperm-donor.html.

90. "Gays to Be Banned."

91. Kotler, "The God of Sperm."

92. See Charles P. Kindregan, Jr., and Maureen McBrien, "Embryo Donation: Unresolved Legal Issues in the Transfer of Surplus Cryopreserved Embryos," *Vill. L. Rev.* 49 (2004): 169; "Changing Realities of Parenthood: The Law's Response to the Evolving American Family and Emerging Reproductive Technologies," *Harv. L. Rev.* 116 (May 2003): 2052, 2068–69; Mary Lyndon Shanley, "Collaboration and Commodification in Assisted Procreation: Reflections on an Open Market and Anonymous Donation in Human Sperm and Eggs," *L. & Soc'y Rev.* 36 (2002): 257.

93. Dawn R. Swink and J. Brad Reich, "Caveat Vendor: Potential Property, Paternity, and Product Liability Online," *BYU L. Rev.* 857 (2007): 8743–44.

94. See Lisa Hird Chung, "Free Trade in Human Reproductive Cells: A Solution to Procreative Tourism and the Unregulated Internet," *Minn. J. Int'l L.* 15 (2006): 263, 284–85.

95. RSA § 168-B: 13 (2007); Alvare, "The Case for Regulating Collaborative Reproduction," 31; Alexander N. Hecht, "The Wild, Wild West: Inadequate Regulation of Assisted Reproductive Technology," *Hous. J. Health L. & Pol'y* 1 (2001): 227, 240–41 (reporting that Delaware, Georgia, Illinois, Maryland, and Oklahoma require only HIV testing while California, Florida, and Indiana legislatures also require screening for syphilis and hepatitis).

96. Hecht, "Wild, Wild West," 243.

97. Andrews and Elster, "Regulating Reproductive Technologies," 51.

98. Weldon E. Havins and James J. Dalessio, "The Ever-Widening Gap between the Science of Artificial Reproductive Technology and the Laws Which Govern That Technology," *DePaul L. Rev.* 48 (1999): 825, 846.

99. Va. Code Ann. § 54.1-2971.1 (2007)

100. Conn. Gen. Stat. § 19a-32d(c)(1)–(2) (2007); Cal. Health & Safety Code § 125315 (a)–(b) (2007); Mass. Ann. Laws ch. 111L, § 4(a) (2007); N.J. Stat. Ann. § 26: 2Z-2(b)(1) (2007).

101. Conn. Gen. Stat. § 19a-32d(c)(2); Cal. Health & Safety Code § 125315 (b); Mass. Ann. Laws ch. 111L, § 4(a); N.J. Stat. Ann. § 26: 2Z-2(b)(2).

102. A.L.M. GL ch. 111L § 4 (2007).

103. Havins and Dalessio, "The Ever-Widening Gap," 846.

104. Alvare, "The Case for Regulating Collaborative Reproduction," 29.

105. 18 Pa.C.S. § 3213(e) (2007).

106. Alvare, "The Case for Regulating Collaborative Reproduction," 31.

107. Ibid., 21.

108. Ibid., 31.

109. Chung, "Free Trade in Human Reproductive Cells," 281.

110. N.H. R.S.A. 168-B: 19 (2007).

111. COMAR § 10.50.01.08. It seems that the code of Maryland regulations applies the same standards to donated eggs.

112. La. R.S. § 40:1062.1(A) (2008); 16 Del. C. § 2801(a) (2008).

113. O.R.C. Ann. § 3111.93 (2007).

114. Idaho Code § 39-5402 (2007) ("Only physicians . . . and persons under their supervision may select artificial insemination donors and perform artificial insemination.")

115. KRS § 311.281 (2007).

116. COMAR § 10.50.01.04(B) (2007).

117. Ibid., § 10.50.01.08.

118. Ibid.

119. Surrey, "What Is SART?"; see David Adamson, "Regulation of Assisted Reproductive Technology in the United States," *Fam. L.Q.* 39 (2005): 727, 732–33 (discussing the accrediting bodies; "two-thirds of SART programs are accredited through this [College of American Pathologists] program. The other one-third are accredited through New York State or through the Joint Commission on Accreditation of Healthcare Organizations (JCAHO)").

120. CDC, "Assisted Reproductive Technology Success Rates," 88.

121. Surrey, "What Is SART?"

122. American Association of Tissue Banks, "Accreditation," http://www.aatb. org/content.asp?contentid=430; American Association of Tissue Banks, "Accreditation Policies" (Nov. 2007), 5, available at http://aatb.timberlakepublishing.com/files/2007accreditationpolicies.pdf.

123. Rachel Hull, "Little Swimmers, Big Problems: The Uncertain State of Sperm Bank Regulations," unpublished paper (2006), 17. For information on AATB certification, see AATB, "Accreditation by Operation," http://www.aatb.org/content. asp?pl=430&sl=458&contentid=655; Denise Grady, "As the Use of Donor Sperm Increases, Secrecy Can Be a Health Hazard," *N.Y. Times,* June 6, 2006, p. F5.

124. American Association of Tissue Banks, "Final Approved Standards Changes for 11th Edition as Amended," *2006 Bulletin,* 06-44, available at http:// www.aatb.org/content.asp?pl=616&sl=621&contentid=690.

125. Northwest Andrology and Cryobank, "Donor Standards," http://www. nwcryobank.com/donor_standards.html.

126. Fairfax Cryobank, "Sperm Bank Comparison," http://www.fairfax-cryobank.com/SpermBankComparisons.aspx.

127. Fairfax Cryobank, "Quality Assurance," http://www.fairfaxcryobank. com/qualassur.aspx?menu=2&turn=on.

128. Practice Committee, ASRM, "Revised Minimum Standards for Practices Offering Assisted Reproductive Technologies," *Fertility & Sterility* 80 (Dec. 2003): 1556.

129. Evan Pondel, "A Booming Baby Business," *Daily News of L.A.*, Apr. 23, 2006, p. B1.

130. "Sperm Donors Valued Less than Egg Donors," *Science Daily*, May 26, 2007, available at http://www.sciencedaily.com/releases/2007/05/070525204143.htm.

131. Cryogenic Laboratories, "Medical/Genetic Screening," http://www.cryolab.com/Default.aspx?section=selection&page=screening.

132. Daniel J. Penofsky, "Sperm Bank Liability for Donor Semen Transmitted AIDS," *Amer. Juris. Proof of Facts* 25 (2007): 1.

133. Joshua Kleinfeld, "Comment: Tort Law and In Vitro Fertilization: The Need for Legal Recognition of 'Procreative Injury,'" *Yale L.J.* 115 (Oct. 2005): 237, 242.

134. *United States v. Jacobson*, 1993 U.S. App. LEXIS 22534 1, 15 (4th Cir. 1993), cert. denied, 1994 U.S. LEXIS 3343.

135. Cal. Penal Code § 367g (2008).

136. LEXIS search, Jan. 22, 2008 (statute is not annotated with any reported cases).

137. See Susan L. Crockin, "Reproductive Genetics: Conceiving New Wrongs?" *Sexuality, Reprod. & Menopause* 3 (2005): 37, available at http://www.dnapolicy.org/resources/ReproGenConceivingWrongs.pdf.

138. The following discussion is based on *Harnicher v. Univ. of Utah Med. Ctr.*, 962 P.2d 67 (Utah 1998).

139. Ibid., 72.

140. *Perry-Rogers v. Obasaju*, 723 N.Y.S.2d 28, 29 (App. Div. 2001).

141. *Paretta v. Medical Offices for Human Reproduction*, 760 N.Y.S.2d 639, 646–47 (Sup. Ct. 2003).

142. *Andrews v. Keltz*, 2007 N.Y. Misc. LEXIS 2229 (S.Ct. 2007).

143. Restatement (Second) of Torts § 46 cmt. b (1965).

144. See Robert Rhee, "A Principled Solution for Negligent Infliction of Emotional Distress Claims," *Ariz. St. L.J.* 36 (2004): 805, 829–30.

145. Fred Norton, "Note: Assisted Reproduction and the Frustration of Genetic Affinity: Interest, Injury, and Damages," *NYU L. Rev.* 74 (June 1999): 793; Kleinfeld, "Tort Law and In Vitro Fertilization," 237.

146. Kleinfeld, "Tort Law and In Vitro Fertilization," 244.

147. Norton, "Assisted Reproduction and the Frustration of Genetic Affinity," 815.

148. This discussion is drawn from *Jeter v. Mayo Clinic Arizona*, 121 P.3d 1256 (Ariz. App. 2005); and Carol Sowers, "Court Rules in Embryo Lawsuit: Couples Can Sue for Egg Damages," *Arizona Republic*, Dec. 8, 2005, p. 1B.

149. Kleinfeld, "Tort Law and In Vitro Fertilization," 241.

150. Felice J. Freyer, "State Review Finds No Misuse of Embryos," *Providence Journal-Bulletin*, Oct. 7, 1995, p. 1A.

151. Andrew R. LaBarbera, "Mishaps: How and Why Mistakes Occur in the Embryology Lab and How to Prevent Them," PowerPoint presentation (2007), available at http://www.ialsnet.org/documents/ASRM/LaBarbera_PPT.pdf.

152. Ibid.; Ethics Committee of the ASRM, "Disclosure of Medical Errors Involving Gametes and Embryos," *Fertility & Sterility* 86 (Sept. 2006): 513.

153. Ibid.

Notes to Chapter 4

1. *Guardianship of I.H.*, 834 A.2d 922 (Me. 2003).

2. See Richard Storrow, "Rescuing Children from the Marriage Movement: The Case against Marital Status Discrimination in Adoption and Assisted Reproduction," *U.C. Davis L. Rev.* 39 (2006) 305, 311–13.

3. *Tioga County v. South Creek Township*, 75 Pa. 433, 436–37 (1874).

4. William Blackstone, *Commentaries on the Laws of England* (Chicago: University of Chicago Press, 1979), 457.

5. See Lynne Marie Kohm, "Marriage and the Intact Family: The Significance of *Michael H. v. Gerald D.*," *Whittier L. Rev.* 22 (2000): 327, 335.

6. Harry D. Krause, "Bringing the Bastard into the Great Society: A Proposed Uniform Act on Legitimacy," *Tex. L. Rev.* 44 (1966): 829, 844–45 n. 34.

7. "Comment: The Law of Adoption," *Amer. L. Rev.* 9 (1874): 74, 77 (quoting Mass. Gen. Laws, ch. 110, 7 (1851).

8. The status of children changed dramatically during the nineteenth century. See, e.g., Janet Dolgin, "Transforming Childhood: Apprenticeship in American Law," *New Engl. L. Rev.* 31 (1997): 1113, 1163.

9. Janet Hopson Dickson, "Comment: The Emerging Rights of Adoptive Parents: Substance or Specter?" *UCLA L. Rev.* 38 (Apr. 1991): 917, 938.

10. Burton Z. Sokoloff, "Antecedents of American Adoption," *The Future of Children* 3, no. 1 (1993): 18, available at http://www.futureofchildren.org/usr_doc/vol3no1ART1.PDF.

11. See ibid., 23 (agencies tried for the "best fit" between parent and child through matching practices).

12. See Naomi Cahn, "Perfect Substitutes or the Real Thing?" *Duke L.J.* 52 (2003): 1077, 1152; E. Wayne Carp, ed., *Adoption in America: Historical Perspectives* (Ann Arbor: University of Michigan Press, 2002), 126.

13. Cheryl Wetzstein, "Qualms Temper Americans' Favorable View of Adoption: Demographics Have Big Effect on People's Views," *Washington Times*, Nov. 19, 1997, p. A2.

14. *Hood v. McGehee*, 237 U.S. 611 (1915).

15. *Brown v. Finley*, 157 Ala. 424 (1908); *Lingen v. Lingen*, 45 Ala. 410 (1871).

16. *In re Edwards Estate*, 273 N.W.2d 118 (S.D. 1978).

17. *MacCallum v. Seymour*, 686 A.2d 935 (Vt. 1996).

18. Rick Pyper, "Comment: Why Mississippi Should Give Adopted Children the Same Intestate Succession Rights Which Natural-Born Children Enjoy," *Miss. L.J.* 64 (Fall 1994): 201, 202.

19. Ralph C. Brashier, "Children and Inheritance in the Nontraditional Family," *Utah L. Rev.* (1996): 93, 153–54 n. 199; Jan Ellen Rein, "Symposium: The Winds of Change in Wills, Trusts and Estate Planning Law: Relatives by Blood, Adoption, and Association: Who Should Get What and Why," *Vand. L. Rev.* 37 (May 1984): 711, 731–33.

20. Colo. Rev. Stat. § 15-11-103(6) (2007).

21. 20 Pa. Cons. Stat. § 2108 (2007). See also statutes listed in Brashier, "Children and Inheritance in the Nontraditional Family," 153 n. 195.

22. Me. Rev. Stat. Ann. Tit. 18-A, § 2-109(1) (2007).

23. Unif. Probate Code § 2-114(b)(2006), available at http://www.law.upenn.edu/bll/archives/ulc/upc/final2005.htm.

24. Walter Wadlington, "The Adopted Child and Intra-Family Marriage Prohibitions," *Va. L. Rev.* 49 (1963): 478.

25. See, e.g., *State of Missouri ex rel. Miesner v. Geile*, 747 S.W.2d 757 (Mo. Ct. App. 1988).

26. *Bagniardi v. Hartnett*, 81 Misc. 2d 323 (N.Y. 1975).

27. Ibid. (citing *Matter of Enderle Marriage License*, 1 Pa. D&C2d 114 (Ct. Com. Pl. 1954)).

28. 493 N.E.2d 1265 (Ind. Ct. App. 1986); see also *State v. Burney*, 455 A.2d 1335 (Conn. 1983). But see *Bohall v. State*, in which the Indiana Supreme Court upheld an incest conviction against a man who sexually molested his biological daughter, who had been adopted by another family. 546 N.E.2d 1214 (Ind. 1989).

29. On the other hand, in *State v. Sharon Holden*, a Delaware court allowed an incest prosecution to proceed against a half brother and half sister who had the same mother. 429 A.2d 1321 (Super. Ct. 1981). The sister had been adopted when she was ten days old, and her brother had been raised as a ward of the state; although the adoption statute eliminated any ties between the biological parents and the children, the blood relationship continued. Ibid.

30. *State v. Lee*, 17 So. 2d 277 (Miss. 1944);

31. *State v. Bale*, 512 N.W.2d 164 (S.D. 1994).

32. Jacquelyn Mitchard, "Legal Squabble over Baby Tears Family Apart," *Chattanooga Times*, Feb. 21, 1998, p. D6.

33. Mary Beth Murphy, "Blood Relative Adoption Ruling Is Overturned," *Milwaukee Journal Sentinel*, Sept. 9, 1998, sec. News, p. 1.

34. U.S. Congress, Office of Technology Assessment (OTA), "Artificial Insemination: Practice in the United States: Summary of a 1987 Survey—Background Paper," OTA-13P-BA-48 (Washington, DC: U.S. Government

Printing Office, Aug. 1988)," 10, available at http://www.princeton.edu/~ota/disk2/1988/8804/8804.PDF.

35. *Gursky v. Gursky*, 39 Misc. 2d 1083, 1086 (N.Y. 1963).

36. *Orford v. Orford*, 49 Ont.L.R. 15, 58 D.L.R. 251 (1921).

37. Alfred Koerner, "Medicolegal Considerations in Artificial Insemination," *La. L. Rev.* 8 (1948): 484, 494.

38. Ann T. Lamport, "The Genetics of Secrecy in Adoption, Artificial Insemination, and In Vitro Fertilization," *Amer. J. L. & Med.* 14 (1988): 109, 116.

39. Blackstone, *Commentaries on the Laws of England*, 447.

40. *Levy v. Louisiana*, 391 U.S. 68 (1968).

41. *Glona v. American Guarantee & Liability Ins. Co.*, 391 U.S. 73 (1968).

42. *Levy*, 391 U.S. at 72.

43. See *In re Estate of Jensen*, 162 N.W.2d 861 (N.D. 1968) (stating right of illegitimate descendants to take property through their mother in intestacy); *R v. F.*, 273 A.2d 808 (N.J. Juv. & Dom. Rel. Ct. 1971) (holding that visitation rights must be extended to putative father of illegitimate children); *Storm v. None*, 291 N.Y.S. 513 (N.Y. Fam. Ct. 1968) (ruling on illegitimate child's right to support from his father).

44. Longshoremen's and Harbor Worker's Compensation Act: *Ingalls Shipbuilding Co. v. Neuman*, 322 F. Supp. 1229, 1244–45 (S.D. Miss. 1970); Federal Employees Group Life Insurance Act: *Haley v. Metropolitan Life Ins. Co.*, 434 S.W.2d 7 (Mo. App. 1968); Jones Act: *Herbert v. Petroleum Pipe Inspectors, Inc.*, 396 F.2d 237 (5th Cir. 1968); Servicemen's Group Life Insurance Act: *Prudential Ins. Co. v. Willis*, 182 S.E.2d 420 (1971); Copyright Act: *Jerry Vogel Music Co. v. Edward B. Marks Music Co.*, 425 F.2d 834 (2nd Cir. 1969).

45. Harry D. Krause, "The Uniform Parentage Act," *Fam. L.Q.* 8 (1974): 1.

46. Harry D. Krause, "Bringing the Bastard into the Great Society: A Proposed Uniform Act on Legitimacy," *Tex. L. Rev.* 44 (1966): 829.

47. Ibid., 833.

48. Unif. Parentage Act, prefatory note (1973), available at http://www.law.upenn.edu/bll/archives/ulc/fnact99/1990s/upa7390.htm.

49. Krause, "The Uniform Parentage Act," 1.

50. Unif. Parentage Act § 2 (1973).

51. Ibid., § 4(a)(1), § 4(a)(4).

52. Krause, "The Uniform Parentage Act," 12.

53. Unif. Parentage Act, § 5 (1973).

54. Ibid. See comment to § 5.

55. Alabama, California, Colorado, Delaware, Hawaii, Illinois, Kansas, Minnesota, Missouri, Montana, Nevada, New Jersey, New Mexico, North Dakota, Ohio, Rhode Island, Washington, and Wyoming. See Table of Jurisdictions Where Act Has Been Adopted, Uniform Parentage Act (1973), 9B U.L.A. 378 (2001).

56. S.J. Ventura and C.A. Bachrach, "Nonmarital Childbearing in the United States, 1940–99," *National Vital Statistics Reports* 48, no. 16 (2000): 2, available at http://www.cdc.gov/nchs/data/nvsr/nvsr48/nvs48_16.pdf; Centers for Disease Control, National Center for Health Statistics, Health E-Stats, "Births: Preliminary Data for 2005 Tables for E-Stat," http://www.cdc.gov/nchs/data/hestat/prelimbirths05_tables.pdf#1, table 3.

57. National Conference of Commissioners on Uniform State Law, "A Few Facts about the . . . Uniform Status of Children of Assisted Conception Act," http://www.nccusl.org/Update/uniformact_factsheets/uniformacts-fs-uscaca.asp. See also Unif. Parentage Act, Art. 7, § 706 (amended 2002) (stating that the two states took opposite approaches: "Virginia chose to regulate such agreements, while North Dakota opted to void them"), available at http://www.law.upenn.edu/bll/archives/ulc/upa/final2002.htm.

58. See Unif. Parentage Act, Art. 5.

59. Ibid., Art. 7 prefatory comment.

60. Ibid., Art. 3a (1997 draft), available at http://www.law.upenn.edu/bll/archives/ulc/upa/par1197.htm.

61. Ibid., Art. 7, § 704 (2000), available at http://www.law.upenn.edu/bll/archives/ulc/upa/upasty1020.htm.

62. Ibid., Art. 7, § 706 (amended 2002).

63. Ibid., prefatory note.

64. Ibid.

65. Ibid. See John J. Sampson, Preface to the Amendments of the Uniform Parentage Act (2002), *Fam. L.Q.* 37 (2003): 1, 2.

66. Sampson, Preface to the Amendments, 2.

67. See ibid., 3.

68. Unif. Parentage Act, Art. 7, §§ 703–4.

69. Ibid., Art. 1 § 102(4) and Art. 7 § 702.

70. Ibid., Art. 7, § 702 comment.

71. Delaware, North Dakota, Oklahoma, Texas, Utah, Washington, and Wyoming. See National Conference of Commissioners on Uniform State Law, "A Few Facts about the Uniform Parentage Act," http://www.nccusl.org/Update/uniformact_factsheets/uniformacts-fs-upa.asp (accessed Jan. 22, 2008).

72. Unif. Parentage Act (amended 2002), Art. 7 § 702 prefatory comment.

73. Ibid., Art. 7 § 704.

Notes to Chapter 5

1. When state laws have not addressed these issues or are ambiguous, judges have sometime decided cases that significantly affect the rights of donors, recipients, and children. Although cases from a state's highest court are binding on all other courts in that state, they (of course) do not control decisions in other states.

2. Lori Andrews and Nanette Elster, "Regulating Reproductive Technologies," *J. Leg. Med.* 21 (2000): 35, 49.

3. See generally Kira Horstmeyer, "Note: Putting Your Eggs in Someone Else's Basket: Inserting Uniformity into the Uniform Parentage Act's Treatment of Assisted Reproduction," *Wash. & Lee L. Rev.* 64 (2007): 671, 684–91 (discussing five categories of states).

4. E.g., *E.G. v. K.M,* 37 Cal. 4th 130 (Cal. 2005); *Serpico v. Urso,* 469 N.E.2d 355 (Ill. App. Ct. 1984).

5. Ohio requires both husband and wife to consent in writing before the woman can be inseminated with donor sperm. ORC Ann § 3111.92 (2006). In Kansas, the consent of a husband and wife can be filed with the court, and it is treated just like consent to an adoption:

> The consent provided for in this act shall be executed and acknowledged by both the husband and wife and the person who is to perform the technique, and an original thereof may be filed under the same rules as adoption papers in the district court of the county in which such husband and wife reside. The written consent so filed shall not be open to the general public, and the information contained therein may be released only to the persons executing such consent, or to persons having a legitimate interest therein as evidenced by a specific court order.

K.S.A. § 23-130 (2006).

6. The following facts are drawn from *Alexandria S. v. Pacific Fertility Medical Center, Inc.,* 55 Cal. App. 4th 110 (1997).

7. 10 Okl. Stat. Ann. §§ 552–53 (2007).

8. Conn. Gen. Stat. §§ 45a-772–73 (2007).

9. N.J. Stat. § 9: 17-44b (2007).

10. John Bowe, "Gay Donor or Gay Dad?" *N.Y. Times,* Nov. 19, 2006, sec. 6, p. 66.

11. See *In re K.M.H,* 169 P.3d 1025 (Kan. 2007).

12. *In re Sullivan,* 157 S.W.3d 911, 913 (Tex. Ct. App. 2005).

13. Michael Serazio, "Seminal Case: How Donated Sperm Spawned a Child," *Houston Press,* Mar. 10, 2005, available at http://www.houstonpress.com/2005-03-10/news/seminal-case (accessed Nov. 5, 2007).

14. See, e.g., *Thomas S. v. Robin Y.,* 209 A.D.2d 298, 299 (N.Y. App. Div. 1994).

15. *Steven S. v. Deborah D.,* 25 Cal. Rptr. 3d 482 (Cal. Ct. App. 2005). The court found that "[t]here was nothing in the statute that precluded its application given the facts of the case, which included the facts that the mother knew the male individual was the donor; after the initial impregnation failed, the parties engaged in sexual intercourse in an attempt to impregnate the mother; the mother acknowledged the male individual as the father of the child; and the mother allowed the male individual to celebrate in the joy of the child's birth."

16. Helen M. Alvare, "The Case for Regulating Collaborative Reproduction: A Children's Rights Perspective," *Harv. J. on Legis.* 40 (2003): 1, 15 (citing voluntary ASRM guidelines advising that "[d]onors and recipients and their partners should execute documents that define or limit their rights and duties with regard to any offspring").

17. Ibid., 27 (noting Florida statute requires donors to relinquish all rights and obligations with respect to resulting children and citing that North Dakota, Oklahoma, Texas, and Virginia make the intended mother the legal mother while relieving the egg donor of all rights and obligations). Laura M. Katers, "Arguing the 'Obvious' in Wisconsin: Why State Regulation of Assisted Reproductive Technology Has Not Come to Pass, and How It Should," *Wis. L. Rev.* (2000): 441, 448 (stating the legal relationship of the egg donor to the child is uncertain in most states).

18. The statutory provisions relating to the parental status of sperm donors, however, have been applied in court. See, e.g., *Lamaritata v. Lucas*, 823 So.2d 316 (Fla. Dist. App. 2d 2002) (holding sperm donor was not a parent and had no parental rights under state law); *L.A.L. v. D.A.L.*, 714 So.2d 595 (Fla. Dist. App. 2d 1998) (applying statute to foreclose parental rights to sperm donor); *In re Sullivan*, 157 S.W.3d 911, 922 (Tex. App. 2005) (interpreting plain and common meaning of applicable statute such that one's status as a sperm donor does not establish in and of itself the existence of a parent-child relationship between the donor and the child resulting from assisted reproduction).

19. Fl. Stat. Ann. § 742.11. (2007).

20. See Fla. Stat. Ann. § 742.14 (2007).

21. N.D. Cent. Code §§ 14-20-02(8), 14-20-60 (2007); Tex. Fam. Code Ann. §§ 160.102(6), 160.702 (2007).

22. N.D. Cent. Code § 14-20-02(8)(a).

23. Ibid., § 14-20-02(8)(b).

24. Ibid., § 14-20-02(8)(d).

25. Ibid., § 14-20-60.

26. Ibid., § 14-20–07(1)(a)–(c).

27. Ibid., § 14-20-07(2)(e).

28. Okla. Stat. Ann. tit. 10, ch. 24 (2007).

29. Ibid., §§ 554, 556(B)(1).

30. Ibid., §§ 555, 556(B)(2), (C), (D).

31. Ibid., § 556(A)(1), (2). See also § 556(A)(3) (requiring the original written consent of the husband and wife donating the human embryo to be filed with the court by the physician).

32. Tex. Fam. Code Ann. § 160.702.

33. Ibid., § 160.102(2)(B), (C).

34. Ibid., § 160.703.

35. Ibid., § 160.704(a).

36. Ibid., § 160.102(6).

37. Ibid., § 160.102(6)(A), (B).

38. Ibid., § 160.706(a) (stating that if a marriage is dissolved before the placement of eggs, the former spouse is not a parent of the resulting child unless the former spouse consented in a record that if assisted reproduction were to occur after a divorce, the former spouse would be a parent of the child); ibid., § 160.707 (providing that if a spouse dies before the placement of eggs, the deceased spouse is not a parent of the resulting child unless the deceased spouse consented in a record that if assisted reproduction were to occur after death, the deceased spouse would be a parent of the child).

39. Va. Code. Ann. § 20-158 (2007).

40. Ibid., tit. 20, ch. 9.

41. Ibid., § 20-158(1).

42. Ibid., § 20-158(2).

43. Ibid., § 20-156.

44. Ibid., § 20-158(3).

45. Wyo. Stat. Ann. § 14-2-406 (2007).

46. See John A. Robertson, "Gay and Lesbian Access to Assisted Reproductive Technology," *Case W. Res. L. Rev.* 55 (Winter 2004): 323, 348.

47. Utah Code Ann. § 78-45g-704 (2007).

48. See N.D. Cent. Code § 14-20-61 (2007) (stating that "[a] man who provides sperm for, or consents to, assisted reproduction by a woman as provided in section 14-20-62 with the intent to be the parent of her child, is a parent of the resulting child.")

49. See Utah Code Ann. § 78-45g-704 ("If a *husband* provides sperm for, or consents to, assisted reproduction by his wife . . . , he is the father of a *resulting child born to his wife*"; emphasis added). Compare to Wyo. Stat. Ann. § 14-2-903 (2007) ("A *man* who provides sperm for, or consents to, assisted reproduction by a woman . . . , with the intent to be the parent of her child, is the parent of the *resulting child*"; emphasis added).

50. Okla. Stat. tit. 10 § 556 (2007). However, the Oklahoma statute only explicitly addresses assisted reproduction in the husband-wife scenario, even when referring to the donors. See ibid. § 556(6) (establishing that "[t]he *husband* and *wife* donating the embryo shall have no right, obligation or interest with respect to [the resulting] child"; emphasis added).

51. Del. Code Ann. tit. 13, § 8-702 (2007).

52. Conn. Gen. Stat. § 19a-32d(c)(2) (2007).

53. La. Rev. Stat. Ann. § 9: 122 (2007). See also ibid. § 9: 129.

54. Ibid., § 9: 130.

55. Olga Batsedis, "Embryo Adoption: A Science Fiction or an Alternative to Traditional Adoption?" *Fam. Ct. Rev.* 41 (2003): 565 (citing Isabel Sanchez, "Parenting Puzzle," *Albuquerque Journal*, May 5, 2002).

56. "Ben and Jerry's Co-Founder Blasts Wasteful Government Spending," *Donahue* (MSNBC television broadcast, Aug. 28, 2002), available at http://www. lexis.com/research/retrieve?_m=b61bf9108d1b8428a695e9550e41b3cc&new StartCite=1&crnCh=0&crnCt=ALLCASES&docnum=1&_fmtstr=VKWIC&_ startdoc=1&wchp=dGLbVzb-zSkAA&_md5=33514e59f42214a45454b348aff38 e19&focBudTerms=donahue%20and%20adoption%20w/20%20embryo%20 and%20date%20bef%202003%20and%20people&focBudSel=all; WHDH-TV, "Extra Embryos" (television broadcast, May 6, 2003), available at http://www3. whdh.com/features/articles/specialreport/A243/ (quoting attorney Susan Crockin).

57. Batsedis, "Embryo Adoption."

58. *In re Baby M.,* 537 A.2d 1227, 1248 (N.J. 1988).

59. This discussion of the trial court's opinion is based on *In re Baby M.,* 525 A.2d 1128 (N.J. Super. 1987).

60. See Elizabeth J. Samuels, "Time to Decide? The Laws Governing Mothers' Consent to the Adoption of Their Newborn Infants," *Tenn. L. Rev.* 72 (2005): 509, 541–45.

61. Katharine K. Baker, "Bargaining or Biology? The History and Future of Paternity Law and Parental Status," *Cornell J. L. & Pub. Pol'y* 14 (2004): 1, 26.

62. Ca. Family Code, Uniform Parentage Act § 7610(a) (2002 (enacted 1992)).

63. *Johnson v. Calvert,* 851 P.2d 781 (Cal. 1993).

64. Ibid., 782.

65. *J.F. v. D.B.,* 897 A.2d 1261 (Pa. Super. Ct. 2006).

66. Ibid.

67. John Horton, "Triplets' Custody Awarded to Father, Toddlers in Tug of War between Dad, Surrogate," *Cleveland Plain Dealer,* Apr. 22, 2006, p. A1.

68. *Rice v. Flynn,* 2005 Ohio 4667 (Ct. App. 2005).

69. *J.F. v. D.B.,* 848 N.E.2d 873, 881 (Ohio Ct. App. 2006) (Slaby, Presiding Judge, concurring); aff'd & rev'd, 2007 WL 4531973 (Ohio 2007).

70. See John Horton, "Surrogate Awarded Custody of Triplets: CSU Professor Who Fathered Babies Gets Visitation," *Cleveland Plain Dealer,* Jan. 8, 2005, p. A1; compare Barbara White Stack, "Surrogate Mother Gets Custody of 3; Judge Criticizes Sperm Donor, Cuts Back His Visitation Rights," *Pittsburgh Post-Gazette,* Jan. 8, 2005, p. A1.

71. *Nemcek v. Paskey,* 849 N.E.2d 108 (Ohio Com. Pl. 2006).

72. *In re Roberto d.B.,* 923 A.2d 115, 122–23 (Md. Ct. App. 2007).

73. Ibid., 125 n. 15.

74. Jennifer Hendricks, "Essentially a Mother," *Wm. & Mary J. of Women & L.* 13 (2007): 429, 479.

75. Vermont Statute, Title 15: Domestic Relations § 124(f) (2007 (enacted 1999)).

76. See Adam Liptak, "Parental Rights Upheld for Lesbian Ex-Partner," *N.Y. Times,* Aug. 5, 2006, available at http://www.nytimes.com/2006/08/05/us/05gay.html?_r=1&oref=slogin.

77. *Miller-Jenkins v. Miller-Jenkins,* 912 A.2d 956 (Vt. 2006).

78. Ibid., 951.

79. *Finstuen v. Crutcher,* 496 F.3d 1139, 1142–43 (10th Cir. 2007).

80. See Joan H. Hollinger et al., *Adoption Law and Practice* (New York: Matthew Bender, 2006), vol. 1, § 3.06(6).

81. *Lofton v. Kearney,* 358 F.3d 804 (11th Cir. 2004), cert. denied, 543 U.S. 1081 (2005). Utah Code § 78-30-1(3)(b) (2007); Miss. Code Ann. § 93-17-3(2) (2004).

82. Robert F. Kelly and Shaun L. Ward, "Allocating Custodial Responsibilities at Divorce," *Family Court Review* 40 (2002): 350.

83. Defense of Marriage Act, 28 USC § 1738(c)(2008).

84. Uniform Child Custody Jurisdiction and Enforcement Act, Art. 1 § 102(7) (2007).

Notes to Chapter 6

1. Amy Harmon, "Hello, I'm Your Sister," *N.Y. Times,* Nov. 20, 2005, p. A1; Michael Leahy, "Family Vacation," *Washington Post Magazine,* June 19, 2005, p. W12; Kay Miller, "The Legacy of Donor 1047," *Minnesota Star Tribune,* Aug. 21, 2005, p. 1E; Amy Harmon, "Are You My Sperm Donor? Few Clinic Will Say," *N.Y. Times,* Jan. 20, 2006, p. A3; Amy Harmon, "Sperm Donor Father Ends His Anonymity," *N.Y. Times,* Feb. 14, 2007, p. A18; Dena Potter, "Bill Would Forbid Anonymous Sperm and Egg Donors," Associated Press, Jan. 29, 2007, available at http://press.jrc.it/NewsExplorer/clusteredition/en/20070129,washtimes-575 b99ad98739db45484bc521fe4eff0.html.

2. Lucy R. Dollens, "Note: Artificial Insemination: Right of Privacy and the Difficulty in Maintaining Donor Anonymity," *Ind. L. Rev.* 35 (2001): 213, 216–17.

3. David Plotz, *The Genius Factory: The Curious History of the Nobel Prize Sperm Bank* (New York: Random House, 2005).

4. Elizabeth J. Samuels, "The Idea of Adoption: An Inquiry into the History of Adult Adoptee Access to Birth Records, *Rutgers L. Rev.* 53 (2001): 367, 368.

5. Lucy Frith, "Gamete Donation and Anonymity: The Ethical and Legal Debate," *Human Reproduction* 16 (2001): 818, 821.

6. Human Fertilisation and Embryology Authority, "HFEA Register: An Introduction," http://www.hfea.gov.uk/en/1212.html.

7. Hayley Mick, "Who's Your Donor?" *Globe and Mail,* July 24, 2007, p. L1.

8. It appears that state law did not actually regulate this promise of nondisclosure. Similarly, in the adoption context, state law never guaranteed complete anonymity to the biological parents.

9. George J. Annas, "Fathers Anonymous: Beyond the Best Interests of the Sperm Donor," *Child Welfare* 60 (Mar. 1981): 161–74.

10. Plotz, *Genius Factory*, 170–71.

11. The Sperm Bank of California, "Identity-Release Program," http://www.thespermbankofca.org/idrelease.html.

12. Ibid.

13. Jennifer Egan, "Wanted: A Few Good Sperm," *N.Y. Times*, Mar. 19, 2006, sec. 6, p. 46.

14. Michael Leahy, "Family Vacation," *Washington Post*, June 19, 2005, p. W12.

15. Amy Harmon, "Sperm Donor Father Ends His Anonymity," *N.Y. Times*, Feb. 14, 2007, p. A18.

16. "Anonymous Sperm Donor Meets Kid," *CBS News: The Early Show* (CBS television broadcast, Aug. 23, 2005), available at http://www.cbsnews.com/stories/2005/08/23/earlyshow/living/main791690.shtml.

17. *Johnson v. Superior Court*, 80 Cal. App. 4th 1050 (2d Dist., 2000), *rev. denied*, 2000 Cal. LEXIS 6741 (2000); see also David Kravets, "Court Limits Sperm Donors' Rights," *AP Online*, Aug. 24, 2000.

18. *Johnson*, 80 Cal. App. 4th 1050.

19. The contract between the sperm recipients and the Cryobank stated that the Johnsons would "not now, nor at any time, require nor expect [Cryobank] to obtain or divulge . . . the name of said donor, nor any other information concerning characteristics, qualities, or any other information whatsoever concerning said donor, . . . it being the intention of all parties that the identity of said donor shall be and forever remain anonymous." Ibid., 1064–65.

20. Ibid., 1057.

21. Joanna E. Scheib, Maura Riordan, and Phillip R. Shaver, "Choosing between Anonymous and Identity-Release Sperm Donors: Recipient and Donor Characteristics," *Reproductive Technologies* 10 (2000): 50.

22. Leigh Woosley, "Invisible Legacy," *Tulsa World*, Jan. 5, 2006, available at http://www.tulsaworld.com/news/article.aspx?articleID=060105_Fa_D1_Invis32261.

23. "Moral Issues of Sperm Donation, Religion and Ethics," *Newsweekly* (PBS television broadcast, WNET-TV, Aug. 25, 2006).

24. SpermCenter.com, "ID Release Donors: What Does 'ID Release' Really Mean?" http://www.spermcenter.com/id-release-donors.htm.

25. Sperm Bank of California, "Identity-Release Program."

26. Lois Romano, "Multiple Single Moms, One Nameless Donor," *Washington Post*, Mar. 27, 2006, p. A2.

27. Cary Tennis, "Should We Two Mommies Tell Our Child Who the Sperm Donor Was?" *Salon.com*, Jan. 3, 2007, http://www.salon.com/mwt/col/tenn/2007/01/03/lesbian_parents/index.html.

28. Y. Wang and A. Leader, "Non-Anonymous (ID-Release) Donor Sperm Is Not the Preferred Choice of Women Who Are Undergoing Assisted Human Reproduction," *Fertility & Sterility* 84, supp. 1 (2005): S204, S205.

29. A. Brewaeys, J.K. de Bruyn, L.A. Louwe, and F.M. Helmerhorst, "Anonymous or Identity-Registered Sperm Donors? A Study of Dutch Recipients' Choices," *Human Reproduction* 20, no. 3 (Jan. 27, 2005): 820–24, available at http://humrep.oxfordjournals.org/cgi/content/abstract/20/3/820.

30. Wang and Leader, "Non-Anonymous (ID-Release) Donor Sperm Is Not the Preferred Choice," S205.

31. Kristen MacDougall, Gay Becker, Joanna E. Scheib, and Robert D. Nachtigall, "Strategies for Disclosure: How Parents Approach Telling Their Children That They Were Conceived with Donor Gametes," *Fertility & Sterility* 87 (2007): 524; Patricia Hershberger, Susan C. Klock, and Randall B. Barnes, "Disclosure Decisions among Pregnant Women Who Received Donor Oocytes: A Phenomenological Study," *Fertility & Sterility* 87 (2007): 288, 289.

32. E. Lycett, K. Daniels, R. Curson, S. Golombok, "School-Aged Children of Donor Insemination: A Study of Parents' Disclosure Patterns," *Human Reproduction* 20 (2005): 810; Hershberger, Klock, and Barnes, "Disclosure Decisions among Pregnant Women Who Received Donor Oocytes," 289.

33. ASRM Ethics Committee, "Informing Offspring of Their Conception by Gamete Donation," *Fertility & Sterility* 81 (2004): 527.

34. S. Golombok, F. MacCallum, E. Goodman, and M. Rutter, "Families with Children Conceived by Donor Insemination: A Follow-Up at Age 12," *Child Development* 73 (2002): 952.

35. J.E. Scheib, M. Riordan, and S. Rubin, "Choosing Identity-Release Sperm Donors: The Parents' Perspective 13–18 Years Later," *Human Reproduction* 18 (2003): 1115, 1122.

36. J.E. Scheib, M. Riordan, and S. Rubin, "Adolescents with Open-Identity Sperm Donors: Reports from 12–17 Year Olds," *Human Reproduction* 20 (2005): 239, 244.

37. Scheib, Riordan, and Rubin, "Choosing Identity-Release Sperm Donors," 1120.

38. Donor Sibling Registry, "Frequently Asked Questions," http://www.donorsiblingregistry.com/FaqPage.php.

39. MacDougall et al., "Strategies for Disclosure," 526–27.

40. Ibid., 527–28.

41. Ibid., 528.

42. Ibid.

43. Ellen Sarasohn Glazer and Evelina Weidman Sterling, *Having Your Baby through Egg Donation* (Indianapolis: Perspectives, 2005), 293.

44. S. Golombok, F. MacCallum, E. Goodman, and M. Rutter, "Families Created by Gamete Donation: Follow-Up at Age 2," *Human Reproduction* 20 (2005):

286; Joanne E. Scheib and Alice Ruby, "Impact of Sperm Donor Information on Parents and Children," *Sexuality, Reprod. & Menopause* 4 (2006): 17.

45. Gay Becker, Anneliese Butler, and Robert D. Nachtigall, "Resemblance Talk: A Challenge for Parents Whose Children Were Conceived with Donor Gametes in the US," *Social Science and Medicine* 61 (2005): 1300, 1308.

46. Ibid., 1304.

47. S. Golombok, S. Brewaeys, M.T. Giavazzi, D. Guerra, F. MacCallum, and J. Rust, "The European Study of Assisted Reproduction Families: The Transition to Adolescence," *Human Reproduction* 17, no. 3 (Mar. 1, 2002): 830–40; S. Golombok, C. Murray, V. Jadva, E. Lycett, F. MacCallum, and J. Rust, "Non-genetic and Non-gestational Parenthood: Consequences for Parent-Child Relationships and the Psychological Well-Being of Mothers, Fathers and Children at Age 3," *Human Reproductions* 21, no. 7 (July 1, 2006): 1918–24.

48. A.J. Turner and A. Coyle, "What Does It Mean to Be a Donor Offspring? The Identity Experience of Adults Conceived by Donor Insemination and the Implication for Counseling and Therapy," *Human Reproduction* 15 (2000): 2041, 2050 (contrasting their study, which did find such psychological issues, with other studies that did not).

49. Celia Hall, "Torment of Children with Donors for Fathers," *Daily Telegraph*, Aug. 31, 2000, p. 5 (Donor Conception Network provides support for parents and some children).

50. Ibid.

51. Katy Guest, "It's Difficult to Say This and Not Shock People," *Independent on Sunday*, July 9, 2006, p. 46.

52. J.E. Scheib, M. Riordan, and S. Rubin, "Adolescents with Open-Identity Sperm Donors: Reports from 12–17 Year Olds," *Human Reproduction* 20 (2005): 239, 248.

53. Ibid.; K. Vanfraussen, I. Panjaert-Kristofferson, and A. Brewaeys, "Why Do Children Want to Know More about the Donor? The Experience of Youngsters Raised in Lesbian Families," *J. Psychom. Obstet. Gynecol.* 24 (2003): 31.

54. Katrina Clark, "Who's Your Daddy? Mine Was an Anonymous Sperm Donor. That Made Me Mad. So I Decided to Find Him," *Washington Post*, Dec. 17, 2006, p. B1.

55. Scheib and Ruby, "Impact of Sperm Donor Information on Parents and Children," 18.

56. Glazer and Sterling, *Having Your Baby through Egg Donation*, 293.

57. Nina Burleigh, "Are You My Father? Donor-Inseminated Children," *Redbook* 192 (Mar. 1999) (discussing identity issues for children conceived through donor sperm). Although not all of these questions are answered through meeting gamete providers or adoptive parents—does a sense of humor really come from biology?—these meetings can provide a sense of security, knowledge, and identity.

58. Naomi Cahn and Jana Singer, "Adoption, Identity, and the Constitution: The Case for Opening Closed Records," *U. Penn. J. Const. L.* 2 (1999): 150, 175.

59. Scheib, Riordan, and Rubin, "Adolescents with Open-Identity Sperm Donors," 239.

60. Hall, "Torment of Children with Donors for Fathers" (Donor Conception Network provides support for parents and some children); Roy Eccleston, "Dear Dad (Whoever You Are . . .)," *Australian,* Apr. 19, 1998 (providing contact information for the Donor Conception Support Group of Australia).

61. People Conceived via Donor Insemination, Yahoo group, http://groups.yahoo.com/group/pcvai/.

62. Corky Siemaszko, "Boy Finds Dad with Web Savvy and Spit," *N.Y. Daily News,* Nov. 4, 2005, p. 2.

63. Donor Sibling Registry, http://www.donorsiblingregistry.com/.

Notes to Chapter 7

1. This description is drawn from the following sources: *North Coast Women's Care Medical Group, Inc. v. San Diego Superior Court* (Ca. Sup. Ct. 2008), available at www.cacourtinfo.ca.gov/opinions/documents/S142892.doc.; Greg Moran, "Lesbian's Wish for Child at Odds with M.D.s' Faith," Copley News Service, Aug. 9, 2005; Rob Stein, "Seeking Care, and Refused," *Washington Post,* July 2006, p. A6; Jacob M. Appel, "May Doctors Refuse Infertility Treatments to Gay Patients?" *Hastings Center Report* 36 (July 2006): 20; Elizabeth Weil, "Breeder Reaction: Does Everybody Have the Right to Have a Baby? And Who Should Pay When Nature Alone Doesn't Work?" *Mother Jones* 31 (July 2006): 32.

2. Fertility4Life.com, http://www.fertility4life.com/hi/qa.asp (2006).

3. Andrea D. Gurmankin, Arthur L. Caplan, and Andrea M. Braverman, "Screening Practices and Beliefs of Assisted Reproductive Technology Programs," *Fertility & Sterility* 83 (Jan. 2005): 61–67.

4. Centers for Medicine and Medicaid, "Excluded Drug Coverage by State Medicaid Program" (2008), http://www.cms.hhs.gov/States/EDC/list.asp.

5. See, e.g., Richard Storrow, "The Bioethics of Prospective Parenthood: In Pursuit of the Proper Standard for Gatekeeping in Infertility Clinics," *Cardozo Law Review* 28 (2007): 2283–84.

6. Gurmankin, Caplan, and Braverman, "Screening Practices and Beliefs," 63–65.

7. Storrow, "Bioethics of Prospective Parenthood," 2314–16.

8. Stephen Jay Gould, "Carrie Buck's Daughter," *Const. Comment.* 2 (1985): 331, 332.

9. *Buck v. Bell,* 274 U.S. 200, 207 (1927).

10. *Buck v. Bell,* 130 S.E. 516, 517 (Va. 1925).

11. Gould, "Carrie Buck's Daughter," 336.

12. See Victoria F. Nourse, *In Reckless Hands: Skinner v. Oklahoma and the Near-Triumph of American Eugenics* (New York: Norton, 2008), 21–24.

13. See *Skinner v. Oklahoma,* 316 U.S. 535, 541 (1942); Carter J. Dillard, "Rethinking the Procreative Right," *Yale Human Rights & Dev. L.J.* 10 (2007): 1, 13–14.

14. Fran Smith, "How Bad Does the Health-Care Crisis Have to Get?" *Redbook* 166 (July 2007), available online at http://www.redbookmag.com/your/health-care-crisis-yl.

15. See John A. Robertson, "Commerce and Regulation in the Assisted Reproduction Industry," *Tex. L. Rev.* 85 (2007): 665, 674; Jessica Arons, Center for American Progress, "Future Choices: Assisted Reproductive Technologies and the Law" (2007), 8–11, available at http://www.americanprogress.org/issues/2007/12/pdf/future_choices_section1.pdf.

16. For example, the Illinois statute (215 ILC 5/356m (2008)) provides,

> Infertility coverage. (a) No group policy of accident and health insurance providing coverage for more than 25 employees that provides pregnancy related benefits may be issued, amended, delivered, or renewed in this State after the effective date of this amendatory Act of 1991 unless the policy contains coverage for the diagnosis and treatment of infertility including, but not limited to, in vitro fertilization, uterine embryo lavage, embryo transfer, artificial insemination, gamete intrafallopian tube transfer, zygote intrafallopian tube transfer, and low tubal ovum transfer.

17. See American Society for Reproductive Medicine, "State Infertility Insurance Laws," http://www.asrm.org/Patients/insur.html (accessed Jan. 11, 2008).

18. See ibid.

19. American Fertility Association, "Understanding the New York State Mandate for Insurance Coverage of Infertility," http://www.afafamilymatters.com/conceive/nysmandate.html.

20. See Arons, "Future Choices," 8.

21. Ibid., 43 n. 49.

22. "In Vitro Veritas," *Economist,* July 26, 2007, available at http://www.economist.com/science/displaystory.cfm?story_id=9539788.

23. See Arons, "Future Choices," 10–11.

24. See *Castle Rock v. Gonzales,* 545 U.S. 748 (2005); Susan Bandes, "The Negative Constitution: A Critique," *Mich. L. Rev.* 88 (1990): 2271, 2318–20; Anita Bernstein, "Treating Sexual Harassment with Respect," *Harv. L. Rev.* 111 (1997): 486; Isaiah Berlin, "Two Concepts of Liberty," in *Liberty: Incorporating Four Essays on Liberty* (New York: Oxford University Press 1969), 122–23.

25. See John A. Robertson, *Children of Choice: Freedom and the New Reproductive Technologies* (Princeton, NJ: Princeton University Press, 1994), 22–42; John A. Robertson, "Liberty, Identity, and Human Cloning," *Tex. L. Rev.* 76 (1998):

1371, 1389–90. Robertson argues, "the interest in using ARTs to overcome infertility or achieve other reproductive goals should presumptively be protected against limitation without the strong showing ordinarily needed to limit the reproductive rights of fertile persons." John A. Robertson, "Procreative Liberty and Harm to Offspring in Assisted Reproduction," *Amer. J. L. & Med.* 30 (2004): 7, 20.

26. See Radhika Rao, "Equal Liberty: Assisted Reproductive Technology and Reproductive Equality," *Geo. Wash. L. Rev.* (forthcoming 2008); Cass Sunstein, "Is There a Constitutional Right to Clone?" *Hastings L.J.* 53 (2002): 994. Sunstein notes, "But none of this means that there is a presumptive right to do whatever might be done to increase the likelihood of having, or not having, a child: to enter into surrogacy arrangements, or to use in vitro fertilization, or to attempt to clone a child. The central point is that a ban on cloning, or on surrogacy arrangements, leaves open numerous other channels by which most people may bear a child."

27. See Rao, "Equal Liberty."

28. Nanette R. Elster, "ART for the Masses? Racial and Ethnic Inequality in Assisted Reproductive Technologies," *DePaul J. Health Care L.* 9 (2005): 724 (citing Lisa M. Kerr, "Can Money Buy Happiness? An Examination of the Coverage of Infertility Services under HMO Contracts," *Case West. Res. L. Rev.* 49 (1999): 605).

29. U.S. Department of Health and Human Services, "Fertility, Family Planning, and Women's Health: New Data from the 1995 National Survey of Family Growth" (1997), 61.

30. Ibid.

31. E.g., E.C. Feinberg, F.W. Larsen, W.H. Catherino et al., "Comparison of Assisted Reproductive Technology Utilization and Outcomes between Caucasian and African American Patients in an Equal-Access-to-Care Setting," *Fertility & Sterility* 85 (2006): 891; Jennifer Ach Green, Jared C. Robins, Michael Scheiber, et al., "Racial and Economic Demographics of Couples Seeking Infertility Treatment," *Amer. J. Obst. & Gyn.* 184 (2000): 1082.

32. U.S. Census Bureau, "Income, Poverty, and Health Insurance" (2004), 16, available at http://www.census.gov/prod/2004pubs/p60-226.pdf.

33. Feinberg et al., "Comparison of Assisted Reproductive Technology," 890.

34. Marianne Bitler and Lucie Schmidt, "Health Disparities and Infertility: Impacts of State-Level Insurance Mandates," *Fertility & Sterility* 85 (2006): 858.

35. Feinberg et al., "Comparison of Assisted Reproductive Technology," 893.

36. Bitler and Schmidt, "Health Disparities and Infertility," 858.

37. See Elizabeth Hervey Stephen and Anjai Chandra, "Use of Infertility Services in the United States: 1995," *Fam. Plan. Persp.* 32 (2000).

38. J.C. Robins, J. Ach-Green, M. Scheiber, et al., "Racial and Economic Demographics of Couples Seeking Infertility Treatments," *Fertility & Sterility* 74, no. 3, supp. 1 (2000): S182.

39. Elster, "ART for the Masses?" 728 (citing Families of Color Initiative, "The Hidden Problem of Infertility in the African American Community," http://www.ferre.org/foci/hidden.html). See also Angela Hooton, "A Broader Vision of the Reproductive Rights Movement: Fusing Mainstream and Latina Feminism," *Amer. U. J. Gend., Soc. Pol'y & L.* 13 (2005): 59.

40. See Dorothy Roberts, *Killing the Black Body: Race, Reproduction and the Meaning of Liberty* (New York: Random House, 1997), 259.

41. See Infertility Education, "Is Infertility Stopping You?" http://www.infertilityeducation.org/familiesofcolor.html (accessed Aug. 13, 2007).

42. See Roberts, *Killing the Black Body,* 259.

43. Elster, "ART for the Masses?" 729.

44. See Hooton, "Broader Vision," 73.

45. See Robertson, "Commerce and Regulation," 674; Arons, "Future Choices," 11–13.

46. *Bragdon v. Abbott,* 524 U.S. 624, 638 (1998).

47. See *Saks v. Franklin Covey,* 117 F.Supp.2d 318 (S.D.N.Y. 2000), modified, 316 F.3d 337 2d Cir. 2003); Arons, "Future Choices," 11.

48. *Krauel v. Iowa Meth. Med. Ctr.,* 95 F.3d 674, 679 (8th Cir. 1996).

49. *Saks,* 316 F.3d at 345–46.

50. Robertson, "Commerce and Regulation," 676.

51. See Robertson, "Commerce and Regulation," 677; Richard F. Storrow, "Rescuing Children from the Marriage Movement: The Case against Marital Status Discrimination in Adoption and Assisted Reproduction," *U.C. Davis L. Rev.* 39 (2006): 313–14.

Notes to Chapter 8

1. Craigslist ad, http://www.craigslist.org/nby/etc/388748037.html (accessed Aug. 2007).

2. See Ami S. Jaeger, "Assisted Reproductive Technologies, Collaborative Reproduction, and Adoption," in *Adoption Law and Practice,* ed. Joan Hollinger (New York: Matthew Bender, 2008), § 14.05; see generally National Conference of State Legislatures, "State Laws on Frozen Embryos," http://www.ncsl.org/programs/health/embryodisposition.htm (listing state laws and legislation regarding the use and storage of frozen embryos) (updated July 2007).

3. UAGA (2006), § 16, available at http://www.law.upenn.edu/bll/archives/ulc/uaga/2006final.htm (accessed Feb. 18, 2008).

4. Virginia Code Annotated § 32.1-291.16 (2007).

5. Fla. Stat. § 742.14 (2007).

6. Michele Goodwin, *Black Markets: The Supply and Demand of Body Parts* (New York: Cambridge University Press, 2006), 181.

7. ASRM Ethics Committee, "Financial Incentives in Recruitment of Oocyte Donors," *Fertility & Sterility* 74 (2000): 219.

8. J. Luk and J. Petrozza, "Evaluation of Compliance and Range of Fees by ASRM: Listed Egg Donor and Surrogacy Agencies," *Fertility & Sterility* 86, supp. 1 (Sept. 2006): S190.

9. Ibid.

10. X and Y Consulting, Inc., "Fee Schedule," http://www.eggdonorsnow.com/FeeSched.htm (accessed Mar. 11, 2007).

11. George Washington University Medical Faculty Associates, "Become an Egg Donor," http://www.washivf.com/GWIVF-GWIVF_Content_C-Index_Page_Template_1143644787796.html (accessed Mar. 11, 2007).

12. Genetics and IVF Institute, "How to Become a Donor," http://www.givf.com/donoregg/becomingadonor.cfm (accessed Mar. 11, 2007).

13. Choices Donations, Inc., "Donor Page," http://www.choicesdonations.com/donorpage.htm (accessed Mar. 11, 2007).

14. ASRM Ethics Committee, "Financial Incentives in Recruitment of Oocyte Donors," *Fertility & Sterility* 74 (2000): 216.

15. President's Council on Bioethics, *Reproduction and Responsibility: The Regulation of New Biotechnologies* (2004), ch. 9.

16. SpermCenter.com, "How Much Does Donor Sperm Cost?" http://www.spermcenter.com/tutfees.htm (accessed Mar. 11, 2007).

17. Sperm Bank of California, "Fee Schedule for Recipient Services," http://www.thespermbankofca.org/pdf/feeschedule2006.PDF (accessed Mar. 11, 2007).

18. Fairfax Cryobank, "Fees," http://www.fairfaxcryobank.com/fees.aspx?menu=4&turn=on (accessed Mar. 11, 2007).

19. Fertility4Life.com, "Price Plans," http://www.fertility4life.com/mni/price.asp (accessed Mar. 12, 2007).

20. Will Pavia, "The Vikings Are Coming," *Times* (London), Nov. 27, 2006, p. 4.

21. California Cryobank Sperm Bank, "Fee Schedule," http://www.cryobank.com/fees_ds.cfm?page=9 (accessed Mar. 12, 2007).

22. Penn Fertility Care, "Donor Embryo Program," http://pennhealth.com/fertility/embryo_donor.html (accessed Mar. 12, 2007).

23. "World's First Donor Created Human Embryo Bank—The Abraham Center of Life—Opening in San Antonio," *EWorldwire Press,* July 28, 2006, available at http://www.eworldwire.com/pressreleases/15132 (accessed Mar. 12, 2007).

24. Nicole Foy, "Embryo Broker Gets Federal Once-Over," *San Antonio Express-News,* Jan. 13, 2007, p. 3B; William Saletan, "The Embryo Factory," *Slate,* Jan. 15, 2007, http://www.slate.com/id/2157495 (accessed Mar. 12, 2007).

25. Nightlight Christian Adoptions, "Snowflakes Program," http://www.nightlight.org/snowflakeadoption.htm (accessed Mar. 12, 2007).

26. Nightlight Christian Adoptions, "Snowflakes Embryo Adoptions Fact Sheet," http://www.nightlight.org/Snowflakesfacts.pdf.

27. Abraham Center of Life, "Embryo Donation," http://www.theabraham-centeroflife.com/embryodonation.html (embryos can be made to order or can be made available through donation).

28. These four concerns are nicely articulated in Martha Ertman, "What's Wrong with a Parenthood Market? A New and Improved Theory of Commodification," *N.C. L. Rev.* 82 (2003): 1, 26–34.

29. Mary Lyndon Shanley, *Making Babies, Making Families: What Matters Most in an Age of Reproductive Technologies, Surrogacy, Adoption, and Same-Sex and Unwed Parents' Rights* (Boston: Beacon, 2001), 94–95, 98.

30. Joan Williams and Viviana Zelizer differentiate between *commodification,* which "blurs the distinction between proposals to bring market institutions and strategic, self-interested behavior into family life, and proposals to end domesticity's erasure of women's economic contribution," and *marketization,* which "allocate[s] a certain set of social relations to the market." Joan C. Williams and Viviana A. Zelizer, "To Commodify or Not to Commodify: That Is Not the Question," in *Rethinking Commodification,* ed. Martha Ertman and Joan Williams (New York: New York University Press, 2005), 362, 376 (allowing a market to exist in games is marketization).

31. June Carbone and Paige Gottheim, "Markets, Subsidies, Regulation, and Trust: Building Ethical Understandings into the Market for Fertility Services," *J. Gend., Race & Just.* 9 (2005): 509. In discussing the possibilities for private ordering of reproductive-tissue sales, there are critical issues involving nondiscriminatory market access as well as commodification of babies. The access issues are more easily addressed than the commodification issues; for example, expanding insurance coverage of infertility, an approach used in some other countries, would enhance equity within the system and allow more people of color to use gametic reproduction.

32. See Goodwin, *Black Markets,* 10–16.

33. Ertman, "What's Wrong with a Parenthood Market?" 22–23; Martha M. Ertman, "Marriage as a Trade: Bridging the Private/Private Distinction," *Harv. Civ. Rights–Civ. Lib. L. Rev.* 36 (2001): 79 (Ertman fears the imposition of majoritarian norms on gay, lesbian, and single-parent families).

34. Goodwin, *Black Markets,* 20–22.

35. See Viviana A. Zelizer, *The Social Meaning of Money* (Princeton, NJ: Princeton University Press, 1997); Naomi Cahn, "The Coin of the Realm: Poverty and the Commodification of Gendered Labor," *J. Gend., Race & Just.* (2001): 1–20.

36. Zelizer, *Social Meaning of Money,* 204.

37. Ibid.

38. John A. Robertson, "Commerce and Regulation in the Assisted Reproduction Industry," *Tex. L. Rev.* 85 (2007): 671.

39. Ibid., 671, 691.

40. Ellen Glazer and Evelina Sterling, *Having Your Baby through Egg Donation* (Indianapolis: Perspectives, 2005), 125.

41. See Goodwin, *Black Markets*.

42. See ibid.; see also Williams and Zelizer, "To Commodify or Not to Commodify," 304.

43. Ertman, "What's Wrong with a Parenthood Market?" 55–56.

44. Viviana Zelizer, *Pricing the Priceless Child: The Changing Social Value of Children* (Princeton, NJ: Princeton University Press, 1994), 173–74.

45. Joan Heifetz Hollinger, "State and Federal Adoption Law," in *Families by Law: An Adoption Reader,* ed. Naomi Cahn and Joan Hollinger (New York: New York University Press, 2004), 37, 39.

46. Child Welfare Information Gateway, "Use of Advertising and Facilitators in Adoptive Placements" (2006), available at http://www.childwelfare.gov/systemwide/laws_policies/statutes/advertising.cfm.

47. Michele Goodwin, "The Free-Market Approach to Adoption: The Value of a Baby," *B.C. Third World L.J.* 26 (2006): 61, 66–67.

48. U.S. Department of Health and Human Services, "Trends in Organ Donation and Transplantation in the United States, 1996–2005" (2006), available at http://www.optn.org/AR2006/chapter_i_AR_cd.htm.

49. Goodwin, *Black Markets*, 10–14.

50. Viviana A. Zelizer, "The Purchase of Intimacy," *L. & Soc. Inq.* 25 (2000): 817, 818–19.

51. Mary Lyndon Shanley, "Collaboration and Commodification in Assisted Procreation: Reflections on an Open Market and Anonymous Donation in Human Sperm and Eggs," *L. & Soc'y Rev.* 36 (2002): 257, 279.

52. Ibid., 280.

53. Kari L. Karsjens, "Boutique Egg Donations: A New Form of Racism and Patriarchy," *DePaul J. Health Care L.* 5 (2002): 84.

54. Margaret Radin, "Contested Commodities: The Trouble with Trade in Sex, Children, Body Parts and Other Things," *U. Toronto L.J.* 48 (Winter 1998): 151–55.

55. Ibid., 148.

56. Cahn, "Coin of the Realm," 9.

57. Oliver E. Williamson, "Calculativeness, Trust, and Economic Organization," *J. L. & Econ.* 36 (1993): 453, 483 (attempting to define trust through calculative economic reasoning).

58. Lawrence E. Mitchell, "Understanding Norms," *U. Toronto L.J.* 49 (1999): 177, 232.

59. See Cahn, "Coin of Realm," 25–26.

60. Rene Almeling, "Selling Genes, Selling Gender: Egg Agencies, Sperm Banks and the Medical Market in Genetic Material," *Amer. Soc. Rev.* 72 (June 2007): 334–35.

61. Brooke Lea Foster, "The Hunt for Golden Eggs: Young Women Donating Eggs," *Washingtonian*, July 1, 2007, p. 101.

62. Barry Schwartz, "Money for Nothing," *N.Y. Times*, July 2, 2007, p. A19.

63. See, e.g., Theresa Erickson, "Are Egg Donations Solely about Money?" Associated Press, Feb. 20, 2007, available at http://www.surrogacyissuesblog.com/index.php?s=lorna+marshall&submit=Search.

64. Julia Derek, *Confessions of a Serial Egg Donor* (New York: Adrenaline Books, 2004), 5.

65. Ibid., 6, 8.

66. Ibid., 47.

67. Lorna Marshall, "Issues Physicians Encounter in Third Party Reproduction," PowerPoint presentation, available at http://www.ialsnet.org/documents/ASRM/Marshall_PPT.pdf.

68. Margaret Radin, *Contested Commodities* (Cambridge, MA: Harvard University Press, 1996), 138.

69. Ibid., xiii, 107.

70. E.g., Zelizer, "Purchase of Intimacy," 832.

71. Goodwin, "Free-Market Approach," 76.

72. Ibid., 77.

73. See Radhika Rao, "Property, Privacy, and the Human Body," *B.U. L. Rev.* 80 (2000): 359, 458–59. Rao suggests that the right of privacy protects individuals' relationship to their frozen embryos when the individuals attempt to establish a personal relationship with the embryos, whereas the law of property applies more appropriately when individuals want to sell frozen embryos because they have no personal relationship to the embryos.

74. See Zelizer, *Social Meaning of Money*; Cahn, "Coin of the Realm," 1.

Notes to Chapter 9

1. J. Budziszewski, "So-Called Marriage," *Boundless Webzine* (2004), http://www.boundless.org/regulars/office_hours/a0000865.html.

2. Helen Kennedy, "Oh, Baby! Veep's Kid Expecting: Cheney's Gay Daughter to Deliver in Spring," *N.Y. Daily News*, Dec. 7, 2006, p. 3.

3. See David Blankenhorn, *The Future of Marriage* (New York: Encounter Books, 2007); *Goodridge v. Dept. of Pub. Health*, 440 Mass. 309, 367, 391 (Mass. 2003).

4. Commission on Parenthood's Future (Elizabeth Marquardt, principal investigator), "The Revolution in Parenthood: The Emerging Global Clash between Adult Rights and Children's Needs" (2006), 33, available at http://www.americanvalues.org/parenthood/parenthood.htm.

5. Ibid., 15.

6. Robert P. George and Ryan T. Anderson, "Our Marital Future: One Democrat Gets It," *National Review Online*, Apr. 23, 2007, http://article.nationalreview.com/?q=ODZiOTNhYmYyZTE1MjZmOGZkMjExZGI0MGExMzNhNGY.

7. David Blankenhorn, "The Rights of Children and the Redefinition of Parenthood" (2005), available at http://www.americanvalues.org/html/danish_institute.htm.

8. One of the most forceful advocates within the legal academy is Brigham Young University J. Reuben Clark Law School professor Lynn Wardle. See, e.g., Lynn D. Wardle, "Global Perspective on Procreation and Parentage by Assisted Reproduction," *Cap. U. L. Rev.* 35 (2006): 413.

9. Marsha Garrison, "Law Making for Baby Making: An Interpretive Approach to the Determination of Legal Parentage," *Harv. L. Rev.* 113 (2000): 906, 910.

10. Ibid.

11. Maggie Gallagher, "The Marriage Debate and Reprotech," The Volokh Conspiracy weblog, Oct. 18, 2005, http://volokh.com/archives/archive_2005_10_16-2005_10_22.shtml#1129693131.

12. Margaret F. Brinig and Steven L. Nock, "Legal Status and Effects on Children," Notre Dame Legal Studies Paper No. 07-21 (Mar. 16, 2007), available at http://ssrn.com/abstract=973826.

13. See Judith Stacey and Timothy Biblarz, "(How) Does the Sexual Orientation of Parents Matter?" *Amer. Soc. Rev.* 66 (Apr. 2001), available at http://papers.ssrn.com/sol3/papers.cfm?abstract_id=276907.

14. Laura Hamilton, Simon Cheng, and Brian Powell, "Adoptive Parents, Adaptive Parents: Evaluating the Importance of Biological Ties for Parental Investment," *Amer. Soc. Rev.* 72 (Feb. 2007): 111, available at http://www.asanet.org/galleries/default-file/Feb07ASRAdoption.pdf.

15. ASRM Ethics Committee, "Access to Fertility Treatment by Gays, Lesbians, and Unmarried Persons," *Fertility & Sterility* 86 (2006): 1333, 1335, available at http://www.asrm.org/Media/Ethics/fertility_gaylesunmarried.pdf.

16. Judy Peres, "In-Vitro New Front in Embryo War," *Chicago Tribune*, July 6, 2005, p. C1.

17. Catechism of the Catholic Church, 2376–2377, available at http://www.vatican.va/archive/catechism/p3s2c2a6.htm.

18. Associated Press, "Teacher Says She Was Fired over In Vitro," Sept. 28, 2006, available at http://www.msnbc.msn.com/id/12738144/.

19. Quoted in Piet Levy, "Birth of Twins Costs Woman Her Job," *Religion News Service*, May 17, 2006.

20. Focus on the Family, "Contact Us: Custom Help," *Family.org*, http://family.custhelp.com/cgi-bin/family.cfg/php/enduser/std_adp.php?p_faqid=1190.

21. Deborah Wald, "Thank God for Angelina and Brad!" Waldlaw Blog, Aug. 10, 2006, http://debwald.blogspot.com/2006_08_01_debwald_archive.html.

Wald has also written an extremely useful brochure, "Protecting Your Family: A Legal Guide for Lesbian Couples Using Donor Insemination," available at http://www.waldlaw.net/brochure_women.pdf.

22. Susannah Baruch, David Kaufman, and Kathy L. Hudson, "Genetic Testing of Embryos: Practices and Perspectives of U.S. IVF Clinics," *Fertility & Sterility* (July 10, 2007): 4, available at http://www.dnapolicy.org/resources/PGD-SurveyReportFertilityandSterilitySeptember2006withcoverpages.pdf.

23. Genetics and IVF Institute, "PGD," http://www.givf.com/pgd/pgd.cfm.

24. Baruch, Kaufman, and Hudson, "Genetic Testing of Embryos," 7.

25. Harvard Law Review Association, "Regulating Pre-Implantation Genetic Diagnosis: The Pathologization Problem," *Harv. L. Rev.* 118 (June 2005): 2772–73.

26. See generally Jeffrey R. Botkin, "Ethical Issues and Practical Problems in Preimplantation Genetic Diagnosis," *J. L., Med. & Ethics* 26 (Spring 1998): 25.

27. Beth Kohl, *Embryo Culture: Making Babies in the Twenty-First Century* (New York: Farrar, Straus, and Giroux, 2007), 101.

28. Michael J. Sandel, *The Case against Perfectionism: Ethics in the Age of Genetic Engineering* (Cambridge, MA: Belknap, 2007), 9.

29. Ibid., 27, 95.

30. Nicholas D. Kristof, "Birth without the Bother?" *N.Y. Times,* July 23, 2007, p. A19.

31. Vitae Caring Foundation, "Human Egg Donation and Stem Cell Research," http://www.stemcellresearchfacts.com/commercials.html.

32. Commission on Parenthood's Future, "Revolution in Parenthood," 27–28.

33. Ibid., 27.

34. "UK Court Denies IVF Appeal: Woman's Frozen Embryonic Children Must Die," *LifeSiteNews.com,* June 25, 2004, http://www.lifesite.net/ldn/2004/jun/04062508.html.

35. Sandel, *Case against Perfectionism,* 116.

36. Ibid., 118–19.

37. International Society for Stem Cell Research, "Frequently Asked Questions," http://isscr.org/science/faq.htm.

38. Eve Herold, *Stem Cell Wars: Inside Stories from the Frontlines* (New York: Palgrave Macmillan, 2006), 123.

39. Joseph Russell Falasco, "Frozen Embryos and Gamete Providers' Rights: A Suggested Model for Embryo Disposition," *Jurimetrics J.* 45 (Spring 2005): 282–83; John A. Robertson, "In the Beginning: The Status of Early Embryos," *Va. L. Rev.* 76 (April 1990): 437.

40. Robertson, "In the Beginning," 515.

41. Liza Mundy, "A Debate's Tiny Casualties: Multiple Births Raise a Key Issue for Embryo Research," *Washington Post,* June 5, 2007, p. A17.

42. Radhika Rao, "Property, Privacy, and the Human Body," *B.U. L. Rev.* 80 (April 2000): 444.

43. Guido Calabresi and Douglas Melamed, "Property Rules, Liability Rules, and Inalienability Rules: One View of the Cathedral," *Harv. L. Rev.* 85 (1972): 1089.

44. Robyn Shapiro, "Who Owns Your Frozen Embryo? Promises and Pitfalls of Emerging Reproductive Organs," ABA website, http://www.abanet.org/irr/hr/spring98/sp98shapiro.html. Other states are considering such legislation. See generally Shelley Emling, "Frozen Embryos Creating Legal, Ethical Dilemma," Cox News Service, Mar. 3, 2001 (reporting that New Jersey legislators were considering a statute that would require couples to sign a contract prior to undergoing in vitro fertilization procedures but that many states "have been hesitant to take up the issue because it could stir passions on both sides of the thorny abortion debate"); see Randy Diamond, "Court Won't Allow Forced Motherhood," *Record*, Aug. 15, 2001 (reporting on New Jersey League of American Families arguing for preservation of zygotes in recent New Jersey Supreme Court case).

45. Fla. Stat. Ann. § 742.17(2) (West 2007).

46. Ibid., § 742.17(3). Florida is one of the few states that addresses the postdeath disposition of gametic material in any detail. Its statute provides in § 742.17,

> A commissioning couple and the treating physician shall enter into a written agreement that provides for the disposition of the commissioning couple's eggs, sperm, and preembryos in the event of a divorce, the death of a spouse, or any other unforeseen circumstance.
>
> (1) Absent a written agreement, any remaining eggs or sperm shall remain under the control of the party that provides the eggs or sperm.
>
> (2) Absent a written agreement, decisionmaking authority regarding the disposition of preembryos shall reside jointly with the commissioning couple.
>
> (3) Absent a written agreement, in the case of the death of one member of the commissioning couple, any eggs, sperm, or preembryos shall remain under the control of the surviving member of the commissioning couple.
>
> (4) A child conceived from the eggs or sperm of a person or persons who died before the transfer of their eggs, sperm, or preembryos to a woman's body shall not be eligible for a claim against the decedent's estate unless the child has been provided for by the decedent's will.

47. Tex. Fam. Code Ann. § 160.706(b) (Vernon 2007).

48. La. Rev. Stat. Ann. § 9: 130 (2007). The *Davis* trial court found that eggs become human beings at the moment of fertilization and awarded custody of them to the wife. *Davis v. Davis*, 842 S.W.2d 588, 589 (Tenn. 1992).

49. La. Rev. Stat. Ann. § 9: 130 (2007).

50. Ibid.

51. Ibid., § 9: 126.

52. Ibid., § 9: 131.

53. See Nicole L. Cucci, "Constitutional Implication of In Vitro Fertilization Procedures," *St. John's L. Rev.* 72 (Spring 1998): 434–35.

54. See generally *Planned Parenthood of Southeastern Pa. v. Casey*, 505 U.S. 833, 901 (1992); *Stenberg v. Carhart*, 530 U.S. 914, 945–46 (2000); *Gonzales v. Carhart*, 127 S.Ct. 1610 (2007).

55. See Kathryn Venturatos Lorio, "From Cradle to Tomb: Estate Planning Considerations of the New Procreation," *La. L. Rev.* 57 (Fall 1996): 41–43; Jennifer M. Stolier, "Disputing Frozen Embryos: Using International Perspectives to Formulate Uniform U.S. Policy," *Tulane J. Int'l & Comp. L.* 9 (Spring 2001): 477–79.

56. Cal. Penal Code § 367g (2001).

57. Mass. Gen. Laws ch. 111L, § 4 (2007).

58. Russell Korobkin, "Buying and Selling Human Tissues for Stem Cell Research," *Ariz. L. Rev.* 49 (Spring 2007): 50.

59. See John A. Robertson, "Decisional Authority over Embryos and Control of IVF Technology," *Jurimetrics J.* 28 (1988): 290.

60. *Davis*, 842 S.W.2d at 588.

61. Ibid., 590.

62. 696 N.E.2d 174 (N.Y. 1998).

63. Ibid., 176–77.

64. *Davis*, 842 S.W.2d at 595–96 (citing *York v. Jones*, 717 F. Supp. 421 (E.D. Va. 1989) (discussing bailment of preembryos)).

65. Ibid., 597. In the court's speculation on whether it would enforce an agreement, it says that initially such an agreement would be presumed valid but that the parties' initial "informed consent" to IVF procedures "will often not be truly informed because of the near impossibility of anticipating . . . all the turns that events may take as the IVF process unfolds. Providing that the initial agreements may later be modified *by agreement* will, we think, protect the parties against some of the risks they face in this regard. But, in the absence of such agreed modification, we conclude that their prior agreements should be considered binding." Ibid.

66. Ibid., 598.

67. Ibid., 604.

68. *Kass*, 696 N.E.2d at 176–77.

69. Ibid., 178.

70. See *A.Z. v. B.Z.*, 725 N.E.2d 1051, 1057 (Mass. 2000); *J.B. v. M.B.*, 751 A.2d 613, 619 (N.J. Super. Ct. App. Div. 2000), *aff'd as modified*, 783 A.2d 707, 720 (N.J. 2001); *Litowitz v. Litowitz*, 10 P.3d 1086, 1093 (Wash. Ct. App. 2000).

71. *A.Z.*, 725 N.E.2d at 1054. The court also found that the contract itself was not necessarily binding, terming the agreement less of a contract than an effort by the clinic to provide information about the reproductive technologies at issue and observing that the husband had signed blank forms, with the wife filling in the relevant details. Ibid., 1057–58.

72. Ibid., 1056.

73. Ibid., 1055.

74. Ibid., 1057–58.

75. Ibid., 1059.

76. Ibid., 1057–58.

77. *J.B.*, A.2d at 619 (further citations omitted).

78. Ibid., 616.

79. Ibid., 615.

80. Ibid.

81. Ibid., 619. "Even if the wife were relieved of the financial and custodial responsibility for her child, the fact that her biological child would exist in an environment controlled by strangers is understandably unacceptable to the wife." Ibid.

82. Ibid.

83. *Litowitz*, 10 P.3d 1086 (Wash. Ct. App. 2000).

84. Ibid., 1087.

85. Ibid., 1091.

86. Ibid., 1089.

87. Ibid., 1091.

88. Ibid., 1093.

89. Ibid., 1091.

90. Ibid.

91. Ibid.

92. Chi Steve Kwok, "Note: Baby Contracts—*Litowitz v. Litowitz*, 10 P.3d 1086 (Wash. Ct. App. 2000)," *Yale L.J.* 110 (May 2001): 1289. Kwok compares *Litowitz* to a custody dispute rather than a dispute over the right to procreate.

93. *Litowitz*, 10 P.3d at 1088.

94. *In re Marriage of Witten*, 672 N.W.2d 768 (Iowa 2003).

95. *Roman v. Roman*, 193 S.W.3d 40 (Tex. App. 2006, pet. denied), petition for certiorari filed Jan. 9, 2008.

96. BBC News, "Woman Loses Final Embryo Appeal," Apr. 10, 2007, available at http://news.bbc.co.uk/1/hi/health/6530295.stm.

97. *J.B.*, 751 A.2d at 619 (further citations omitted).

98. See Howard Fink and June Carbone, "Between Private Ordering and Public Fiat: A New Paradigm for Family Law Decision Making," *J. L. & Fam. Stud.* 5 (2003): 1, 67 (suggesting that, although courts differ on the enforceability of embryo-disposition agreements, the decisions indicate that "courts will enforce such agreements where they provide for the donation or destruction of the frozen

gametic material, but not where they provide for the implantation of the embryos over the objection of one of the parties").

99. *Roe v. Wade*, 410 U.S. 113, 158 (1973).

100. Ibid., 163.

101. Ibid., 150.

102. Ibid., 162.

103. Lori B. Andrews, "The Stork Market: The Law of the New Reproduction Technologies, *ABA J.* 70 (Aug. 1984): 50.

104. *Casey*, 505 U.S. at 846.

105. *Gonzales*, 127 S.Ct. at 1633.

106. Ibid.

107. Jack M. Balkin, "How New Genetic Technologies Will Transform *Roe v. Wade*," *Emory L.J.* 56 (2007): 845.

108. *Gonzalez*, 127 S.Ct. at 1626.

109. Liza Mundy, *Everything Conceivable: How Assisted Reproduction Is Changing Our World* (New York: Knopf, 2007).

110. David Barnhizer suggests that the law, including courts, is at the center of the "seismic" cultural conflict and that there has been little reasoned discourse from intellectuals on these issues. David Barnhizer, "Ideology, Propaganda and Legal Discourse in the Argument Culture," Cleveland-Marshall Leg. Stud. Paper No. 07-141, Mar. 20, 2007, available at http://papers.ssrn.com/sol3/papers.cfm?abstract_id=975256. Although law is central to cultural conflicts—control of national appropriations on teen education, for example, helps determine what teens actually learn—I see law as the result, rather than the catalyst, of such conflicts. The laws that exist reflect certain values; while those laws may promote the development of, or revolution against, those values, they exemplify the values of the winning position. Moreover, I see more reasoned analysis from within and outside the academy than does Barnhizer.

111. Cultural Cognition Project at Yale Law School, http://research.yale.edu/culturalcognition/.

112. Donald Braman, Dan M. Kahan, and James Grimmelmann, "Modeling Facts, Culture, and Cognition in the Gun Debate," *Soc. Just. Res.* 18 (Sept. 2005): 283.

113. Dan M. Kahan and Donald Braman, "Cultural Cognition and Public Policy," *Yale L. & Pol'y Rev.* 24 (Winter 2006): 163.

114. Ibid., 165.

115. See generally ibid.; Cultural Cognition Project at Yale Law School, "Culture and Political Attitudes," http://research.yale.edu/culturalcognition/content/view/91/100/.

116. See Braman, Kahan, and Grimmelmann, "Modeling Facts, Culture, and Cognition"; Donald Braman and Dan M. Kahan, "Overcoming the Fear of Guns, the Fear of Gun Control, and the Fear of Cultural Politics: Constructing a Better Gun Debate," *Emory L.J.* 55 (2006): 586–88.

117. Kahan and Braman, "Cultural Cognition and Public Policy," 166; Braman and Kahan, "Overcoming the Fear of Guns," 595–98.

118. George Lakoff, *Don't Think of an Elephant* (White River Junction, VT: Chelsea Green, 2004), 115.

Notes to Chapter 10

1. June Carbone and Paige Gottheim, "Creating Life? Examining the Legal, Ethical, and Medical Issues of Assisted Reproductive Technologies: Markets, Subsidies, Regulation, and Trust: Building Ethical Understandings into the Market for Fertility Services," *J. Gend., Race & Just.* 9 (2006): 544.

2. Judith Daar, "Regulating Reproductive Technologies: Panacea or Paper Tiger?" *Hous. L. Rev.* 34 (1997): 637, 638.

3. Debora Spar, *The Baby Business: How Money, Science and Politics Drive the Commerce of Conception* (Boston: Harvard Business School Press, 2006), 224–31.

4. E.g., Kathryn Venturatos Lorio, "The Process of Regulating Assisted Reproductive Technologies: What We Can Learn from Our Neighbors—What Translates and What Does Not," *Loyola L. Rev.* 45 (1999): 247, 267.

5. Karen M. Ginsberg, "Note: FDA Approved: A Critique of the Artificial Insemination Industry in the United States," *U. Mich. J. L. Ref.* 30 (1997): 823, 824.

6. Practice Committee of the Society for Assisted Reproductive Technology and the American Society for Reproductive Medicine, "Guidelines for Advertising by ART Programs," *Fertility & Sterility* 82 (2004): 527.

7. For examples, see a search of the FTC's web archive, http://search.ftc.gov/query.html?qt=infertility+services&col=hsr&col=news&col=full.

8. Mary E. Abusief, Mark D. Hornstein, and Tarun Jain, "Assessment of United States Fertility Clinic Websites According to the American Society for Reproductive Medicine (ASRM)/Society for Assisted Reproductive Technology (SART) Guidelines," *Fertility & Sterility* 87 (2007): 88, 92.

9. Human Fertilisation and Embryology Authority, "Infertility: the HFEA Guide" (2007–2008): 13, available at http://www.hfea.gov.uk/docs/Guide2.pdf.

10. Martha M. Ertman, "What's Wrong with a Parenthood Market?" *N.C. L. Rev.* (2003): 1, 37.

11. David Frankfurter, "To Insure or Not to Insure: That Is the Question," *Fertility & Sterility* 80 (2006): 24.

12. Leland Traiman, "Creating Life? Examining the Legal, Ethical, and Medical Issues of Assisted Reproductive Technologies: Guidelines but No Guidance: GaySpermBank.com vs. FDA," *J. Gend., Race & Just.* 9 (Spring 2006): 619.

13. American Association of Tissue Banks, "Standards for Tissue Banking, 11th Edition" (2007), 25–26.

14. ASRM Ethics Committee, "Financial Compensation of Oocyte Donors," *Fertility & Sterility* 88 (2007): 305.

15. Ginsberg, "FDA Approved?" 844.

16. See American Society for Reproductive Medicine, "Guidelines on Numbers of Embryos Transferred," *Fertility & Sterility* 86, supp. 4 (2006): S51–S52 (additionally the guidelines suggest no more than three embryos for a woman with a regular prognosis between the ages of thirty-five and thirty-seven or a woman between the ages of thirty-eight and forty with a "more favorable" prognosis). In response to the risks posed by multiple births, "clinics are focusing on transferring fewer embryos and on developing more sophisticated ways to identify the healthiest embryos with the greatest chance of success." Laurie Tarkan, "Lowering Odds of Multiple Births," *N.Y. Times*, Feb. 19, 2008, p. F1.

17. See Caroline Jones, "The Changing Face of Family: A Controversial New Proposal Would Mean a Special Stamp on the Birth Certificates of Babies from Donor Eggs or Sperm," *Mirror* (London), Jan. 10, 2008, p. 40.

18. Daniel J. DeNoon, "IVF Risks Mostly Due to Multiple Births: Single-Embryo Transfer May Cut Risk of In-Vitro Fertilization," *WebMD Medical News*, July 26, 2007, http://www.webmd.com/infertility-and-reproduction/news/20070726/ivf-risks-mostly-due-to-multiple-births?page=1; Hilary White, "More Health Risks Found in IVF Babies: Scientist Suggests IVF Children Should Be Monitored into Adulthood," *LifeSiteNews.com*, July 27, 2007, http://www.lifesite.net/ldn/2007/jul/07072709.html.

19. Tarkan, "Lowering Odds of Multiple Births."

20. Brooke Lea Foster, "The Hunt for Golden Eggs: Young Women Donating Eggs," *Washingtonian* (July 2007): 101, available at http://www.washingtonian.com/articles/health/4722.html.

21. Linda Guidice, Eileen Santa, and Robert Pool, eds., *Assessing the Medical Risks of Human Oocyte Donation for Stem Cell Research: Workshop Report* (Washington, DC: National Academies Press, 2007), 18.

22. Ruth Farrell, Susannah Baruch, and Kathy Hudson, "IVF, Egg Donation, and Women's Health" (2006), Genetics & Public Policy Center, available at http://www.dnapolicy.org/resources/IVF_Egg_Donation_Womens_Health_final.pdf.

23. See ASRM, "Guidelines on Numbers of Embryos Transferred."

24. See Farrell, Baruch, and Hudson, "IVF, Egg Donation, and Women's Health," 2.

25. See Guidice, Santa, and Pool, *Assessing the Medical Risks*, 34–36.

26. L. Brinton, K. Moghissi, B. Scoccia, C. Westhoff, and E. Lamb, "Ovulation Induction and Cancer Risk," *Fertility & Sterility* 83 (2005): 261–74.

27. See Guidice, Santa, and Pool, *Assessing the Medical Risks*, 24–26.

28. ASRM, "Guidelines on Numbers of Embryos Transferred," S159.

29. The New York Department of Health explains, "Programs are required, by the American Society for Reproductive Medicine and the State Health Department, to limit the number of children created using the same donor," although

the informational brochure does not specify the limit. New York State Task Force on Life and the Law, *Thinking of Becoming an Egg Donor?* (2002), 23, available at http://www.health.state.ny.us/community/reproductive_health/infertility/eggdonor.htm#often.

30. See Ova the Rainbow, "FAQs for Egg Donors," http://www.ovatherainbow.com/FAQs%20egg%20donors.htm.

31. See Julia Derek, *Confessions of a Serial Egg Donor* (New York: Adrenaline Books, 2004).

32. ASRM, "Guidelines on Numbers of Embryos Transferred," S158.

33. Ibid., S42–43.

34. N. Adsuar, J. Zweifel, E. Pritts, M. Davidson, D. Olive, and S. Lindheim, "Assessment of Wishes Regarding Disposition of Oocytes and Embryo Management among Ovum Donors in an Anonymous Egg Donation Program," *Fertility & Sterility* 84 (2005): 1514; Derek, *Confessions.*

35. ASRM, "Guidelines on Numbers of Embryos Transferred," S46; American Bar Association Family Law Section Committee, "Proposed Model Code Governing Assisted Reproduction" (2007), available at http://www.abanet.org/family/committees/artmodelcode_november2007.pdf.

36. See B. Lo, V. Chou, M. Cedars, E. Gates, R. Taylor, R. Wagner, L. Wolf, and K. Yamamoto, "Informed Consent in Human Oocyte, Embryo, and Embryonic Stem Cell Research," *Fertility & Sterility* 82 (2004): 559.

37. There are a few exceptions to this rule, in cases in which women addicted to drugs have been ordered to stop having children until they are no longer addicted. These cases are the exception to the rule, and they are controversial precisely because of the public's distaste for government officials' deciding who can give birth.

Notes to Chapter 11

1. Janet L. Dolgin, "Just a Gene: Judicial Assumptions about Parenthood," *UCLA L. Rev.* 40 (Feb. 1993): 637 (in discussing the Supreme Court's unwed-father cases, Dolgin shows that courts support traditional family forms by awarding custody to the biological mother, when she is married). *Stanley v. Illinois,* 405 U.S. 645 (1972), and *Quilloin v. Walcott,* 435 U.S. 918 (1978), concerned the rights of nonmarital fathers, without an in-depth examination of the corresponding rights of married fathers or nonmarital mothers.

2. Marsha Garrison, "Law Making for Baby Making: An Interpretive Approach to the Determination of Legal Parentage," *Harv. L. Rev.* 113 (2000): 882.

3. Ibid., 908–10.

4. Larry Alexander, "Bad Beginnings," *U. Penn. L. Rev.* 145 (1996): 57, 82–85 (arguing, however, that legal principles do not have "the virtue of correct moral principles, since they are not necessarily morally correct").

5. Ibid., 86.

6. *Belsito v. Clark*, 67 Ohio Misc. 2d 59 (1994).

7. Martha Fineman, *The Neutered Mother, the Sexual Family and Other Twentieth Century Tragedies* (New York: Routledge, 1995), 233; see E. Gary Spitko, "The Constitutional Function of Biological Paternity," *Ariz. L. Rev.* 48 (2006): 97.

8. Martha A. Fineman, "Intimacy Outside of the Natural Family: The Limits of Privacy," *Conn. L. Rev.* 23 (1991): 971 (emphasis added).

9. Joseph Goldstein, Anna Freud, and Albert J. Solnit, *Beyond the Best Interests of the Child* (New York: Free Press, 1984).

10. I am here speaking of the problem of essentializing women. See, e.g., Elizabeth Spelman, *Inessential Woman: Problems of Exclusion in Feminist Thought* (Boston: Beacon, 1990); Katherine Bartlett and Carol Stack, "Joint Custody, Feminism, and the Dependency Dilemma," *Berkeley Women's L.J.* 2 (1986): 9, 21.

11. For an analysis of intent, see Jennifer Hendricks, "Essentially a Mother," *Wm. & Mary J. of Women & L.* 13 (2007): 478–80.

12. Marjorie Maguire Shultz, "Reproductive Technology and Intent-Based Parenthood: An Opportunity for Gender-Neutrality," *Wis. L. Rev.* (1990): 297, 323.

13. Vicki C. Jackson, "Baby M and the Question of Parenthood," *Georgetown L.J.* 76 (1988): 1811, 1814.

14. Lyria Bennett Moses, "Understanding Legal Responses to Technological Change: The Example of In Vitro Fertilization," *Minn. J. L., Sci. & Tech.* 6 (2005): 505, 517–18; Gaia Bernstein, "The Socio-Legal Acceptance of New Technologies: A Close Look at Artificial Insemination," *Wash. L. Rev.* 77, no. 4 (2002): 1035.

15. This was the situation in *In re Nicholas H.*, 46 P.3d 932, 935 (Cal. 2002).

16. For example, in one New York case, a sperm donor for a lesbian couple successfully sought additional visitation rights beyond those to which he had previously agreed in writing because, in the court's judgment, it was in the best interests of the child. *In re Tripp v. Hinkley*, 736 N.Y.S.2d 506, 508 (App. Div. 2000).

17. Martha M. Ertman, "What's Wrong with a Parenthood Market? A New and Improved Theory of Commodification," *N.C. L. Rev.* 82 (2003): 1.

Notes to Chapter 12

1. Liza Mundy, *Everything Conceivable: How Assisted Reproduction Is Changing Our World* (New York: Knopf, 2007), 180.

2. Robert Nachtigall, "Secrecy: An Unresolved Issue in the Practice of Donor Insemination," *Amer. J. Obst. & Gyn.* 168 (1993): 1846.

3. Ellen Goodman, "Kids' Right to Know Trumps Sperm Donors' Right to Anonymity," *Baltimore Sun,* Dec. 22, 2006, p. 25A.

4. See Anne Reichman Schiff, "Frustrated Intentions and Binding Biology: Seeking Aid in the Law," *Duke L.J.* 5 (Dec. 1994): 567 ("Procreation by means of sperm donation ought to entail some minimal level of responsibility, even though the donor may have no intention of being the rearing parent.") (she advocates the good-cause standard).

5. See Jennifer A. Baines, "Gamete Donors and Mistaken Identities: The Importance of Genetic Awareness and Proposals Favoring Donor Identity Disclosure for Children Born from Gamete Donations in the United States," *Fam. Court Rev.* 45 (2007): 119.

6. See Richard Woods and Claire Newell, "Foetal Attraction," *Sunday Times* (London), Jan. 13, 2008, p. 12.

7. Dorothy Nelkin and M. Susan Lindee, *The DNA Mystique: The Gene as a Cultural Icon* (New York: Freeman, 1995), 2.

8. See Anne Magurran, "Backseat Drivers," *N.Y. Times,* Dec. 10, 2000, p. 26 (reviewing Evelyn Fox Keller, *The Century of the Gene* (Cambridge, MA: Harvard University Press, 2000)).

9. See E. Wayne Carp, ed., *Adoption in America: Historical Perspectives* (Ann Arbor: University of Michigan Press, 2002), 229 ("One of the central tenets of the [Adoption Rights Movement]'s ideology rests on the superiority of blood ties and the denigration of adoptive kinship."); Elizabeth Bartholet, *Family Bonds: Adoption, Infertility, and the New World of Child Production* (Boston: Beacon, 1993), 59. See also Nelkin and Lindee, *DNA Mystique,* 70 ("The preoccupation with genetic relationships can stigmatize the experience of adoption.").

10. Ellen Herman, "We Have a Long Way to Go," *Boston Globe,* Nov. 25, 1997, p. A13.

11. Carp, *Adoption in America,* 229; see Bartholet, *Family Bonds,* 57–58. Bartholet explains, "The pressure for openness is coming from a movement that is profoundly hostile to adoption as a family form." Ibid., 60. On the other hand, she believes that sealing records tries to avoid the complexities of adoptive families. Ibid., 59–60.

12. Wendy Kramer, "Donor Family Connections," Donor Sibling Registry, July 25, 2007, http://www.donorsiblingregistry.com/DSRblog/index.php.

13. See also Lori B. Andrews and Lisa Douglass, "Alternative Reproduction," *S. Cal. L. Rev.* 65 (1991): 623, 650–51 (opposing the release of the identity of biological parents for the sole purpose of allowing adoptees to obtain current genetic information).

14. Sonia M. Suter, "A Brave New World of Designer Babies?" *Berkeley Tech. L.J.* 22 (Spring 2007): 962.

15. Ibid.

16. Ruth Hubbard and Elijah Wald, *Exploding the Gene Myth: How Genetic Information Is Produced and Manipulated by Scientists, Physicians, Employers, Insurance Companies, Educators, and Law Enforcers* (Boston: Beacon, 1993), 100.

17. Ibid., 101.

18. See Suter, "Brave New World?"

19. James Lindemann Nelson, "Cloning, Families, and the Reproduction of Persons," *Va. L. Rev.* 32 (Spring 1998): 719; see also Joan H. Hollinger, "From Coitus to Commerce: Legal and Social Consequences of Noncoital Reproduction," *U. Mich. J. L. Ref.* 18 (Summer 1985): 874 ("Much of this demand [for non-coital reproduction] follows from the social and psychological importance people attach to the ideal of having children who are genetically theirs.").

20. See Sperm Bank of California, "Become a Sperm Donor: How to Qualify," http://thespermbankofca.org/pages/page.php?pageid=11&cat=11; see also American Society for Reproductive Medicine, "Third Party Reproduction: A Guide for Patients," 5, 10, available at http://www.asrm.org/Patients/patient-booklets/thirdparty.pdf.

21. See generally John Lawrence Hill, "What Does It Mean to Be a 'Parent'? The Claims of Biology as the Basis for Parental Rights," *NYU L. Rev.* 66 (May 1991): 359.

22. See Cryogenic Laboratories, Inc., "Choosing a Donor," http://www.cryolab.com/Default.aspx?section=selection&page=choosingADonor.

23. Leslie Milk, "Looking for Mr. Good Genes," *Washingtonian* (May 1999): 65. Until the widespread use of sperm banks, physicians performing AID matched the recipients and the providers.

24. *If These Walls Could Talk 2* (HBO television broadcast, Mar. 5, 2000).

25. See Joanna E. Scheib, Maura Riordan, and Phillip R. Shaver, "Choosing between Anonymous and Identity-Release Sperm Donors: Recipient and Donor Characteristics," *Reproductive Technologies* 10 (2000): 50, 56–57. The authors of this study speculate that matching helps lesbian couples because

> matching the donor to one's partner may increase the non-genetic parent's involvement with the DI process, the recipient's pregnancy, and eventually the child. . . . it may be especially important to a lesbian couple, in which the non-genetic mother's role as a parent may be repeatedly questioned by some segments of society.

Ibid., 57.

26. Also, the information available at the time of adoption or gamete provision will be outdated by the time the offspring reaches adulthood.

27. See *Matter of Baby Boy "SS" v. Rosemarie "TT,"* 719 N.Y.S.2d 311 (App. Div. 2001).

28. Ulrich Mueller, book review of Victor Groza and Karen F. Rosenberg, eds., *Clinical and Practice Issues in Adoption: Bridging the Gap between Adoptees Placed as Infants and as Older Children, Adoption Q.* 3 (1999): 99.

29. Jed Rubenfeld, "The Right of Privacy," *Harv. L. Rev.* 102 (Feb. 1989): 737, 741–42.

30. *Eisenstadt v. Baird*, 405 U.S. 438, 453 (1972).

31. *Wyman v. James*, 400 U.S. 309, 312n. 4 (1971).

32. Ibid., 341–42 (Marshall, J., dissenting).

33. Daniel Solove, "A Taxonomy of Privacy," *U. Penn. L. Rev.* 154 (2006): 477, 490–91.

34. For a discussion of the relevant cases, see Naomi Cahn and Jana Singer, "Adoption, Identity, and the Constitution: The Case for Opening Closed Records," *U. Penn. J. Const. L.* 2 (1999): 150; Elizabeth Samuels, "The Idea of Adoption: An Inquiry into the History of Adult Adoptee Access to Birth Records," *Rutgers L. Rev.* 53 (2001): 428–30.

35. Jeffrey Rosen, *The Unwanted Gaze: The Destruction of Privacy in America* (New York: Vintage, 2000), 15. Rosen's formulation echoes an earlier concept that was also claimed to be a form of privacy, the "right to personhood." These varying conceptualizations of privacy show its amorphous nature as a term with constitutional dimensions that is used to cover a broad range of situations that have little in common.

36. This third type of privacy could also be called a right to self-expression, to individual fulfillment. Cf. Robert W. Tuttle, "Reviving Privacy," *Geo. Wash. L. Rev.* 67 (1999): 1183 (questioning whether self-expression is an ultimate good).

37. See *Doe v. Sundquist*, 118 S. Ct. 51 (1997).

38. See generally Catherine J. Ross, "An Emerging Right for Mature Minors to Receive Information," *U. Penn. J. Const. L.* 2 (1999): 223; Emily Buss, "What Does Frieda Yoder Believe?" *U. Penn. J. Const. L.* 2 (1999): 53.

39. *Johnson v. Superior Court*, 80 Cal. App. 4th 1050, 1066 (2d Dist. 2000), *modified*, 101 Cal. App. 4th 869 (2d Dist. 2002).

40. Ibid., 1067.

41. Murray Davis, "Child Should Have Right to Know Genetic Information," *Detroit Free Press*, Mar. 6, 2007, p. 9; Christina Stolarz, "Teen Fighting to Find Real Dad," *Detroit News*, Nov. 20, 2006, p. 1B.

42. Elizabeth Suh and Ashbel S. Green, "Who Gets the Baby?" *Oregonian*, Sept. 22, 2006, p. A1.

43. Ashbel S. Green, "Judge Rules in OHSU Sperm Sample Mix-Up," *Oregonian*, Apr. 17, 2007, p. B2.

44. Thomas Anthony Donahoe, "I Made Him What He Is, but Who Is He?" *N.Y. Times*, July 29, 2007, available at http://www.nytimes.com/2007/07/29/fashion/29love.html?_r=1&scp=1&sq=i+made+him+but+who+is+he&st=nyt&oref=slogin.

45. Daniel J. Solove, *Understanding Privacy* (Cambridge, MA: Harvard University Press, forthcoming 2008), draft p. 56.

46. See Eric D. Blyth, Lucy Frith, and Abigail Farrand, "Is It Possible to Recruit Gamete Donors Who Are Both Altruistic and Identifiable?" *Fertility & Sterility* 84, supp. 1 (2005): S21, available at http://www.sciencedirect.com/science?_ob=ArticleURL&_udi=B6T6K-4H88108-1T&_coverDate=09%2F30%2F2005&_alid=451336191&_rdoc=1&_fmt=&_orig=search&_qd=1&_cdi=5033&_sort=d&view=c&_acct=C000031558&_version=1&_urlVersion=0&_userid=1193445&md5=628 9394e3d8fced9e1f6f37fa5acc030.

47. M.M. Fusillo and A. Shear, "Motivations, Compensation and Anonymity in Oocyte Donors from 38 ART Centers in the United States," *Fertility & Sterility* 88, supp. 1 (2007): S10.

48. See K. Daniels and O. Lalos, "The Swedish Insemination Act and Availability of Donors," *Human Reprod.* 10 (1995): 1871.

49. June Carbone and Paige Gottheim, "Markets, Subsidies, Regulation, and Trust: Building Ethical Understanding into the Market for Fertility Services," *J. Gend., Race & Just.* 9 (2006): 509, available at http://papers.ssrn.com/sol3/papers.cfm?abstract_id=802325.

50. Daniels and Lalos, "Swedish Insemination Act"; F. Shenfield, "Privacy versus Disclosure in Gamete Donation: A Clash of Interest, of Duties, or an Exercise in Responsibility?" *J. Assisted Reprod. and Genetics* 14 (1997): 371; A. Lalos, K. Daniels, C. Gottlieb, and O. Lalos, "Recruitment and Motivation of Semen Providers in Sweden," *Human Reprod.* 18 (2003): 212.

51. Shenfield, "Privacy versus Disclosure," 371.

52. Marilyn Gardner, "Sperm Donors No Longer Bank on Anonymity," *Christian Science Monitor,* Mar. 30, 2005, available at http://www.csmonitor.com/2005/0330/p11s02-lifp.html.

53. Bourn Hall Clinic website, http://www.bourn-hall-clinic.co.uk/index.php.

54. Mark Henderson, "More Sperm Donors Volunteer Despite the Removal of Anonymity," *The Times* (London), May 4, 2007, p. 32.

55. Blyth, Frith, and Farrand, "Is It Possible to Recruit Gamete Donors?"

56. Joan H. Hollinger, "Aftermath of Adoption: Legal and Social Consequences," in *Adoption Law and Practice,* ed. Joan H. Hollinger (New York: Matthew Bender, 2006), § 13.01.

57. Joanna E. Scheib and Alice Ruby, "Impact of Sperm Donor Information on Parents and Children," *Sexuality, Reprod. & Menopause* 4 (2006): 17.

58. "Sperm Donor Shortage Hits Canadian Fertility Clinics," *CBC News,* Dec. 19, 2006, available at http://www.cbc.ca/health/story/2006/12/19/sperm-shortage.html.

59. In the adoption context, the two states—Alaska and Kansas—that never prevented disclosure have experienced higher-than-average adoption rates. See Cahn and Singer, "Adoption, Identity, and the Constitution," 187.

60. John A. Robertson, "Embryos, Families, and Procreative Liberty: The Legal Structure of the New Reproduction," *S. Cal. L. Rev.* 59 (1986): 1018.

61. George J. Annas, "Fathers Anonymous: Beyond the Best Interests of the Sperm Donor," *Fam. L.Q.* 14 (1980): 13.

62. Uniform Parentage Act § 5 (1973), available at http://www.law.upenn.edu/bll/archives/ulc/fnact99/1990s/upa7390.htm.

63. See Elizabeth Samuels, "The Idea of Adoption: An Inquiry into the History of Adult Adoptee Access to Birth Records," *Rutgers L. Rev.* 53 (2001): 428–30; Kristine Cordier Karnezis, "Restricting Access to Judicial Records of Concluded Adoption Proceedings," *Amer. L. Reports,* 3rd ed., 83 (1978): 800 (superseded by Shannon Clark Kief, "Restricting Access to Judicial Records of Concluded Adoption Proceedings," *Amer. L. Reports,* 5th ed., 103 (2002): 255.

64. Samuels, "Idea of Adoption," 429.

65. See Lucy Frith, "Gamete Donation and Anonymity: The Ethical and Legal Debate," *Human Reprod.* 16 (2001): 818; Christopher de Jonge and Christopher L.R. Barratt, "Gamete Donation: A Question of Anonymity," *Fertility & Sterility* 85 (2006): 500.

66. "UK's High Court Gives Hope to Sperm Donor Campaign," *Transplant News,* Sept. 27, 2002, available at http://findarticles.com/p/articles/mi_m0YUG/is_12/ai_n18614239.

67. Mark Henderson, "Donor Children Win Right to Find Biological Parents," *Times,* Jan. 22, 2004, p. 4 (quoting Suzi Leather).

68. See Frith, "Gamete Donation and Anonymity."

69. See Caroline Jones, "The Changing Face of Families: A Controversial New Proposal Would Mean a Special Stamp on the Birth Certificates of Babies from Donor Eggs or Sperm; How Will This—and Other New Laws—Affect Families?" *Mirror* (London), Jan. 10, 2008, p. 40.

70. "Assisted Conception," letter, *Times,* Aug. 3, 2007, p. 16.

71. See American Adoption Congress, "Legislation: Reform Materials: Abortion and Adoption Data from States Who Have Enacted Access," http://www.americanadoptioncongress.org/reform_adoption_data.php.

72. Lucy Frith, "Beneath the Rhetoric: The Role of Rights in the Practice of Non-Anonymous Gamete Donation," *Bioethics* 15 (2001): 476.

73. Sara Cotton, Sara Hill, Anne F. Hirstein, et al., "Model Assisted Reproductive Technology Act," *J. Gend., Race & Just.* 9 (2005): 79–80.

74. Pino D'Orazio, "Half of the Family Tree: A Call for Access to a Full Genetic History for Children Born by Artificial Insemination," *J. Health & Biomedical L.* 2 (2006): 267.

75. Wendy Kramer, Donor Sibling Registry, http://www.donorsiblingregistry.com/chicagotalk.pdf, 6.

76. See, e.g., Baines, "Gamete Donors and Mistaken Identities," 126.

77. See Judith S. Modell, *Kinship with Strangers: Adoption and Interpretations of Kinship in American Culture* (Berkeley: University of California Press, 1995).

78. See Alison Harvison Young, "Reconceiving the Family: Challenging the Paradigm of the Exclusive Family," *Amer. U. J. Gend., Soc. Pol'y & L.* 6 (1998): 554–55; Naomi R. Cahn, "Reframing Child Custody Decisionmaking," *Ohio St. L.J.* 58 (1997): 1 (arguing that it may be appropriate to recognize the caretaking rights of more than two adults).

79. See Rickie Solinger, *Wake Up Little Susie: Single Pregnancy and Race before Roe v. Wade* (New York: Routledge, 1992), 13.

Index

About the Author

NAOMI R. CAHN is John Theodore Fey Research Professor of Law at the George Washington University Law School and a Senior Fellow at the Evan B. Donaldson Adoption Institute. She is coauthor, with Douglas E. Abrams, Catherine J. Ross, and David D. Meyer, of *Contemporary Family Law*, coeditor with Joan Heifetz Hollinger, of *Families by Law: An Adoption Reader* (NYU Press, 2004), and, with Helena Michie, coauthor of *Confinements: Fertility and Infertility in Contemporary Culture* (Rutgers University Press).